The Leyden Papyrus

The Leyden Papyrus

AN EGYPTIAN MAGICAL BOOK

EDITED BY F. Ll. GRIFFITH
AND HERBERT THOMPSON

DOVER PUBLICATIONS, INC.
NEW YORK

This Dover edition, first published in 1974, is an unabridged and unaltered republication of the work originally published by H. Grevel & Co., London, in 1904 under the title *The Demotic Magical Papyrus of London and Leiden.*

International Standard Book Number: 0-486-22994-7
Library of Congress Catalog Card Number: 73-90639

Manufactured in the United States of America
Dover Publications, Inc.
180 Varick Street
New York, N.Y. 10014

PREFACE

THE MS., dating from the third century A.D., which is here edited for the first time in a single whole, has long been known to scholars. Its subject-matter—magic and medicine—is not destitute of interest. It is closely connected with the Greek magical papyri from Egypt of the same period, but, being written in demotic, naturally does not reproduce the Greek hymns which are so important a feature of those papyri. The influence of purely Greek mythology also is here by comparison very slight—hardly greater than that of the Alexandrian Judaism which has supplied a number of names of Hellenistic form to the demotic magician. Mithraism has apparently contributed nothing at all: Christianity probably only a deformed reference to the Father in Heaven. On the other hand, as might have been expected, Egyptian mythology has an overwhelmingly strong position, and whereas the Greek papyri scarcely go beyond Hermes, Anubis, and the Osiris legend, the demotic magician introduces Khons, Amon, and many other Egyptian gods. Also, whereas the former assume a knowledge of the *modus operandi* in divination by the lamp and bowl, the latter describes it in great detail.

But the papyrus is especially interesting for the language in which it is written. It is probably the latest Egyptian MS. which we possess written in the demotic script, and it presents us with the form of the language as written—almost as spoken—by the pagans at the time when the Greek alphabet was being adopted by the Christians. It must not be forgotten, too, that this is the document which contributed perhaps more than any other to the decipherment of demotic, partly through its numerous Greek glosses.

We have therefore thought that a complete edition, with special reference to its philological importance, would be useful. The vocabulary is extensive, comprising about a thousand words. The present volume, containing the introduction, the transliteration, translation, and notes, will be followed by a complete glossary, with separate indices of Greek words, invocation names, names of animals, plants, and minerals, and a list of the glosses, &c., besides a chapter dealing with the principal grammatical forms met with in the MS., and a hand-copy of the text; the photographic reproduction by Hess of the pages in the British Museum and Leemans' facsimile of those at Leiden will of course preserve their independent value for reference, as, for instance, in judging the condition of the MS. and the precise forms of the signs in particular passages.

There is considerable inconsistency in the spelling of words in the papyrus itself. So much having to be rendered more or less conventionally, while fresh light is thrown daily on the intricacies of demotic, it is probable that there are a good many inconsistencies in our transliterations, translations, and notes, in spite of the watchfulness of the excellent reader at the Clarendon

Press. Those, however, who have dealt with the subject at all will probably not judge these too hardly.

In conclusion, we have to record our gratitude, first, to our predecessors in publication and decipherment of the papyrus—to Reuvens, Leemans, and Hess, to Brugsch, Maspero, Revillout, and W. Max Müller—but for whose varied contributions our task would have been infinitely more laborious even in the present advanced state of the study: and secondly, to the authorities of the Egyptian department in the British Museum, and of the Rijksmuseum in Leiden, for their courtesy in affording every facility for studying the original MS., and more especially to Dr. Boeser of the Leiden Museum for much kindness and assistance.

F. Ll. G.

H. T.

CONTENTS

The Leyden Papyrus

INTRODUCTION

I. HISTORY OF THE MS.

The demotic magical papyrus of London and Leiden was discovered at Thebes with other papyri, principally Greek but dealing with subjects of a like nature, in the early part of the last century, and was bought by Anastasi, who was at that time Swedish consul at Alexandria, and made a large collection of Egyptian MSS. When Anastasi obtained the MS. it must already have been torn into two parts, and it is even probable that he obtained the two parts at different times, since he sold his Egyptian collections, including the Leiden MS., to the Dutch government in 1828, while the London portion was bought at the sale of his later collections at Paris in 1857 for the British Museum (No. 1072 in Lenormant's Catalogue).

The Leiden fragment was made known to the world much earlier than that in the British Museum. Its importance for the deciphering of the demotic script by the help of the numerous glosses in Graeco-Coptic characters was at once perceived by the distinguished scholar Reuvens, at that time Director of the Leiden Museum of Antiquities, who proceeded to study it carefully, and in 1830 published an admirable essay[1] in which he sketched the principal contents of the MS. and indicated its value for the progress of demotic

[1] Lettres à M. Letronne sur les papyrus bilingues et grecs, par C. J. C. Reuvens. Leide, 1830. (Première lettre, Papyrus bilingues.)

studies. He then took in hand its reproduction, and the MS. was lithographed in facsimile under his direction, and he had corrected the proofs of the first plate when he was cut off by a premature death in 1835; his work was carried to completion and published by his successor in the Directorship of the Museum, Leemans, in 1839[1]. Heinrich Brugsch studied it closely, and drew from it most of the examples quoted in his Demotic Grammar published in 1855; but, although later scholars have frequently quoted from it and translated fragments of it, the MS. has hitherto remained without complete translation, commentary, or glossary.

The London MS., however, lay from 1857 onwards almost unnoticed in the British Museum. To the late Dr. Pleyte, Leemans' successor at Leiden, belongs the credit of discovering that the two MSS. originally formed one. He had studied the Leiden portion, and at once recognized the handwriting of its fellow in London. Without publishing the fact, he communicated it to Professor Hess of Freiburg, when the latter was working in Leiden on the MS. there. Professor Hess went on to London, and, having fully confirmed Dr. Pleyte's statement, published in 1892 a reproduction of the British Museum MS. with an introduction, including the translation of one column, and a glossary[2].

Reuvens in his essay dwelt at some length on the 'gnostic' character of the MS. He devoted his attention mainly to the parts which contain the glosses, and those are almost exclusively magical invocations, among which occur the names of gods, spirits, and demons, Egyptian, Syrian, Jewish, &c., strung together in a manner similar

[1] Monuments égyptiens du Musée d'Antiquités des Pays-Bas à Leide: papyrus égyptien démotique à transcriptions grecques I. 383, publié par le Dr. Conrad Leemans. Leide, 1839.

[2] Der gnostische Papyrus von London, Einleitung, Text u. Demotisch-deutsches Glossar von J. J. Hess. Freiburg, 1892.

to those found in gnostic writings and on gnostic gems. He even went so far as to associate them with the name of a particular gnostic leader, Marcus, of the second century, chiefly on the ground of his recorded use of Hebrew and Syriac names in his invocations and the combinations of vowels. In consequence the MS. has acquired the name of the 'Leiden Gnostic,' and the term 'Gnostic' has been passed on to the London MS. But as will be seen from the complete translation here published, there is nothing in the work relating to the gnostic systems—it deals with magic and medicine, and it seems a misnomer to call the MS. gnostic merely because part of the stock-in-trade of the magician and medicine-man were a number of invocation names which he either picked up from the gnostics or derived from sources common to him and them. Hence it has been thought desirable to abandon the epithet 'gnostic,' and to call the work the 'Magical papyrus of London and Leiden' (Pap. mag. LL.).

II. CONDITION OF THE MS.

The London portion is in far better condition than the Leiden portion. The papyrus is pale in colour and the ink very black; consequently where the MS. has not suffered material damage it is easy to read, as the scribe wrote a beautiful and regular hand.

The Leiden papyrus, on the other hand, has unfortunately suffered much, as Leemans, with a view to protecting the surface, covered both recto and verso with 'vegetable' paper, which probably could not be removed now without serious injury to the MS.; but either the paper or the adhesive matter employed with it has darkened and decayed, rendering the writing illegible in places.

In 1829, while the MS. was still in charge of Reuvens and before it had been subjected to the operation above described, he took a tracing of it which has been preserved, and which, though of little assistance in points of minute detail, may be relied on for filling up with certainty many groups which are now wholly lost in the original.

The main body of the writing is on the recto (horizontal fibres) of the papyrus, while on the verso are written memoranda, medical prescriptions, and short invocations.

The London MS. is Pap. No. 10070 of the British Museum (formerly Anast. 1072).

The Leiden MS. is known as I. 383 (reckoned among the Anastasi MSS. as A. 65).

The London portion forms the initial part of the MS. and joins on to the Leiden portion without a break, the tenth and last column of the London MS. and the first of the Leiden forming one column.

The first London column is imperfect, and it is not possible to say with certainty whether the MS. began with it or whether there was an anterior part now lost. It is quite possible that it began here. On the other hand, it is certain that the MS. is imperfect at the end, since the broken edge of the papyrus at Leiden shows traces of a column of writing succeeding the present final column.

It is impossible to estimate how much is lost, as the MS. is not an original composition on a definite plan, but a compilation of heterogeneous material collected together without any logical order.

The two portions, if joined together, would measure, roughly speaking, some 5 m. (about 16½ feet) in length. In height it averages nearly 25 cm. (10 in.). The writing is in columns, of which there are twenty-nine on the recto, while on the verso are thirty-three small columns or portions of columns; but these are not marked off, as are the recto columns, by vertical and horizontal framing lines[1], nor are they written continuously, but they seem to have been jotted down there on account of their brevity and discontinuous character.

The recto columns vary somewhat in size, but average 20 × 20 cm. (8 in. square). The writing is frequently carried beyond the framing lines.

In each column of the recto the number of lines is on the average about thirty to thirty-three; but the number is very irregular, ranging from forty-three in one column to five in another.

III. CONTENTS.

As has been stated above, the MS. is a compilation. An analysis of the contents will be found on page 14. From this it will be seen to consist mainly of directions for divination processes involving numerous invocations, together with erotica and medical prescriptions, in which, however, magic plays as large a part as medicine.

The MS. is far from being unique in regard to its contents. Fragments of similar works in demotic exist at Paris (Louvre, No. 3229, published by Maspero, Quelques papyrus du Louvre, 1875), and at Leiden (I. 384 verso, Anast. 75, published by Leemans, Mons. du musée de Leide, 1842, pl. ccxxvi–vii) a MS. partly demotic and partly Greek, the latter portion being published by Leemans in Pap. graeci mus. lugd. bat. 1885, ii. Pap. V, and re-edited by Dieterich, Pap. Mag. Mus. Lugd. Bat. The Greek papyri containing similar texts are numerous, many examples having been pub-

[1] The horizontal lines on the recto are continuous for the whole length of the papyrus.

lished from the museums of Berlin, Leiden, London, and Paris by Goodwin, Parthey, Leemans, Wessely, and Kenyon.

The well-known codex of the Bibliothèque Nationale published by Wessely, Denkschr. Kais. Ak. Wiss. Wien, xxxvi. 1888, contains a few invocations in Old Coptic along with the Greek (cf. Griffith, A. Z. 1901, p. 85, and bibliography, ibid. p. 72).

Magic was from the earliest times largely developed by the Egyptians in relation both to the dead and the living. Under the former head fall both the pyramid texts and other texts found in the tombs, including most of the Book of the Dead, which consists mainly of magical invocations intended to make smooth the path of the deceased in the next world.

Magical texts for the use of the living are found in the Harris magical papyrus (ed. Chabas, 1860), the Metternich stela (ed. Golenischeff, 1877) and kindred stones, the Berlin papyrus edited by Erman (Zaubersprüche für Mutter u. Kind, 1901), &c. Reference may be made to the volume on Egyptian magic by Dr. Wallis Budge, 1899, and to a special study on vessel-divination by E. Lefébure, 'Le vase divinatoire,' in Sphinx, 1902, VI. 61 seq. Cf. also Dieterich, 'Abraxas'; Kenyon in Cat. Greek Pap. in B. M., I. 62 seq.; Miss Macdonald in P. S. B. A., xiii. 160 seq.; Wünsch, Sethianische Verfluchungstafeln aus Rom, &c.

In the closely allied department of medicine, it is sufficient to refer to the Ebers papyrus, the Kahun papyri, and the Berlin medical papyrus (ed. Brugsch, Rec. Mon. pl. 87–107), which offer many parallels. Among the Greek medical writers it is noticeable that Alexander of Tralles seems much more closely allied to the Egyptian school, if that be represented by our MS., than Galen.

But though the subject-matter of the MS. is not without its interest for the history of magic and medicine, its chief claim to publication lies in its philological interest. From the first its numerous glosses have attracted the attention of scholars, and have been the means of fixing the value of a large number of demotic groups. Further it is in date probably the latest known papyrus written in the demotic script; most of the glosses are really Coptic transcriptions, and under this head may likewise be included all the Egyptian words written in cipher; so that the MS. in these furnishes us with a series of very early Coptic words, including several grammatical forms of great interest. Possibly too the text may be of importance in relation to the question of dialects in pagan Egypt; but that is a subject too little worked out at present to allow of definite statements. The vocabulary is very extensive, and includes a number of Greek words, the names of over 100 plants, besides numerous animals and minerals.

IV. PREVIOUS WORK ON THE MS.

It may be useful to record here the names of those who have dealt with the MS. at greater length than a mere passing reference or quotation, and to whom we are indebted for many suggestions:—

REUVENS. Supra, p. 1.
LEEMANS. Mons. &c., texte; Aegyptische Papyrus in demotischer Schrift, &c. 1839.
MASPERO. Rec. trav., i. 18–40 (1870).
REVILLOUT. Setna, introd. pp. 3–48 (1877); Rev. Égypt., i. 163–172 (1880), ii. 10–15, 270–2 (1881); Poème satyrique (1885).
PLEYTE. P. S. B. A., 1883, 149.
BRUGSCH. Wtb. pass., A. Z., 1884, 18 seq.
MAX MÜLLER. Rec. tr., viii. 172 (1886), xiii. 149 (1890).

HESS. Setna pass. (1888), Zur Aussprache des Griechischen, in the *Indo-germanische Forschungen*, vi. 123; Der gnostische Papyrus von London, Einleitung, Text u. Demotisch-deutsches Glossar, 1892.

GROFF. Mém. de l'Institut Égypt. iii. 337 seq. (1897), and Bulletin du même, 1897, 1898.

As the London portion of the MS., which in the order of contents is the first part, was published fifty years later than the second part at Leiden, it follows that each publication has an independent numbering of the columns, starting from I. In view of the fact that there are many references in demotic literature already to the columns by their numbers as established by the publications of Leemans and Hess, it would have been desirable to retain the existing numbering if possible. But, as will be seen by comparison of the hand copy of the whole MS. which accompanies this edition with the former publications, the changes in the way of consolidation of the columns, and in some cases necessary re-numbering of the lines, have made it compulsory to introduce a new and continuous numbering of the columns. For instance, Hess col. X and Leemans col. I form a single column, and the same is the case with Leemans cols. II and III and cols. IV and V, and with verso, cols. XVI and XVII, XXII and XXIII. A comparative table of the old and new numbers will be found at the end.

V. THE GLOSSES.

There are about 640 words with transcriptions in Coptic characters in addition to a few inserted in the text.

Besides all the letters of the Greek alphabet we find the following used:—

ft (= ⲕ 26/15).
ɕ (= ⲕ 7/33, 25/34).
h (= ⲗ 25/34, 35 text).
ⳃ (= ⲱ 2/13, 5/23, 8/8).
ʒ (= ϣ 1/25, 8/9, 13, V. 5/9).
ⲗ (= ϣ 2/18).
ϭ (= ϯ : ϣ 9/11).
ϥ (= ϥ 2/10, 9/14).
ʌ (= ϩ 9/14, 25/34).
ϑ (= ϩ 2/4).
ƅ (= ϧ 9/6, 29/10).
ɗ (= ϫ 2/26, 29/10).

The glosses were undoubtedly written by the same scribe who wrote the demotic text. And it seems that he wrote the glosses before he filled in the rubrics. For the handwriting of the demotic text and of the rubrics is unquestionably the same; and in filling up in red the empty spaces he had left for rubrication, the scribe took occasion to fill in with his red ink occasional lapses in the black writing. In the text this can be observed in e.g. 24/1, the omitted ꞩ— of the second *str* (?) has been filled up in red, and also the omitted determinative in the last word of 28/8, an omitted letter in *pẖr* 29/11, an omitted word *šn* interlineated in 29/12, and a plural sign in 25/26; and so too the gloss ⲉⲱⲉ in 28/8, overlooked when the glosses were originally inserted in black ink.

It is a fact that there is often a considerable difference between the Greek letters in the passages written in Greek and in the glosses (e.g. *παπιπετου* in 15/25 and 15/29), but this may be accounted for by the fact that the former are written in a cursive hand with ligatures, while the glosses are carefully written with separately formed letters without ligatures for distinctness' sake in the narrow space between the lines.

The above considerations, however, only show that the text and glosses were written by the same hand in our existing MS. It does not follow that they were written by the original compiler. Max Müller has argued (Rec. tr., viii. 175) that they must be due to another individual since they are mostly in the Fayumic dialect, while the dialect of the demotic text is 'Untersahidisch' (i. e. Achmimic, so called by Stern). In Rec. tr., xiii. 152 *n.*, he replaces the latter term by a more precise definition: 'Die Mundart steht zwischen Fayumisch u. dem Mittel-ägyptischen von Akhmîm, letzterem näher.' But it is very doubtful whether this distinction between the text and the glosses can be maintained. The only example quoted by Max Müller that distinctly suggests Fayumic is the gloss **ⲗⲱ** and **ⲗ** over a group in 16/5 and 25/34, which he reads as = (ⲉ)**ⲣⲟⲟⲩ**, regarding the interchange of **ⲣ** and **ⲗ** as evidence of Fayumic dialect. But the demotic group in question does not read *er-w*, but *mr* as in *mr-ʾḥ* (1/17, 2/7, 14/6, 28), and the gloss **ⲗⲱ** represents the absolute form of the late Egyptian word which we see in its construct form in Sahidic **ⲗⲉⲙⲏⲏϣⲉ** and in λεσωνις. From the detailed examination of the dialect (in vol. ii) it appears probable that the dialect of the text does not show any distinction from that of the glosses, and it is not necessary to go behind the scribe of the present MS. and place the compiler earlier. He may well have been one and the same.

VI. DATE.

Reuvens (u. s. p. 151) placed the date of the MS. in the first half of the third century A. D., and this was repeated by Leemans.

Groff and Hess attributed it on palaeographical grounds to the second century; but in the light of recent additions to the knowledge of Greek palaeography, and the opinions based on them of Kenyon, Grenfell, and Hunt (see A. Z., xxxix. (1901) p. 78), the third century must be accepted as the date of the MS. But this, of course, is the date at which the papyrus was written, and merely furnishes a *terminus ad quem* for deciding as to the date of the contents.

That the whole of the papyrus, in its present state, was written by one and the same scribe—with the possible exception of verso XXVIII—can scarcely be a matter of doubt to any one who has studied closely the handwriting of the original MSS. It must be stated, however, that Reuvens and Leemans were of opinion that the glosses were written by a later hand than that of the body of the text: but this question has been discussed above (p. 9), and apart from the identity of ink, and the material proof given there, it may be added that the hieratic glosses in 27/8 are certainly written by the same hand as the numerous hieratic passages scattered through the text.

The date of the contents is a much more complicated question. Written partly in hieratic, partly in demotic, and partly in Greek, they wear the aspect of a compilation, which is borne out by the varied and disconnected nature of the subject-matter.

It has been suggested that the work is a translation into demotic of a Greek original, and perhaps this is the first question demanding discussion. Prima facie it may be said to be likely, as so many similar works exist in Greek. The introduction of three invocations of considerable length written in Greek characters almost compels us to accept that origin for those particular sections, viz. 4/1–19, 15/24–31, 23/7–20. It seems probable that the translator felt he could transfer to Egyptian the prescriptions and preparations, while the formula of incantation had to be left in the original language. Had these sections been written in Egyptian originally, it is not likely that an incantation in a foreign tongue would be inserted in the place presumably of an Egyptian one.

And in the first named instance there is the additional evidence of two true Greek glosses, i.e. not *Coptic transcriptions* of the demotic words, but Greek equivalents of the two words 'table' and 'goose,' which seem to be inserted clearly to prevent a misunderstanding of the original terms. In the second instance 15/24–31, the original Greek lines 25–28 are immediately followed by a demotic translation of the same passage (ll. 29–31), which points in the same direction. Translation from the Greek is rendered probable, outside the passages already referred to, by the transcription of Greek prescriptions and substances in 24/1–25, and verso I, II, VIII, IX. According to an ingenious suggestion of Max Müller, in verso II the otherwise unintelligible phrase *mʿnes n rm* is almost certainly a mistranslation of μαγνησία ἀνδρεία. Max Müller has also (Rec. tr., viii. 175–6) given strong reasons for regarding the passage 25/23–37 as being translated from a Greek original. However, even where there are reasons for believing that the demotic is a translation from the Greek, the original source, in relation to magic at any rate, was probably Egyptian—certainly so in the case of the Greek passage in 15/25–28, which has itself clearly an Egyptian origin.

On the other hand, some of the chief sections of the MS. show no traces of Greek influence, e.g. cols. VI and XV. 1–20; but it would be rash to say that they are older; they may well represent only a purer Egyptian source. Max Müller (Rec. tr., viii. 172) has suggested that some of the magic formulae go back to the period from the Eighteenth to the Twentieth Dynasty. This cannot be true of more than a few phrases. The language indeed is not entirely uniform, but throughout the papyrus the vocabulary and grammar are distinctly not 'Late Egyptian'; they are 'demotic,' and that too of a kind which approaches Coptic much more closely than in any other known papyrus. Certain passages, such as the spell in 13/1–10, show more or less archaism, but in all cases it is mixed with late forms.

The use of hieratic might be thought to indicate some antiquity where it occurs. But the writing is a strange jumble; the hieratic is inextricably though sparingly mixed with the demotic, a single word being often written partly in hieratic, partly in demotic. Where hieratic signs occur the language is not generally more archaic than when the demotic is pure. In 23/24 the word Abrasax is written in hieratic. Now Abrasax is usually regarded as a typical gnostic invocation name, Irenaeus having stated that it was invented by Basilides (fl. 125 A. D.). This statement is now generally regarded as an error, and the name may be earlier; but there is no authority for placing it in pre-Christian times (cf. Hort, s. v. Abrasax, in Smith, Dict. Christ. Biog.; Dieterich, Abrasax, p. 46; C. Schmidt, Gnostische Schriften in Kopt. Spr., 1892, p. 562).

Not many documents written in hieratic have been ascertained to be later than the first century A. D.; but they were plentiful at Tanis amongst the burnt papyri found by Professor Petrie in the house of 'Bakakhuiu' (Asychis), the destruction of which Mr. Petrie was disposed to date to 174 A. D. (Tanis, i. p. 41); and Clemens Alexandrinus (Strom. v. 237) mentions hieratic as still taught in the schools (circa A. D. 160–220). Hieroglyphic inscriptions, with the name of Decius (249–251), are found in the temple of Esneh, and the existence of hieroglyphic almost implies that of hieratic.

Judging by the language, it is difficult to believe that any part of the work in its present redaction is more than a century or two older than the papyrus itself.

The contents of the papyrus may be classified as follows :—

1. Divination—
   (*a*) by the vessel of oil I-III, IX-X. 22, XIV, XVIII. 7-33, XXI. 1-9, XXII (?), XXVIII, verso XXII, verso XXVI.
   (*b*) by a lamp V, VI-VII, VIII. 1-12, XVI, XVII-XVIII. 6, XXV. 1-22, XXVII. 13-36, verso XVIII, verso XXIV, verso XXXI.
   (*c*) by the sun X. 22-end, XXVII. 1-12, XXIX.
   (*d*) by moon XXIII. 21-31.
   (*e*) by the Foreleg constellation (Great Bear) verso XVIII.
   (*f*) by stars ? IV. 23-4.
   (*g*) through the priest Psash (?) VIII. 12-end.
   (*h*) through Imuthes IV. 1-22.
   (*i*) by dreams verso XVII, eye-paint XXI, invocation XXVII ? XXVIII.
   (*k*) for thief-catching III. 29, or shipwreck (?) verso XV.
2. to obtain favour and respect XI, verso XXXII.
   to avert anger of superior XV. 24-31.
3. Erotica—
   by potions XV. 1-21, XXI. 10-43, XXV. 23-XXVI.
   by salves XII, verso III. 14-16, XII-XIII. 9, XIII. 10-11, XIV, XXIII, XXV, XXX, XXXII.
   αγωγιμον verso XVI, XVII, XIX.
   διακοπη XIII. 1-10.
4. Poisons, &c.—
   blinding XIII. 11, XXIV. 30.
   soporifics XXIII. 1-20, XXIV, verso II. 16-III. 3.
   maddening (magic) verso XXIX.
   slaying XXIII. 7, XXIV. 28, verso XXXII.
   uses of the shrew-mouse, &c. (chiefly in erotica) XIII. 11-end and verso XXXII.
5. Healing—
   poison XIX. 10-21.
   sting XX. 1-27.
   dog's bite XIX. 9, 32-40.
   bone in throat XIX. 21-32, XX. 27-33.
   gout and other affections of feet verso VIII-X, XI.
   water in ears verso IV. 1-5.
   ophthalmia (?) verso XX.
   fever verso XXXIII.
   haemorrhage, &c. in woman verso V. 1-3, 9-13, V. 4-8.
   to ascertain pregnancy verso V. 4-8.
6. names or descriptions of plants, drugs, &c. verso I-II. 15, III. 4-13, 17-18, IV. 6-19, V. 14-17.

SYNOPSIS OF CONTENTS

VERSO.

EXPLANATION OF SIGNS

TRANSLATION.

RESTORATIONS are placed in *square* brackets [ ]. Lacunae in the original, for which no restoration is suggested, are represented by dots. Words in *round* brackets ( ) are not in the original, but are added by the translators; those between angular brackets ⟨ ⟩ are intended to be omitted.

The second person singular has been rendered by 'thou, thee' in invocations, by 'you' elsewhere. In the very few instances in which the second person plural occurs, it is indicated by the use of 'ye' or 'you' (plur.); (*bis*) following a word indicates that the word is followed in the original by the sign *sp sn*, implying that the word or phrase is to be repeated.

An accurate transcription of the magic names is given in the transliteration; in the translation we have rendered the sound approximately without strict adherence to any one system, generally following the glosses where they exist, as it was thought that this would be the most useful course for such readers as are not Egyptian scholars.

TRANSLITERATION.

For the system, see note preceding the demotic glossary. Words transliterated with Coptic letters *between asterisks* are written in *cipher* in the original.

REFERENCES.

In referring to the plates of the papyrus in vol. ii, Col. I. l. 1 is quoted as 1/1 and verso, Col. II. l. 3 as V. 2/3, &c.

TRANSLITERATION

Col. I.

1\. . . . . . ẖn p tš n Pr-mze z-mt

2\. . . . . . štte n pe-f ryt ḥtp n Pr- . . . e ḥr-f mw tyk

3\. . . . . . n ʾm t(?) e ne-f(?) sḥ(?)n ʿre·t ʿnẖ·t

4\. . . . . . tkr my p wyn p wstn ẖn pe hn

5\. . . . . . a·wn n-y p t a·wn n-y t ty·t a·wn n-y p nwn

6\. . . . . . ʿo·t n ḥmt n ʾrq-ḥḥ n ntr·w nt n t p·t nt θse ʾm-n

7\. . . . . . wyn p wstn ẖn pe hne pe

8\. . . . . . ẖm-ẖl nte ḥr-f pẖt a py hne (nḥe) my wz

Col. I.

l. 1. Restore from 18/7. The parallel text to ll. 13–17 shows that more than half of the page is lost, but the heading line was probably not of full length. *Pr-mze* is **ⲡⲉⲙϫⲉ** (Oxyrhynchus), capital of the nineteenth nome of Upper Egypt.

l. 2. *Pr- . . . e* (?). The group suggests a reading *Pr-ʾr-ʾmn* for **ⲡⲉⲣⲉⲙⲟⲩⲛ** (Pelusium), but the *ʾr* (?) sign is perhaps too upright, and it is more likely that the two signs following *Pr* are a special group for some divine name. Nothing is known of the religious importance of Pelusium, or even of its name in Egyptian, but the city is mentioned in a Greek invocation quoted below at l. 12.

l. 3. *sḥ* (?). This group, here in the plural, may represent 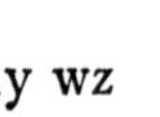 *sʾḥ*, 'toes' (Lange, A. Z., 1896, 76). Cf. Lepsius, Todtenb., c. 42, l. 9 *ìw zbʿ·w-ì sḥ·w-ì m ʿrʿlw* (*sic*) *ʿnẖ·w*, 'my fingers and toes are as rearing serpents.' But the same group recurs in 7/2 as a masc. sing. subst. where the context rather suggests the meaning 'testicles.'

ʿnẖ·t, of a serpent, cf. 12/17; in Egyptian Pleyte, Pap. Tur., cxxxii. 4 and (very late) Mar. Pap. Boul., I. Pl. 9, ll. 5–6. It seems to mean 'darting forward for attack.' Similar meanings, 'rise,' &c., are common, esp. in late texts, Br., Wtb., 198–9; cf. also 9/16, 10/7. But in Griffith, Tell el Yahudiyeh, xxv. 15, an enraged serpent *ʿnẖ nf·w-f* 'breathed its vapour' at a god, *ʿnẖ* being there a transitive verb surviving in Sah. **ⲁⲛϣ-ⲧⲏⲩ** 'breathe,' Bsciai, Rec. tr., vii. 25 (Job ix. 18).

TRANSLATION

Col. I.

(1) [A vessel-divination which a physician?] of the nome of Pemze [gave to me]. Formula: (2) '[O god N.] . . . . . the border of whose girdle (?) rests in Peremoun (?), whose face is like a spark (3) . . . . of (?) an obscene (?) cat, whose toes (?) are a rearing uraeus (4) . . . . quick[-ly?]; put light and spaciousness in my vessel (5) . . . . Open to me the earth, open to me the Underworld, open to me the abyss, (6) . . . . great . . . . . of bronze of Alkhah, ye gods that are in heaven, that are exalted, come ye (7) . . . . [put?] light and spaciousness in my vessel, my (8) . . . . [this] boy, whose face is bent over this vessel

---

l. 4. *p wyn p wstn*, cf. Leyd. Pap. Gr. V. v. 17 (ed. Dieterich) *γενεσθω βα(θος) πλα(τος) μη(κος) αυγη* in an *ονειρου αιτησις*.

l. 5. Or perhaps '[Open to me, O heaven!], open to me, O earth!' &c. Cf. Pap. Bibl. Nat. l. 1180 *ανοιγητι* (sic) *ουρανε*.

ty·t transcribed ΤΗΙ in Gloss. 17/20, O. C. Par. ΤΗ (A. Z., 1883, 94). In II Kham. ii. 10, &c., the judgement of the dead takes place in Tei, which seems convertible with Amenti.

p nwn. It is a question whether this is the hieroglyphic . The latter occurs only twice in this papyrus, but in one of the instances it is clearly parallel to *nwn*. Cf. xxi. 33 *nte-k py k km ḥyt 'r pyr n p* 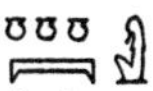 with ix. 15 *'nk p hf 'r pyr n p nwn*.

l. 6. *'rq-ḥḥ*. Brugsch, Dict. Geog., 130, 1121 = [α]λχαι 15/27, O.C. Par. ⲁⲗⲭⲁ̀ⲁ̀ (A. Z., 1883, 104), the necropolis at Abydos where the head of Osiris was preserved. It is spelt with *l*, *'lg-ḥḥ* only once in 15/30, cf. the converse in *gh'l'kter* = χαρακτηρ 5/5.

'm-n. ⲁⲙⲱⲓⲛⲓ, cf. Müller, A. Z., 1893, 50, who suggests that it is cohortative 1st plur. 'let us come,' or for *'m-w n-y*, 'come ye unto me,' with the *n-y* unaccented being reduced to an enclitic, but cf. 11/16 *'m-n n-y*.

l. 8. *nḥe*, 'oil,' and *hne*, 'vessel,' confused in the writing. Parallel passages authorize either.

9\. . . . . . e ze py šn-hne p šn-hne n ᵓS·t pe e-s qte
10\. . . . . . ᵓm n-y a ẖn . . . pe ḥtr ze hb nb . . .
11\. . . . [nte-]k t wn yr·t-f n py ᶜlw a bl ar-w tre-w
12\. . . . . . z ᵓnk pe p pr-ᶜo my-sr sr-my-srpt rn-yt
13\. . . . . . [a]r-k ty n p-hw z ᵓnk pe syt-tᵓ-k stm rn-yt stm
14\. . . . . . hrenwte lᶜppt-t-thᶜ lᵓksnthᶜ sᶜ
15\. . . . . l bwel sp-sn lwtery gᶜsᶜntrᶜ yᶜh-ᶜo
16\. . . . . . [p]šft n t p·t ᵓblᶜnᶜthᶜnᶜlbᶜ p srrf
17\. . . . . . [e·ᵓr-k] zt-f e·ᵓr-k sq n ẖrw-k p mr-ᵓḥ-nfr pe ḥtr

---

l. 10. *ḥtr* here and elsewhere perhaps 'compeller,' meaning him (here Anubis) who compels the gods to do the magician's will.

l. 11. ⲙⲁ. Note this gloss as a variant or correction of *nte-k ty*, also in l. 18.

l. 12. *z ᵓnk.* For the essentially Egyptian identification of the utterer of the spell with his god see DIETERICH, Abraxas, p. 136 note, and cf. Iambl. de Myst. vi. 6.

p pr-ᶜo my-sr, cf. the corrupt *τον μουισδρω τον αναξ* Leyd. Pap. Gr. V. ix. 11–12.

sr-my-srpt. The same signs recur grouped together in varying order as a divine appellative in 9/6 and 11/8. The knife  and hide  are the zodiacal signs of Leo and Aries (BRUGSCH, Nouv. Rech., p. 22); the flower or seed-head is the peculiar determinative of the ⲥⲁⲣⲡⲟⲧ throughout this papyrus. The same divine name, composed of a lotus bud (?)  with lion and spelt-out name of ram (*srìw*), occurs in LEPS., Todt., cap. 162, l. 5, variants giving *srpd* for the lotus bud (?) (BR., Wtb., 1265) and *mᵓy* for the lion (Leyd. Lijkpap., No. 16). Cf. also PLEYTE, Chapitres Suppl., Pl. 14 and 131. The group of a lotus leaf, lion, and ram is figured on several hypocephali, the best example being in BUDGE, Lady Meux Cat., 2nd ed., Pl. VI. Cf. PLEYTE, ib. text, Pl. opp. p. 60. Probably none of these instances are earlier than the Persian invasion. Outside our papyrus the normal order is evidently lotus-lion-ram, and Greek versions agree with this: Brit. Mus. Pap. CXXI. l. 499 *εγω ειμι ο εν τω Πηλουσιω καθϊδρυμενος Σερφουθ: μουϊσρω*: (so facs.), similarly l. 557; in Leyd. Pap. V. col. 3 a, l. 6, the spelling is varied and corrupt. In each case *σερφουθ* is marked off from *μουισρω*, the latter appearing as one word. On a gnostic gem in the Wilson Collection belonging to Aberdeen University is the legend:—*σερφουθ μουισρω λαιλαμ δος μοι χαριν πραξιν νεικην.* In this combination the lotus (ⲥⲁⲣⲡⲟⲧ, see below, 2/17), the lion (ⲙⲟⲩⲓ, see below, 5/11), and the ram (ⲥⲣⲟ, see below, 11/8 and 14/13, and decan names in BR., Wtb. Suppl., 995) probably all represent solar attributes.

rn-yt. This abnormal spelling apparently arises from a combination

(oil); cause to succeed (9) . . . . for this vessel-divination is the vessel-divination of Isis, when she sought (10) . . . . come in to me, O my compeller (?), for everything (11) . . . . and cause the eyes of this child to be opened to them all, (12) . . . . for I am the Pharaoh Lion-ram; Ram-lion-lotus is my name (13) . . . . to thee here to-day, for I am Sit-ta-ko, Setem is my name, Setem (14) [is my true name, &c.] Hrenoute, Lapptotha, Laxantha, Sa-(15)[risa, &c.] . . . . . . Bolbouel (*bis*), Louteri, (Klo-)Kasantra, Iaho (16) [is my name, &c., Balkam the] dread (?) one of heaven, Ablanathanalba, the gryphon (17) [of the shrine of God, &c.].' [You] say it, drawling (?) with your

---

of the earlier *rn-y* and the later form found in O. C. Par. ⲉⲣⲉⲛⲧ (A. Z., 1900, 89, cf. Boh. ⲉⲣⲉⲛⲕ Hyv. Actes, 108). Cf. 14/2 *yrt-yt*.

l. 13. Lines 13–17 are repeated with the missing passages complete in verso XXVII, which is written on the back of this and the following column.

syt-tꜣ-k. The first element is written as the 'serpent' ⲥⲓⲧ in the parallel text and *k* is bull (ⲕⲟ, 7/33), but *tꜣ* seems meaningless. It may possibly be 'the impregnator of the cow,' cf. BUDGE, Nesiamsu, iii. 6, *pꜣ kꜣ sty m kꜣ·wt*. In PARTHEY, Zwei gr. Zauberpap., i. 252, we have practically the same phrase introduced into an O. C. context which gives an entirely different meaning, 'I am Osiris whom Set destroyed,' ⲡⲉⲛⲧⲁⲥⲏⲧ ⲧⲁⲕⲟ(ϥ); see ERMAN, A. Z., 1883, 109 note.

stm, i.e. 'hearing,' or perhaps 'hearer,' but the personal determinative is absent.

l. 15. *Kasantra* alone without ⲕⲗⲟ appears in the demotic of both texts, suggesting a reminiscence of the prophetess Cassandra.

l. 16. *srrf* the hieroglyphic *sfr* of II Beni Hasan, Pl. IV, a winged quadruped with raptorial beak. The *srrf* is described in Kufi, xv. 1 seq., as 'the image (?) of god (?), the king (?) of all that is in the world, the avenger that cannot (himself) be punished; his beak is that of the falcon, his eyes those of a man, his limbs of a lion, his ears of a . . . , his scales of a water- . . . , his tail a serpent's.' Further, he is the mightiest of beings next to God, has authority over everything on earth like Death, and is the instrument of God's vengeance.

l. 17. *sq*, cf. 6/19 for the complete phrase. The meaning 'drawl' is not quite certain. It must be some artificial way of speaking, such as whining or muttering, cf. 7/32 and Leyd. Pap. Gr. W. col. 1, l. 38, col. 3. l. 2, and φθογγος αναγκαστικος, &c., Brit. Mus. Gr. Pap. CXXI. 765 seq.

18. . . . . . a šnt-k ar-f ty n p-hw nte-k t wn yr·t-f n py ʿ[lw]

19. . . . . . nb nte-k nḥm py ʿlw nte ḥr-f pẖ[t a py]

20. . . . . . n ntr ḥry-t p-sepe-n-p-t ḥry-t . . . .

21. . . . . . ank pe Ḥr ʾMn nt ḥms a py šn-hne ty n p[-hw]

22. . . . . . py šn-hne ty n p-hw mʿryghʿry e·ʾr-k . . . .

23. . . . . . nte-w z pe šn n-y z n-w sp-sn n ntr·w nt wʿb n p nwn

24. . . . . . n t n rn nte n ntr·w n Kmy ẖʿ ẖr n gpe·w

25. . . . . . thʿr z ank tʿ-py-šteh-ʿy n t n rn

26. . . . . . t wz-k p pr-ʿo pešʿm-ʿy nt ḥtp ḥr r

27. . . . . . ny ẖpš·w n nb n mʿ·t t mʿ·t n r-y p ʾbye

28. . . . . thʿ z ank pe stel yʿh-ʿo wn-t

Col. II.

1. e·ʾr-k z n p ẖm-ẖl z a·wn n yr·t-k e-f wn yr·t-f nte-f nw a p wyn e·ʾr-k t ʾr-f ʿš

2. z ʿw sp-sn p wyn pyr sp-sn p wyn θse sp-sn p wyn ẖy sp-sn p wyn p nt n bl

3. ʾm a ẖn e-f ẖp nte-f wn yr·t-f nte-f tm nw a p wyn e·ʾr-k t ʾr-f ẖtm yr·t-f

---

p-mr-ʾḫ pronounced *p-le-ehe*, produces the common Ptolemaic proper name Πελαιας, as is proved by a bilingual (Spiegelberg, Strassb. Pap. No. 21, text, pp. 21–2, the reading *P-ers* to be corrected to *p-mr-ʾḫ*; the Greek nominative shown in Grenf. Amh. Pap. LI. 5). The religious significance of this appellation, 'the good oxherd,' is not clear, nor has it been traced in early texts; from 2/7 it is clearly applied to Anubis, and perhaps dogs were used for herding cattle in Ancient Egypt? It is probably equivalent to Gk. *ποιμην*, for which see Goodwin, Cambridge Essays, 1852, p. 26, B. M. Gr. Pap. XLVI, l. 31. If the Good Shepherd is the meaning, we may note the Χριστος Ανουβις of Leyd. Pap. Gr. V. vi. 17.

l. 19. *nḥm* written with the lotus bud, cf. Br., Wtb., 796–7.

l. 20. **ⲣⲉⲧ**. In the writing of the glosses the aspirate is suppressed before **ⲣ**, even in 19/19 **ⲡⲣⲁⲧ** for *p-ḫrt*, so also 16/7 **ⲕⲁⲣⲣⲏ**, 28/9 **ⲣⲟⲇⲟⲣ** 29/14 **ⲣⲁⲃⲱⲧ**, V. 33/3 **ⲁⲣⲁⲉⲓ**. The initial demotic group *ḫry* is seen in

voice: 'O beautiful oxherd, my compeller, (18) . . . . ask thee about here to-day: and do thou cause the eyes of this boy to be opened (19) . . . . and do thou protect this boy whose face is bent down [over this (20) vessel] . . . . . of god, lord of earth, the survivor (?) of the earth, lord of earth . . . . (21) . . . . I am Hor-Amon that sitteth at this vessel-divination here to-day (22) . . . . this vessel-divination here to-day; Marikhari, thou . . . . (23) . . . . and that they tell me my inquiry. Say to them (*bis*) "O holy gods of the abyss (24) . . . . . [I am] . . . . of earth by name, under the soles [of] whose [feet?] the gods of Egypt are placed (25) . . . . thar, for I am Ta-pishtehei of earth by name (26) . . . . preserve thee, O Pharaoh, Pashamei that resteth at the mouth (?) (27) . . . . these shoulders of real gold. Truth is in (?) my mouth, honey (28) [is in my lips?] . . . . . . Ma . . . tha for I am Stel, Iaho, Earth-opener."'

Col. II.

(1) You say to the boy 'Open your eyes'; when he opens his eyes and sees the light, you make him cry out, (2) saying 'Grow (*bis*), O light, come forth (*bis*) O light, rise (*bis*) O light, ascend (*bis*) O light, thou who art without, (3) come in.' If he opens his eyes and does

---

Ptolemaic proper names commencing with Φρι- 'sheikh' = *p-ḥry-*. The pronunciation here would be *ḥri-to* rather than **рєт**, unless the spelling is fanciful.

l. 21. Hor-Amon is known in figures of glazed pottery (Lanzone, Diz. Mit., 601).

l. 23. *sp-sn*. It seems probable that this group may be used simply as a mark of emphasis, e.g. after *m šs*, 'exceedingly,' and here after the imperative 'say to them!' It can hardly mean 'say to them twice.'

l. 26. *ḥr r*, or 'opposite,' as in Coptic **ϩιрєн-**.

l. 27. *'bye*, cf. 9/16: or perhaps, 'The truth of my mouth [is] the honey [of my lips].'

4. e·ʾr-k ʿš ar-f n whm z-mt·t p kke a·ʿl-k n ḥ·t-f p wyn a·ʾny p wyn n-y a ẖn

5. p šʿy nt ẖn p nwn a·ʾny p wyn n-y a ẖn Wsr nt ḥr nšme·t a·ʾny p wyn n-y

6. a ẖn py IV tw nt n bl a·ʾny p wyn n-y a ẖn p nte p šp pa ny wne·t·w n t·t-f a (*sic*)

7. a·ʾny p wyn n-y a ẖn ʾNp p-mr-ʾḥ nfr a·ʾny p wyn n-y a ẖn z e·ʾr-k

8. a t s-ʿo ar-y ty n p-hw z ʾnk Ḥr s ʾS·t p s nfr n Wsr e·ʾr-k a ʾny n ntr·w n t s·t

9. wype e·ʾr-k a t ʾr-w ʾr n pe hb n-se t mšʿe(?) te·t yp·t Ne-tbew e·ʾr-k a ty ʾr-w ʾr nʾm-s

10. z(?) . . . . twrʿm-ne ʿm-ne ʿ·ʿ mes sp-sn ʿo-rnw-ʿo-rf sp-sn ʿo-rnw-ʿo-rf sp-sn pʿh-ʿo-r-f

11. . . . . . pʿh-r-f y-ʿo qwy n stn tw-ḥr my wz py ʿlw nte ḥr-f pḫte a py

12. nḥ[e nte-k(?)] t pḥ(?) n-y Sbk šʿ nte-f pyr stm rn-yt stm pe pe rn n mt z ʾnk

13. l . . [m] . . . . . t twlot tʿt pyntʿt pe rn n mt p ntr ʿo nte ne·ʿw rn-f

---

Col. II.

l. 4. *a·ʿl-k.* The *a* is an addition above the line. *ʿl-k* would be ⲟⲗ=ⲕ, but the *a* prefixed suggests *ⲁⲗⲓ=ⲕ on the analogy of ⲁⲗⲓ, hardly ⲁⲗⲟ=ⲕ 'cease,' cf. St., § 384. The gloss may of course be incomplete, like some others.

a·ʾny, the same formula in O. C. Par. ⲉⲛⲓ ⲥⲁⲃⲁⲱⲑ ⲛⲁⲓ ⲉϩⲟⲩⲛ A. Z., 1900, p. 87.

l. 5. *p šʿy* O. C. Par. ⲡϭⲟⲓ A. Z., 1883, p. 105: 1900, 92 and ⲯⲟⲓ ib. 93 from Pap. Bibl. Nat. l. 1643. A god whose name often occurs in Graeco-Egyptian names, Σενψαις, &c. (cf. Spiegelberg, Demot. Stud., i. p. 57*), and in the titles of Antoninus Pius was translated ἀγαθοδαίμων. In the older texts (*Šʾy*) he seems to be mainly a god of destiny (Lanz., Diz. Mit., 1185).

p šʿy nt ẖn p nwn = ο μεγας δαιμων ο φνουνοχθονιος, B. M. Pap. XLVI. 239.

nšme·t, the bark of Osiris: see Rec. trav., xvi. 105 seq., esp. p. 121.

l. 6. *šp.* The meaning is very uncertain. It might be 'the ruling star,' cf. Leyd. Pap. Gr. W. col. 9, l. 36 ἐπικάλου τὸν τῆς ὥρας καὶ τὸν τῆς ἡμέρας θεόν.

not see the light, you make him close his eyes, (4) you call to him again; formula: 'O darkness, remove thyself from before him (*sic*)! O light, bring the light in to me! (5) Pshoi that is in the abyss, bring in the light to me! O Osiris, who is in the Nesheme-boat, bring in the light to me! (6) these four winds that are without, bring in the light to me! O thou in whose hand is the moment(?) that belongeth to these hours (7) bring in the light to me! Anubis, the good oxherd, bring in the light to me! for thou (8) shalt give protection (?) to me here to-day. For I am Horus son of Isis, the good son of Osiris; thou shalt bring the gods of the place (9) of judgement, and thou shalt cause them to do my business, and they shall make my affair proceed; Netbeou, thou shalt cause them to do it. (10) For [I am ?] Touramnei, Amnei, A-a, Mes (*bis*), Ornouorf (*bis*), Ornouorf (*bis*), Pahorof, (11) . . . . Pahrof, Io, a little (?) king, Touhor; let this child prosper, whose face is bent down to this (12) oil [and thou shalt] escort (?) Souchos to me until he come forth. Setem is my name, Setem is my correct name. For I am (13) L[ot], M[oulo]t, Toulot, Tat,

---

l. 8. cω may be only magical gibberish, but suggests the word for 'protection,' 'amulet.'

l. 9. *wype*, the gods of the place of judgement are presumably the numerous gods of Egypt who assisted at the judgement of the dead. Cf. V. 33/2.

Ne-tbew, a deity (?) unknown except in the proper name Παυετβευς, GRENF. Pap. Tebt. No. 88, l. 20 (B.C. 115–4). There are said to be sixteen of them in V. 33/5 q. v.

mšʿ, of an inanimate object in a transferred sense.

l. 11. *qwy n stn*, perhaps only gibberish, to be pronounced *kouiens* (?).

l. 12. *pḥ* or perhaps *še*.

Sbk. It seems curious that the very well-defined god Souchos should be asked for when Anubis is the one really required: doubtless he might be supposed to dwell in the liquid oil.

rn-yt, &c. Cf. O. C. Par. ερεnτ . . . πε πα ρεn ñ ꞁꞁнт (A. Z., 1884, pp. 23–4, 1900, p. 89). *το ονομα το αληθινον* B. M. Pap. XLVI. 115.

l. 13. Lot Moulot may perhaps be the missing words, cf. 18/13.

14. wnḥ a py ʿlw aph-ʿo-b-ʿo-s ʿpsewst-ʿo-s epʿletsyʿ e·ʾr-k ʿš ny

15. sḫ·w n sp VII e·ʾr-k t ʾr-f wn yr·t-f nte p wyn aʿny nte-f z ʾNp ʾy a ḫn e·ʾr-k ʿš ḥ·t-f

16. z-mt·t ʾy ryz mw ryz ʾy t wr t ʾy py ḥwt nfr a·ms heryew t šr·t n t neme·t

17. ʾm n-y z nte-k py sšn ʾr pyr ḫn t srpt n p nws-t-r nt ʾr wyn a p t tre-f

18. hy ʾNp ʾm n-y p ḫy p zr p ḥry-sšt n na t ty·t p pr-ʿo n na ʾmnt p wr syn

19. . . nfr n Wsr p nḫt ḥr-f ʾwt n ntr·w e·ʾr-k ḫʿ n t ty·t ne-ḥr t·t-f n Wsr e·ʾr-k šms

20. [n] by n ʾBt z e-w ʿnḫ nʾm-k tre·w ny by·w na ty·t tsre·t ʾm a p t wnḥ-k ar-y

---

l. 14. *aph-ʿo-b-ʿo-s*, &c. As the glosses show this is merely a transcription of the Greek words *ἀφόβως ἀψεύστως ἐπ' ἀληθείᾳ*, and to mark this the determinative of that which is foreign is placed at the end of each word. It is interesting to find the initial letter /, here and in 10/30, representing the Gk. *α*, and so indicating that that was its normal pronunciation. In Achm. it corresponds to ⲁ, rarely ⲉ, in Sah. and Boh. to ⲉ, rarely ⲁ. ⲉ is probably a wearing down or shortening of the earlier ⲁ.

l. 15. *aʿny*, a peculiar writing (as if *a·ʿn-y*) for ⲁⲛⲁⲓ, occurring also in I Kham. v. 14 *.

16. *ʾy*. The sign represents  and is transcribed ⲏⲓ twice 7/24, 16/9. This can hardly be the pronunciation of the interjection . The usual interjection in religious texts is 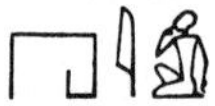 which occurs here frequently spelt , but we consider  to be distinct from *hy*.

ryz mw ryz, cf. 18/13 *lot mw lot*, 27/5 *rw my rw*, V. 12/3 *lyl mw lyl*.

neme·t apparently a goddess, perhaps of destruction: usually this

---

* The group for *ʿny* is that which spells *ne-ʿne* (ⲛⲁⲛⲟⲩ=) in ordinary texts, but here the *ne* is superfluous, and in this papyrus a false *ne* is always written before *ʿne*, so that ⲛⲁⲛⲟⲩ= has to be written out *ne*(*-ne*)*-ʿne*. In other texts as well as this we find *ne-nfr* with a false *ne-*, probably due to the initial sound of *nfr*, and this may have led to the otiose *ne* before *ʿne* in the present text.

Peintat is my correct name. O great god whose name is great, (14) appear to this child without alarming or deceiving, truthfully.' You utter these (15) charms seven times, you make him open his eyes. If the light is good and he says 'Anubis is coming in,' you call before him (Anubis). (16) Formula: 'O Riz Muriz, O To-ur-to, O this beautiful male born of Herieou, the daughter of the Neme, (17) Come to me, for thou art this lotus-flower that came forth from in the lotus of Pnastor, and that illuminates the whole earth; (18) hail! Anubis, come to me, the High, the Mighty, the Chief over the mysteries of those in the Underworld, the Pharaoh of those in Amenti, the Chief Physician, (19) the fair [son ?] of Osiris, he whose face is strong among the gods, thou manifestest thyself in the Underworld before the hand of Osiris. Thou servest (20) the souls of Abydos, for they all live by thee, these souls (namely) those of the sacred Underworld. Come to the earth, show thyself to me

---

name is attached to the execution-block, but here it has the determinative of fire.

l. 17. Cf. Horus on the lotus at Erment L. D. iv. 61, g. 65; and in Greek papyri, *εχεις μορφην νηπιου παιδος επι λωτω καθημενος* PARTHEY, Zwei gr. Zauberpap., ii. 106; *ο επι του λωτου καθημενος και λαμπυριδων την ολην οικουμενην* Leyd. Pap. Gr. V. iii. 15.

sšn, *srpt*, see LORET, Rec. trav., i. 190, for a useful but by no means final discussion of the Egyptian names of the lotus. *srpt* (see 1/12) is a name apparently of late introduction, *sšn* is very ancient, and both words are to be paralleled, with varied meaning, in Semitic languages. From this passage one may conjecture that *srpt* is the lotus bud and *sšn* the flower.

l. 18. *wr syn*, 'chief physician,' an old Egyptian official title (O. K. in P. S. B. A., xi. 306, Persian period BRUGSCH., Thes., 639), but amongst the gods most applicable to Thoth. Apparently Thoth and Anubis are here united, cf. the name Hermanubis and l. 21. *ḥry-sšt*, 'chief over the mysteries,' is another old title appropriate enough for either Thoth or Anubis.

l. 20. 'For they all live by thee.' Apparently Anubis was responsible for the provision of food and attendance on the souls.

21. ty n p-hw nte-k Tḥwt nte-k p e·ʾr pyr n ḥt-f n p šʿy ʿo p yt·w sp-sn n n ntr·w tre·w ʾm a r n r·w

22. n pe hne n p-hw nte-k z n-y wḥ n mt·t mʿ·t ẖr mt·t nb nt e-y šn ẖr-w e·mn mt·t n ʿze nʾm-w z ʾnk ʾS·t

23. t rẖe·t nte n z n r-y ẖp z-mt sp VII e·ʾr-k z n p ẖm-ẖl ze a·zy-s n ʾNp z

24. mšʿ a bl a·ʾny n ntr·w a ẖn e-f mšʿ m-s-w nte-f ʾnyt-w a ẖn e·ʾr-k šn p ʿlw z ḥr n ntr·w

25 ʾy a ẖn e-f z ḥr-w ʾy nte-k nw ar-w e·ʾr-k ʿš ḥ·t-w z-mt·t nhe-k n-y sp-sn p šʿy nhs·t-k merʿ

26. p wr-ty tsytsyw tnnzyw a·ʾry mt ar-y Tḥwt my ʾre qme mḥ p t n wyn hb

27. m ḥr-f šps šps ʿq a p ḥt my t ẖp t mʿ·t p ntr ʿo nte ne·ʿw rn-f z sp VII

28 e·ʾr-k z n p ẖm-ẖl z a·zy-s n ʾNp z a·ʾny wʿ tks a ẖn ẖr n ntr·w my ḥms-w e-w

---

l. 21. *p yt·w sp-sn* is intended to be read *p yt yt·w* as 8/2. Cf. the common appellation *προπατωρ* in the Gk. papyri. 'Father of the fathers of all the gods' occurs perhaps as early as the N. K. in Boul. Pap. No. 17, p. 7, l. 6 (Hymn to Amon-Re).

l. 22. *nte-k z n-y wḥ.* For this formula cf. O. C. Par. ⲡ̄ⲥⲉϫⲓ ⲟⲩⲱ ⲛⲁⲓ ⲁϥⲫⲱϧ ⲉⲧⲓϫⲛⲟⲩ ⲙ̄ⲙⲟⲟⲩ ⲉⲣⲟϩ (*sic*) (A. Z., 1900, 89). *εισελθε και χρηματισον* B. M. Pap. XLVI. 445. *šn*, lit. 'inquire,' is used vaguely, both of the inquiry and of the answer in this papyrus, as *χρηματιζειν* in Greek. ϣⲓⲛⲓ ϭⲁ in Copt. is 'beg for,' not 'ask a question'; possibly it has such a meaning here.

l. 24. *ḥr n ntr·w ʾy*, &c.=*(ϩ)ⲁⲛⲛⲧⲏⲣ ⲉⲓ . . . *(ϩ)ⲁⲩ ⲉⲓ (see chapter on grammar in vol. ii).

l. 25. 'And you see them' is an addition above the line which does not seem appropriate, as the boy, not the magician, is to see them.

nhe-k . . . nhs·t-k: the defective spelling *nhe* is found again in the papyrus, leaving no doubt that it represents *nhse*, 'waken,' 'raise.' The verb is 'ivtae infirmae' according to SETHE, and the suffix form, lost in Coptic, shows here a curious uncertainty as to the retention of the *t*.

l. 26. *wr-ty.* Originally the title of the high priest of Thoth at Hermopolis Magna (Khmun), it was perhaps applied later to the ibis-god himself (e. g. LEGRAIN, Livre des transf., iv. 5). Evidently in connexion with this, Thoth is called 'the god five times great (*ʿo*), the mighty (*wr*) lord of Khmun' (II MAHAFFY, Petrie Pap. Pl. 13, II Kham.

(21) here to-day. Thou art Thoth, thou art he that came forth from the heart of the great Agathodaemon, the father of the fathers of all the gods; come to the mouths (22) of my vessel to-day and do thou tell me answer in truth to everything that I shall inquire about, without falsehood therein; for I am Isis (23) the Wise, the words of whose mouth of mine (*sic*) come to pass.' Formula: seven times. You say to the boy 'Speak to Anubis, saying (24) "Go forth, bring in the gods."' When he goes after them and brings them in, you ask the boy, saying 'Have the gods (25) come in?' If he says 'They have come' and you (*sic*) see them, you cry before them. Formula: 'Raise thyself for me (*bis*), Pshoi; raise thyself, Mera (26), the Great of Five, Didiou, Tenziou, do justice to me. Thoth, let creation (?) fill the earth with light; O (thou who art an) ibis in (27) his noble countenance, thou noble one that enters the heart, let truth be brought forth, thou great god whose name is great.' Say seven times. (28) You say to the boy 'Speak to Anubis, saying "Bring in a table for the

---

5, 7). The common Ptolemaic name Πορτις (cf. GRENFELL, Gk. Pap. I, II; Amherst Pap.; WILCKEN, Gr. Ostr.) in the witnesses of the Grey antigraph (Brit. Mus. Gr. Pap. I. Pl. 27) is *P-wr-ty* in the corresponding Berlin demotic Pap. 3119 verso (Berl. Dem. Pap. Pl. 16). Πορτις is no doubt founded on an abbreviated pronunciation of the name which we have here with its full value *P-wer-tiu*. In V. 33/2 we have the normal orthography of the title, varied here and in 22/1.

my 're qme. Meaning very uncertain; if the dot after *qme* be taken as closing the phrase, the *'r* must be regarded as passive in meaning 'let a creation (?) be made,' cf. 5/22 *my wn yr·t* and GRIFF., High Priests, p. 87, n. to l. 6, and SETHE, Verb., ii. § 247, and *mḥ* following the dot suggests an imperative. Perhaps *Mareqom* (?) is to be taken as a magical name.

l. 27. *ʿq a p ḥt*, perhaps may be participial rather than imperative. *ʿq r ḥt*, lit. 'enter the heart,' is common in early demotic in the sense of 'please.' Cf. ⲁⲕϩⲧⲏ= (SPIEGELB., Rec. trav., xxiii. 201) ⲱⲕ ⲛ̄ ϩⲏⲧ (BSCIAI, ib., vii. 27).

29. ḥms e·ʾr-k z a·ʾny wʿ ʾrp a ẖn klp-f a n ntr·w a·ʾny hyn·w t a ẖn my wm-w my swr-w

Col. III.

1. my wm-w my swr-w my ʾr-w hw nfr e-w wḥ e·ʾr-k z n ʾNp z ʿnn (*sic*) e·ʾr-k šn n-y e-f z t ḥ·t e·ʾr-k z n-f z p ntr nt ne ʾr pe šn

2. n p-hw my ʾr-f ʿḥ e rt-f e-f z ʿḥ-f e·ʾr-k z n-f z a·zy-s n ʾNp z fy n nk n t mte e·ʾr-k ʿš

3. ḥ·t-f ty hte·t z p šʿy n p-hw p nb n p-hw p nte pe-f pe ny wne·t·w e·ʾr-k t ʾr-f zt-s

4. n ʾNp z p ntr nt ne šn n-y n p-hw my ʾr-f z n-y rn-f e-f ʿḥ a rt-f nte-f z rn-f e.ʾr-k šn·t-f

5. a mt·t nb nt e·ʾr-k wẖ-f pe-f swḥ-ʾyẖ ẖr ʾny-k tbe VII nmy e b-ʾr te-w qym nʾm-w a pnʿ-w

6. a p ke ḥr e·ʾr-k fy·t-w e·ʾr-k wʿb n wš n zḥ-w a nte(?) nb n p t nte-k smne·t-w n pe-w ky e·wne-w

7. smne·t nʾm-f ʿn nte-k smne tbe III ẖr p nḥe t k·t tbe·t IV nte-k sʿr-w n p qt n p ẖm-ẖl(?) n wš n

8. zḥ ʿe·t nte-f a p ʾytn nge bʿe VII nte-k ʾr-w n py smte ʿn nte-k ʾny t VII e-w wʿb

9. nte-k sʿr-w n p qte n p nḥe erme tyk VII n ḥm nte-k ʾny wʿ·t bʾtʾne·t nmy nte-k mḥ-s n

---

l. 29. *wʿ ʾrp*, 'a (vessel of) wine,' probably the κεραμιον of the Rosetta stone: cf. the use of *ḥt*, 'silver,' in contracts = *tbn*.

Col. III.

l. 1. *ʾr hw nfr*: from this and other passages it is clear that the actual meaning of this common expression is not to pass a day of pleasure, but simply 'enjoy oneself.'

ʾNp would seem to be an error for *p ẖm-ẖl*, 'the boy.'

t ḥ-t, probably as we say 'the first thing,' 'at once.'

l. 2. *n t mte*, 'from the midst,' i. e. of the gods seated at the meal.

l. 3. *p-hw . . . ny wne·t·w*, cf. note on 2/6.

l. 5. *swḥ-ʾyẖ*, lit. 'spirit-gathering,' is the title for the material arrangements for divination as to locality, censing, salves, &c., to be employed, not the invocations.

Egyptian bricks are crude. The use of burnt brick was introduced by the Romans and increased to Byzantine times, but crude brick remained throughout the principal building material.

gods, and let them sit."' When they (29) are seated, you say 'Bring in a (jar of) wine, broach it for the gods; bring in some bread, let them eat, let them drink,'

Col. III.

(1) 'let them eat, let them drink, let them pass a festal day.' When they have finished, you speak to Anubis (*sic*) saying 'Dost thou make inquiry for me?' If he says 'At once,' you say to him 'The god who will make my inquiry (2) to-day, let him stand up.' If he says 'He has stood up,' you say to him (i.e. the child) 'Say to Anubis "Carry off the things from the midst"'; you cry (3) before him (i.e. the god) instantly saying 'O Agathodaemon of to-day, lord of to-day, O thou whose (possession) these moments are!' You cause him (the boy) to say (4) to Anubis 'The god who will inquire for me to-day, let him tell me his name.' When he stands up and tells his name, you ask him (5) concerning everything that you wish.

Its spirit-gathering. You take seven new bricks, before they have been moved so as to turn them (6) to the other face; you take them, you being pure, without touching them against anything on earth, and you place them in their manner in which they were (7) placed, again; and you place three tiles under the oil; and the other four tiles, you arrange them about the child without (8) touching any part of him against the ground; or seven palm-sticks, you treat them in this fashion also. And you take seven clean loaves (9) and arrange them around the oil, with seven lumps of salt,

---

l. 6. *nte nb.* The reading not quite certain, but extremely probable.

l. 7. *p qt.* The usual group for *qt* is very much abbreviated, and is thus identical with that for *wḥ*, 'wish,' but there can be little doubt of the reading. The meaning must be that the bricks are laid about the boy so that he can stand or sit on them without touching the ground.

l. 9. *tyk* can scarcely be other than Sah. ⲧⲁϭ. The otiose *y* may be

10. nḥe n whe e-f wʿb nte-k t a t bʿtʿne·t ḫm sp-sn n wš n t ḫp hʿyse nte-f ḫp e-f stf

11. m šs sp-sn nte-k ʾny wʿ ḫm-ḫl e-f wʿb e b-ʾr te-f še erme s-ḥm·t e·ʾr-k sze a ḫry ḫn zz-f

12. e-f ʿḥ a rt-f a t ḥ·t z ʿn e-f a ʾr šw n še a p hne e-f ḫp e-f ʾr šw e·ʾr-k t str-f a ḥr ḫe·t-f

13. e·ʾr-k ḥbs-f n wʿ·t šnt·t n ʿyw·t e-s wʿb e·ʾr-k ʿš a ḫry ḫn zz-f e wn wʿ ryt n t ry·t ḥry-f (*sic* ?)

14. n t šnt·t e·ʾr-k ʿš py ʿš nt ḥry a ḫry ḫn zz-f e-f kšp a ḫry nw a ḫn p nḥe šʿ sp VII e yr·t-f

15. ḫtm e·ʾr-k wḥ e·ʾr-k t ʾr-f wn yr·t-f e·ʾr-k šn·t-f a p nte ʾr-k wḥ-f ḫr ʾr-k-f šʿ p nw n p *θ* VII n p hw

16. p ʿš nte ʾr-k ʿš-w (*sic*) a ḫry ḫn zz-f n ḥ·t a znt-f n ne-f msz·w z ʿn e-f a ʾr šw n še ḫr

17. p hne z-mt·t hb šps nšr bk šps apḥte·t my wʿb-y mw ky hb šps nšr

18. bk šps apḥte·t e·ʾr-k ʿš n·y a ḫry ḫn zz-f šʿ sp VII e·ʾr-k t ʾw ny ḫr

19. mt·t ne-f msz·w e-ḫp nte pe-f msz II mt·t (ne)nfr-f m šs sp-sn e-f ḫp e pe-f msz n

20. wnm(?) pe (ne)nfr-f e-f ḫp e p . . . pe ne-bn-f pḫre·t n pḫr p hne n gtg nte n ntr·w ʾy a ḫn nte-w z

---

compared with that in *byl* for ⲃⲁⲗ 13/12, *P-šylem* (21/3) = O. C. ⲡⲁϭⲁⲗⲱⲙ, and is brought about by such forms as *ʾny·t-k* (root *ʾny*) for *ʾn·t-k*, *my* (ⲙⲟⲓ) ⲙⲁ-, *rn-yt* for *rn-t* (1/12).

l. 10. Oasis oil, cf. 6/2, not mentioned elsewhere; a kind of 'real oil,' but not identical with it 25/12.

ḫm sp-sn must be read *ḫmḫm*, C. ϣⲏⲙϣⲏⲙ, cf. 2/21, 18/13, 24/12.

hʿyse, meaning quite uncertain: cf. perhaps *ḥsyse* in I Kham. 6/19, II Kham. 6/16.

l. 12. *a ḥr ḫe·t-f*, a curious expression, 'on the face of (?) his belly,' cf. the use of *ḥr* in l. 6.

l. 13. *šnt·t n ʿyw·t* : Boh. ϣⲉⲛⲧⲱ ⲛⲓⲁϥ (Peyron), cf. *σινδὼν βυσσίνη* Hdt. ii. 86. The Egyptian *šnd·t* was the loin-cloth or tunic, and in this papyrus it still seems to signify a dress, though in Coptic it can be used simply for 'cloth.' Cf. Pap. Bibl. Nat. l. 88 (A. Z., 1883, 99) and Brit. Mus. Pap. Gr. No. XLVI. l. 206, for the use of *σινδων* in magic.

Omit the words 'you call down into his head.'

and you take a new dish and fill it with (10) clean Oasis oil and add to the dish gradually without producing cloudiness (?) so that it becomes clear (11) exceedingly; and you take a boy, pure, before he has gone with a woman, you speak down into his head (12) while he stands, previously, (to learn) whether he will be profitable in going to the vessel. If he is profitable, you make him lie on (?) his belly; (13) you clothe (?) him with a clean linen tunic (?), ⟨you call down into his head⟩, there being a girdle on the upper part (14) of the tunic; you utter this invocation that is above, down into his head, he gazing downwards ⟨looking⟩ into the oil, for seven times, his eyes being (15) closed. When you have finished, you make him open his eyes, you ask him about what you desire; you do it until the time of the seventh hour of the day.

(16) The invocation that you utter down into his head previously to test him in his ears as to whether he will be profitable in going to (17) the vessel. Formula: 'Noble ibis, falcon, hawk, noble and mighty, let me be purified in the manner of the noble ibis, falcon, (18) hawk, noble and mighty.' You utter this down into his head for seven times; when you utter this, then (19) his ears speak. If his two ears speak, he is very good; if it be his right ear, (20) he is good; if it be his left ear, he is bad.

Prescription for enchanting the vessel quickly so that

---

l. 14. Omit 'looking' as corrected by the addition above the line.

l. 15. *n p θ VII*: for the reading *θ*, rather than *θ wne·t*, compare V. 24/6. The phrase is evidently to be connected with the Coptic idiom ⲡⲛⲁⲩ ⲛ̄ ϫⲡ̄ⲯⲓⲧⲉ, 'the ninth hour.' ϫⲡ:ⲁϫⲡ are feminine.

l. 19. *e-ḫp*, probably an unique spelling in demotic instead of the usual *e-f ḫp*, for ⲉϣⲱⲡⲉ.

l. 20. The word for left (sinister) cannot yet be transliterated. In Egyptian we have *ỉby* and *smḥ*, in Sah. ϩⲃⲟⲩⲣ and Boh. ϫⲁϭⲏ: in several passages we have *gbyr*, the Achmim. ϭⲃⲓⲣ (Zach. xii. 6, in

21. n-k wḥ n mt·t mʿ·t e·ʾr-k t qwqe n swḥ·t n *мсєϩ* nge p nt ḫn-s a t st·t ḥr pḫre-f ty hte·t pḫre·t a t ʾr-w

22. sze e·ʾr-k t tp n *кроүр* a p ʿḫ ḫr ʾr-w sze pḫre·t a ʾny n ntr·w a ḫn n kns e·ʾr-k t sḫy

23. n msḥ ḥr ʿnte sq a p ʿḫ e·ʾr-k wḫ a t ʾr-w ʾy a ḫn n tkr ʿn e·ʾr-k t ḫ n *єміс* e p ʿḫ erme t qwqe

24. n swḥ·t nt ḥry ḫr pḫr-f ty hte e·ʾr-k wḫ a ʾny rm e-f ʿnḫ a ḫn e·ʾr-k t gʾlʾgʾntsy a p ʿḫ ḫr ʾw-f a ḫn

25. e·ʾr-k wḫ a ʾny ʾyḫ a ḫn e·ʾr-k t s-wr ḥr ʾny(?) n ylḫ a p ʿḫ ḫr ʾw p ʾyḫ a ḫn e·ʾr-k t ḥt

26. n hyt·t nge wn·t(?) nfr sp·sn e·ʾr-k wḫ a ʾny ḥsy a ḫn e·ʾr-k t gʿlʿb n yʿm a p ʿḫ

27. e·ʾr-k wḫ a ʾny rm e-f mwt a ḫn e·ʾr-k t hs n *єо* ḥr s Nb·t-ḥ·t a p ʿḫ ḫr ʾw-f a ḫn e·ʾr-k

28. wḫ a t še(-w) n-w tre·w e·ʾr-k t hs n *єн* a p ʿḫ ḫr ʾr-w še n-w a pe-w mʿ tre-w nte-k ʿš pe-w r n wt-w ʿn(?)

Pap. Rain. Mitth. ii. 266); *gbyr* may possibly be connected with ϩⲃⲟⲩⲣ and with the demotic ligature here; or *ḫmr* may be the reading of the latter.

l. 22. *tp*. Two portions of the body are written *tp* in the demotic of this papyrus. One has the det. of bone as well as that of flesh, and is undoubtedly ⲧⲁⲡ, 'horn,' Eg.  · Without the det. of bone we have the *tp* of an ass or a hoopoe, which presumably means the head or skull; in other cases, e.g. 19/26, one may doubt whether horn ⲧⲁⲡ is not intended by the same group.

l. 23. *sq*, written with the crocodile, presumably = ⲥⲓⲕⲉ; see the verb in Brugsch, Rec., iv. Pl. 97, l. 16, and as a participle attached to a word meaning incense, ib., Pl. 85 A, ll. 3, 7, and 11; Pl. 96, l. 6.

ⲉⲙⲓⲥ suggests ⲉⲙⲓⲥⲉ : ⲁⲙⲓⲥⲓ, i. e. 'anise,' or according to some MSS. 'mint,' Loret, Flore Phar., 2nd ed. pp. 53, 71; and it seems possible that the tall dry stalks of the anise (as opposed to the commonly prescribed seeds) should be denoted by *ḫ*, lit. 'wood.'

l. 24. *gʾlʾgʾntsy* with gloss ⲕⲁⲗⲁⲕⲁⲛⲑⲓ suggests κολοκύνθις; but as the determinative here indicates a mineral and not a plant, it must be intended for χαλκάνθη, 'sulphate of copper,' which is written χαλάκανθον in Leyd. Pap. X. 1, 3.

l. 25. *ʾyḫ*, 'spirit' of a dead person, or a 'demon': the Gk. δαίμων, which may be good or bad (Pap. Bibl. Nat. passim). On the Bentresh Stela the demon possessing the princess is *ʾḫ*.

the gods enter and tell (21) you answer truthfully. You put the shell of a crocodile's egg, or that which is inside it, on the flame; it will be enchanted instantly.

Prescription to make them (22) speak: you put a frog's head on the brazier, then they speak.

Prescription for bringing the gods in by force: you put the bile (23) of a crocodile with pounded frankincense on the brazier.

If you wish to make them come in quickly again, you put stalks (?) of anise (?) on the brazier together with the (24) egg-shell as above, then the charm works at once.

If you wish to bring in a living man, you put sulphate of copper on the brazier, then he comes in.

(25) If you wish to bring in a spirit, you put *sa-wr* stone with stone of *ilkh* on the brazier, then the spirit comes in. You put the heart (26) of a hyaena or a hare, excellent (*bis*).

If you wish to bring in a drowned man, you put sea-*karab*-stone (?) on the brazier.

(27) If you wish to bring in a murdered (?) man, you put ass's dung with an amulet of Nephthys on the brazier, then he comes in.

If you (28) wish to make (them) all depart, you put ape's dung on the brazier, then they all depart to their place, and you utter their spell of dismissal also.

---

ylḫ. The *ḫ* is written by a sign common enough in other texts, but in this MS. found only here, and in 6/20 *ḫtn* and 23/29 *ḫlby*.

l. 26. *ḥsy*, 'approved,' 'deified,' as an expression for one drowned or devoured by a crocodile (19/24), cf. Hdt. ii. 90, and note to l. 31.

gʿrʿb n yʿm, 'sea-*karab*,' determined as a mineral can scarcely be κάραβος = 'palinurus vulgaris,' unless its shell be treated as such. Cf. καρκινος ποταμιος in Pap. Bibl. Nat. 2458, 2687. In favour of the sense 'crab' or 'crayfish' we might suppose that it was called 'sea-karab' to distinguish it from the καραβος, 'beetle.'

l. 27. *rm e-f mwt*, ⲣⲉϥⲙⲟⲟⲩⲧ, but perhaps meaning 'murdered man,' not merely a 'dead' man.

l. 28. *še n-w*: this ethical dative adds a certain force to the word, of

29. e·ʾr-k wḫ a ʾny ʿze a ḫn e·ʾr-k t ḫqe n grwgws ḥr ʾbn t a p ʿḫ n sḫ nte ʾr-k ʿš e·ʾr-k šʿne

30. wt-w e pe-w(?) mʿ wt nfr wt rše

31. e·ʾr-k wḫ a t ʾre n ntr·w ʾy n-k a ḫn nte p hn pḫr n tkr e·ʾr-k ʾny wʿ mḫrr nte-k t še-f n ḥsy ḫn p(?) ʾrt n ʾḥ·t km·t

32. nte-k ty-f a p ʿḫ ḫr pḫre-f n t wne·t n rn-s nte p wyn ḫp

33. wʿ s a mr-f a ḫ·t-f n p nt ḫr hne a t ʾr-f pḫr n tktk e·ʾr-k ʾny wʿ swt n ʿyw n ʿy XVI IV·t n ḥt IV·t n [wt ?]

34. IV·t sšt IV·t n ʾtme·t nte-k ʾr-w n wʿ swt nte-k sp-w n snf n qwqwpt nte-k mr-f n wʿ mḫrr n ʿḥ-f n p rʿ

35. ḥsy e-f qs n ḥbs(?) n š-stn nte-k mr-f a ḫe·t-f n p ḫm-ḫl nt ḫr p hn ḫr pḫr-f n tkr e [mn mt·t ?] n p [t . . . .] nʾm-f(?)

Col. IV.

1. wʿ sš-(?)mšt e·ḫr ʾr-s p ntr ʿo ʾy-m-ḥtp pe-f swḥ-ʾyḫ ḫr ʾny-k wʿ tks n ḫ n zyt

---

withdrawal into or to oneself, an idea naturally associated with sleeping or lying down (*str n-k* 4/8) and best seen with the verb *še*, which by itself means 'go,' while *še n-f* (ϣⲉ ⲛⲁϥ) means 'go away,' 'go home,' 'withdraw.'

l. 29. *ʾny ʿze a ḫn*, probably = *κλεπτην πιασαι* B. M. Pap. XLVI. 172.

e·ʾr-k šʿne = ⲉⲕϣⲁⲛ-, an isolated instance at present. The following is the *απολυσις* of the Gk. papyri, B. M. Pap. CXXI. 333.

l. 31. *t še-f n ḥsy* = ϫⲟϥ ⲛϩⲁⲥⲓⲉ, cf. Sah. ⲁⲩϣⲉ ⲛϩⲁⲥⲓⲉ *εναυαγησαν* 1 Tim. i. 19, and ⲃⲱⲕ ⲛϩⲁⲥⲓⲉ 'be drowned' (Peyron). The literal meaning is 'thou shalt cause him to go as one praised (pleasing).' Similarly in I Kham. iv. 9, 14, 20 drowning is expressed by *ʾr-f ḥs·t p Rʿ*, 'He did that which pleased Re (the sun god).' *ḥsy* has det. of sun and in some cases the divine det. ˥ prefixed to the word-sign, cf. 15/12. In Gk. our expression is rendered by *ἐκθέωσον*, 'deify,' or possibly 'consecrate,' which proves that the meaning 'blessed dead,' i.e. 'divinised,' was not yet forgotten: *λαβων μυγαλον εκθεωσον πηγαιω υδατι, και λαβων κανθαρους σεληνιακους δυο εκθεωσον υδατι ποταμιω* Pap. Bibl. Nat. l. 2455; *εασον καλαβωτην εις κρινινον εως αν αποθεωθη* B. M. Pap. CXXI. 629; *αποθωσον εις* [*γαλα*, &c.] Berl. Pap. I. 5.

ḥsy—as a proper name = Ασιης (Spiegelberg, Eigennamen, p. 7*), lit. 'praised' or 'blessed'—is an euphemism for 'drowned.' No other meaning is ascertained in demotic for the word as subst.; and that it

(29) If you wish to bring in a thief, you put crocus powder with alum on the brazier.

The charm which you pronounce when you (30) dismiss them to their place: 'Good dispatch, joyful dispatch!'

(31) If you wish to make the gods come in to you and that the vessel work its magic quickly, you take a scarab and drown it in the milk of a black cow (32) and put it on the brazier; then it works magic in the moment named and the light comes.

(33) An amulet to be bound to the body of him who has the vessel, to cause it to work magic quickly. You take a band of linen of sixteen threads, four of white, four of [green], (34) four of blue, four of red, and make them into one band and stain them with the blood of a hoopoe, and you bind it with a scarab in its attitude of the sun-god, (35) drowned, being wrapped in byssus, and you bind it to the body of the boy who has the vessel and it will work magic quickly; there being nothing [in the world better (?)] than it (?).

Col. IV.

(1) A scout-spreader (?), which the great god Imuthes makes. Its spirit-gathering. You bring a table of olive-

---

implies that condition is shown by the determinative of water added to the name on mummy tickets (Spiegelberg, l. c.). We may thus be sure of its meaning in l. 26 q. v. and in l. 35, as well as in the numerous parallels to the passage here under discussion. Applied to Osiris, also, the word 'drowned' is quite appropriate, see 6/12.

l. 33. See the same list of the colours in Br., Wtb. Suppl., p. 173.

l. 34. *n ʿḥ-f n p rʿ*, the κανθαρον ηλιακον τον τας ιβ̄ ακτινας εχοντα of Pap. Bibl. Nat. l. 751: i.e. true scarab with front tarsi drawn to edge of thorax, so displaying 12 spines (4 on head and each leg), fancifully compared to sun's rays; cf. hieroglyph of the sun's glory .

l. 35. The reading at the end is very uncertain: perhaps *ar-f*.

Col. IV.

l. 1. Imuthes, cf. Sethe, Untersuch. II, Imhotep. In B. M. Pap. CXXI. 630 he appears as τον εν Μεμφει Ασκληπιον; and in the demotic of Leyd. I.

2. e-f θ rt·t IV e bnp rm nb n p t ḥms ḥr ʾ·t-f a nḥe nte-k ḫʿ-f e-f wʿb a te-k·t qts(?) e·ʾr-k wḫ

3. a ʾr wḫe(?) nʾm-f n mt·t mʿ·t n wš n mt·t n ʿze tey-s pe-f smte e·ʾr-k ḫʿ p tks ḫn wʿ . . . e-f wʿb

4. n t mt·t n p mʿ e-f ḫn a zz-k nte-k ḥbs-f n wʿ·t šnt·t n zz-f a rt-f nte-k ḫʿ tbe·t

5. IV ḥr rt-f n p tks ne-ḥr-f e t wʿ.t n t rʿ·t ḥry·t n t wʿ·t nʾm-w e wn wʿ·t ḫw·t n sʿn ne-ḥr-f nte-k t zbe·t

6. n ḫ n zyt ar-s nte-k t ʿt n sre·t e-f nt·yt ḥr ḫl ḥr qs-ʿnḫ(?) nte-k ʾr-w n bnn·t

7. nte-k t wʿ·t a p ʿḫ nte-k ḫʿ p sp a te-k·t qts(?) nte-k ʿš py ʿš n mt·t wynn(?) ar-f z-mt·t nte-k str n wš n szy

8. wbe rm nb n p t nte-k str n-k ḫr nw-k a p ntr e-f n p smte n wʿ wʿb e-f θ ḥbs(?) n š-stn ḥr ʾ·t-f e-f θ še a rt-f

9. *επεικαλουμαι σε τον εν τω αορατω σκοτει καθημενον και ανα μεσον*

10. *οντα των μεγαλων θεων δυνοντα και παραλαμβανοντα τας ηλιακας*

11. *ακτεινας και αναπεμποντα την φαεσφορον θεαν νεβουτοσουαληθ*

384, verso I* he is invoked as 'Imhotp-wer (the Great), son of Ptah and Khretankh,' as at Deir el Medineh, Sethe, ib., 24.

tks, elsewhere a 'boat,' but the gloss τραπεσεν defines it as a 'table.' Tertullian, Apol. 23, mentions oracles from tables. *ḥms ḥr ʾt-* in l. 2 can hardly mean anything but 'sit upon,' which rather implies a 'bench,' cf. B. M. Pap. XLVI. 3 *βαθρον*.

l. 2. *a te-k qt* (?)-*s*, cf. ⲕⲟⲧⲥ, 'circulus,' but *wḫ-s* is a possible reading, and it may be conjectured to mean 'at your convenience,' also in l. 7.

l. 3. *wḫe* with prefixed ˥ (?), the reading doubtful. For a word *wḫ*, 'letter,' see II Kham. ii. 28, &c. The meaning here seems always to be a *direct* divination without medium. We have *wḫe* (?) *n p ḫbs*, 'lamp divination,' 27/29; *wḫe* (?) *n Manebai*, 'a divination named Manebai,' 27/32; *wḫe* (?) *a ḫrw Pe-sḫ*, 'divination for the voice of Pasash,' 8/12.

tke for *tks*, like *nhe* for *nhs* cf. 2/25.

'room (?),' the reading and meaning very uncertain.

l. 5. Or 'one by each of them (the feet),' but the expression hardly admits of this.

l. 6. *sre·t* with gloss ϫⲏⲛⲁⲅⲣⲓⲟⲩ, perhaps a wild goose, cf. Br., Wtb. Suppl., 1082. Note the fem. gender, which apparently distinguishes it

wood (2) having four feet, upon (?) which no man on earth has ever sat, and put it, it being clean, beside (?) you. When you wish (3) to make an inquiry-of-god (?) with it truthfully without falsehood, behold (this is) the manner of it. You put the table in a clean room (?) (4) in the midst of the place, it being near your head; you cover it with a tunic (?) from its head to its feet, and you put four bricks (5) under the table before it, one above another (?), there being a censer of clay before it (the table); and you put charcoal (6) of olive-wood on it (the censer) and put wild-goose fat pounded with myrrh and *qs-ankh*, and make them into balls (7) and put one on the brazier, and lay the remainder at your side (?), and pronounce this spell in Greek (?) speech to it—Formula—and you spend the night without speaking (8) to any one on earth, and you lie down and you see the god in the likeness of a priest wearing fine linen and wearing (a) nose at his feet.

(9) 'I invoke thee who art seated in the invisible darkness and who art in the midst (10) of the great gods sinking and receiving the sun's (11) rays and sending forth the luminous goddess Neboutosoualeth,

---

from the domesticated duck called *sr*, found from the O. K. onwards, which is masc.

l. 7. *wynn*(?), cf. V. 3/12. There as well as here the 'foreign' sign after *mt·t* refers to Greek words. In 27/35 the word is spelt out strangely *wʿyʿny*; *wynn* is the usual demotic spelling, **ⲟⲩⲉⲉⲓⲛⲓⲛ** the Coptic, but **ⲟⲩⲉⲉⲓⲉⲛ** is quoted by PEYRON in Sah., and perhaps this is the form indicated in 27/35. In 12/25 we have *wʿyʿnʿyne·t* for the fem.

str n-k, ethical dative: see note to *še n-w* 3/28.

szy wbe, cf. the common phrase in Greek magic *κοιμω μηδενι δους αποκρισιν* B. M. Pap. XLVI. l. 398, CXXI. l. 748, CXXII. 67; *κοιμω αναποκριτος* XLVI. l. 458.

l. 8. *e-f θ še*, apparently as seen in very late sculpture in figures of gods, &c., with jackals' heads on their feet indicating wariness and swiftness (?). Cf. MASPERO, Les Origines, p. 149; PLEYTE, Chap. Supplem., i. p. 133; in Greek papyri *εν τοις ποσιν εχων την ορασιν* (?).

12. *θεον μεγαν βαρζαν βουβαρζαν ναρζαζουζαν βαρζαβουζαθ*

13. *ηλιον αναπεμτον μοι εν τη νυκτι ταυτη τον αρχαγγελον σου*

14. *ζεβουρθαυνην· χρηματισον επ' αληθειας αληθως αψευδως αν-*

15. *αμφιλογως περι τουδε πραγματος οτι εξορκιζω σε κατα του εν τη*

16. *πυρινη χλαμυδι καθημενου επι της αρουρεας κεφαλης του αγα-*

17. *θου δαιμονος παντοκρατορος τετραπροσωπου δαιμονος υψιστου σκο-*

18. *τιου και ψυχαουγεου φωξ μη μου παρακουσης αλλα αναπεμψον*

19. *ταχος τη νυκτι ταυτη επιτα . αιην του θεου τουτο ειπας γ'*

20. ḫr ʾr-f sze wbe-k n r-f wbe r-k n mt·t mʿ·t ḫr hb nb e·ʾr-k wḫ-f e-f wḥ e-f še n-f ʿn

21. ḫr ʾr-k wḥ wʿ pyngs n ʿš wne·t(?) ḥr n tbe·tw(?) nte-k wḥ n syw·w ḥr ʾ·t-f nte-k sḫ pe-k ʿs-sḥne a wʿ zʿm nmy

22. nte-k wḥ-f ḫr p pynʿks ḫr ʾr-f t ʾw ne-k syw·w n-k e-w wz ḫr pe-k ʿš-sḥne

23. n wz ḫyb e-f znt swḥ n *ϧⲉⲥ* ḥr ḫl ḫy t a yr·t-k nʾm-f ḫr ʾr-k wz ḫyb·t

24. k·t ʿn tpe ḥnʿ snf n *ⲕⲟⲩⲕⲟⲩⲡ(?)ⲉⲧ* θ-ḫ-w(?) nte-k ʾr-w n pḫre šwy smt yr·t-k nʾm-f ḫr nw-k ar-w ʿn

---

l. 16. *αρουρεας*. Mr. Kenyon suggests that this may possibly be a corruption of *αργυρεας*.

l. 18. *ψυχαουγεου*. Mr. Kenyon, who has kindly looked at this passage in the original MS., writes: 'I think the fourth letter is *α*, not *λ*, . . . and the only thing I can think of is *ψυγαγωγου*. In this case we should again have *γ* and *ο* confused (as in *αρουρεας* = *αργυρεας*?). This leaves *φωξ* unaccounted for, but a nominative (and from its termination it could be nothing else) is out of place here, so that the corruption must in any case be rather extensive. I do not think anything but *επιταγαιην* can be read in l. 19. Probably *ἐπιταγῇ* is meant.' The word *ψυχαγωγου* is probably to be taken as associated with the idea of necromancy.

(12) the great god Barzan Boubarzan Narzazouzan Barzabouzath, (13) the sun; send up to me this night thy archangel (14) Zebourthaunen; answer with truth, truthfully, without falsehood, without (15) ambiguity concerning this matter, for I conjure thee by him (16) who is seated in the flaming vesture on the silver (?) head of the (17) Agathodaemon, the almighty four-faced daemon, the highest (18) darkling and soul-bringing (?) Phox; do not disregard me, but send up (19) speedily in this night an injunction (?) of the god.' Say this three times.

(20) Then he speaks with you with his mouth opposite your mouth in truth concerning everything that you wish. When he has finished, and goes away again, (21) you place a tablet of reading (?) the hours upon the bricks and you place the stars upon it and write your purpose (?) on a new roll (22) and place it on the tablet; then he (?) makes your stars appear which are favourable for your purpose (?).

(23) [A method] of lucky-shadows (?), that is tested: a hawk's egg with myrrh, pound (?), put on your eyes of it, then it makes lucky-shadows (?). (24) Another again: head and blood of a hoopoe; cook (?) them and make them into a dry medicament and paint your eyes with it; then you see them, again.

φωξ may be an indeclinable magic name, though the customary line has not been drawn over it. Cf. *ο μεγας και ισχυρος θεος φους* . . . B. M. Pap. CXXIV. 20 and *φυξε* below 7/22.

l. 20. *r-f wbe r-k*: *στομα προς στομα* Berl. Pap. I. 39.

l. 23. *wz ḫyb.* The shadow is probably that of the god appearing in the lamp. Cf. 6/6.

l. 24. *θ-ḫ-w*, probably the imperative of some verb *θḫ* (?) followed by the suffix of the object, meaning e. g. 'cook them,' so also Louvre Dem. Mag. vi. 18 *nte-k θ-ḫ-w*.

Col. V.

1. nte-k ty ʿḥ pe-k(?) . . . . nte-k qlhe a p ʾytn n(?) rt-k n sp VII nte-k ʿš ny sẖ·w a p ẖpš [e ḥr(?)]-k st a mẖty n sp VII

2. nte-k st-k a ẖry nte-k še a wʿ·t ry·t n kke

3. wʿ . . . . . . e-f znt nte-k še-k (*sic*) a wʿ·t ry·t n kke e-s wʿb e ḥr-s wn a p-rs nte-k t wʿb-s n mw

4. n ḥsm nte-k ʾny wʿ ẖbs nmy e-f wbẖ e bnp-w t prš mw n qme ar-f nte-k t wʿ šʿl

5. e-f wʿb ar-f nte-k mḥ-f n nḥe n mʿ·t bn-s sẖ py rn ḥnʿ ny ghʿlʿgter a p šʿl n rʾw ẖl n ḥ·t

6. nte-k wḥ-f ḥr wʿ·t tbe·t nmy ne-zz-k e ḥr-f prẖ n šʿ nte-k ʿš ny sẖ a p ẖbs ʿn n ke sp VII e·ʾr-k t ʾlbwnt a ḥry ne-ḥr

7. p ẖbs e·ʾr-k nw m-s p ẖbs ḥr nw-k a p ntr n p qte n p ẖbs nte-k str n-k ḥr wʿ·t tme·t n qme e bnp-k sze

8. wbe rm nb n p t ḥr z-f n-k wḥ n rswe·t tey-s pe-f ʿš z-mt·t (tey-s sẖ·w nt e·ʾr-k sẖ a p šʿl ẖbs ⲃⲁϫϭϫⲥⲓϫϭϫ)

Col. V.

l. 1. There seem to be traces of writing above this line, at least towards the left end: compare the top line in Col. VIII. Lines 1 and 2 are probably to be read in l. 3, before 'thou goest to a dark niche,' the phrase with which l. 2 ends.

Read *e-ḥr-k* (or *e zz-k* as in l. 32?) *st e mẖty*.

mẖty, a word occurring as early as the time of Darius, possibly arising from a confusion of the words *mḥt*, 'north,' and *ẖty*, 'go north.' An instance of careless confusion of *ḥ* and *ẖ* by our scribe, due to both being ϩ, e.g. in Sah., occurs in 21/12, but is on a different footing.

ẖpš, lit. the 'foreleg' = the Great Bear. ϣⲱⲡϣ : ϣⲱⲃϣ corresponds to ἀρκτοῦρος in Job ix. 9 (cf. also Zoega, 650). But in the astronomical texts *ẖpš* as consisting of seven stars evidently is ἄρκτος itself (Brugsch, Thes., 123, Aegyptol., 343).

l. 3. *nte-k še-k* should be either *nte-k še* in continuation of other directions (cf. ll. 1–2), or *ḥr še-k*.

l. 4. *prš*, ⲡⲏⲣϣ, either red earth or red lead. The requirement that the lamp used for divination shall be free from red colour (ἀμίλτωτος) is found in Leiden Pap. Gr. V, col. 1, l. 22, and col. 4, l. 25; Parthey, Zwei

Col. V.

(1) And you set up your [planisphere?] and you stamp on the ground with your foot seven times and recite these charms to the Foreleg, turning (?) to the North seven times (2) and you return down and go to a dark recess.

(3) A question-form, tested. You go to a dark clean recess with its face open to the south and you purify it with (4) natron-water, and you take a new white lamp in which no red earth or gum-water has been put and place a clean wick (5) in it and fill it with real oil after writing this name and these figures on the wick with ink of myrrh beforehand; (6) and you lay it on a new brick before you, its underside being spread with sand; and you pronounce these spells over the lamp again another seven times. You display frankincense in front of (7) the lamp and you look at the lamp; then you see the god about the lamp and you lie down on a rush mat without speaking (8) to any one on earth. Then he makes answer to you by dream. Behold its invocation. Formula: (*In margin*: Behold the spells which you write on the wick: Bakhukhsikhukh, *and figures*)

---

gr. Zauberpap., I. l. 277. As to the use of red earth and gum with pottery cf. the quotation from Sacy, s.v. ϫⲱⲓ, in Peyron, p. 380 a.

l. 5. *r'w ḫl*, 'myrrh ink,' *σμυρνομελαν*, probably somewhat after the recipe given in Parthey, u. s. II. 34[a].

gh'l'gter = *χαρακτῆρες*, a term. techn. for mystic symbols: cf. Wünsch, Sethian. Verfluchungstafeln, p. 98; Schmidt, Gnostische Schriften, p. 54 seq.

l. 6. *ne-zz-k*. It seems probable that  reads *zz*, for apart from any other correspondences we have this compound preposition written out as *ne-zz-* in 14/6 and Louvre Dem. Mag. iv. 19. 22.

'lbwnt, *ⲁⲗⲃⲟⲩⲛⲟⲩⲧ* 22/17, evidently = *λιβανωτός*.

l. 8. ⲃⲁϫȣϫⲥⲓϫȣϫ looks like 'Soul of Khukh, son of Khukh.' The magic-name compounds with *χουχ*, *χυχ*, *χωωχ* are very numerous; cf. P. Sophia, § 361, ⲃⲁⲓⲛϫⲱⲱϫ and elsewhere often *βαιχυχ*. Sethe, Verbum, i. § 417, suggests that the ϫⲟȣϫ is the elemental god *KK*, 'darkness.'

9. hy ank mwrʾy mwryby bʾbel bʾ-ʿo-th bʾ-my p šʿy

10. ʿo mwrʿth-ʿo p . . . ẖbr n by nt ḥtp n ḥry ẖn n p·t n p·t·w (*sic*)

11. tʾtot sp-sn bwlʾy sp-sn my-ḥr . . . sp-sn lʾhy sp-sn b-ʿo-lbwel y sp-sn ʾʿ tt sp-sn bwel sp-sn y-ʿo-hel sp-sn p šmsy ḥyt

12. n p ntr ʿo p nt t wyn m šs sp-sn p ẖber n t st·t p nte t st·t n r-f nte b-ʾre-s ʿẖm p ntr ʿo nt ḥms

13. ẖn t st·t p nt n t mt·t n t st·t nt n p šy n t p·t nte p ʿw erme p nʿš n p ntr n t·t-f wnḥ-k ar-y

14. ty n p-hw mw ky p ky n wnḥ-k a mwses nta e·ʾr-k ʾr-f ḥr p tw nte ḥr-k t ẖp p kke p wyn ne-ḥr-f

15. tg(?)a te-y tbḥ nʾm-k nte-k wnḥ-k ar-y ty n py grḥ nte-k sze erme-y nte-k z n-y wḥ n mt·t mʿ·t n wš n mt·t n ʿze z e-y a šʿš-k

16. n ʾBt e-y a šʿšʿ-k n t p·t ne-ḥr p rʿ e-y a šʿšʿ-k ne-ḥr ʿḥ e-y a šʿšʿ-k

17. ne-ḥr p nt ḥr p bḥt nte b-ʾr-f thm pe p šʿšʿ ʿo petery sp-sn pʿter enphe sp-sn **ⲉⲛⲫⲉ ⲃ̅**

18. p ntr nt n t rʿ ḥry·t n t p·t nte p šbt nt (ne)ʿne-f n t·t-f ʾr t ẖp ntr e bnp ntr t ẖp-f ʾm n-y

19. a ẖry a ẖn n t mt·t n ty st·t nt ty ḥ·t-k pa bwel sp-sn nte-k t mʾ-y p ʿš-sḥne [nt] e-y šll ẖrr-f

20. n py grḥ n mt·t mʿ·t n wš n mt·t n ʿze my mʾ-s my stm-s p ntr ʿo sysyhowt sp-sn ke-z **ⲁⲣⲙⲓⲱⲟⲩⲑ** ʾm

21. a ẖn ẖr zz-y nte-k z n-y wḥ n p nt e-y šn ẖrr-f n mt·t mʿ·t n wš n mt·t n ʿze p ntr ʿo nt ḥr p tw

---

l. 10. Read *ẖn t p·t n n p·tw* or *ẖn p·t p·tw.*

l. 11. In the demotic there is one uncertain sign that may correspond to ⲧⲁⲩⲓ of the gloss.

l. 12. Lines 12–22 are parallel to 7/8–18, 17/1–10, 17/27–32.

l. 14. Moses was a popular hero with many legends in Jewish circles, both before and after Christ (Wiedemann in P. S. B. A. xi. 29, 267). Note that the form of the name employed is Greek and not Hebrew; cf. V. 12/6.

nta eʾr-k: cf. note to 15/13.

(9) 'Ho! I am Murai, Muribi, Babel, Baoth, Bamui, the great Agathodaemon, (10) Muratho, the . . . form of soul that resteth above in the heaven of heavens, (11) Tatot (*bis*), Bouel (*bis*), Mouihtahi (?) (*bis*), Lahi (*bis*), Bolboel, I (*bis*), Aa, Tat (*bis*), Bouel (*bis*), Yohel (*bis*), the first servant (12) of the great god, he who giveth light exceedingly, the companion of the flame, he in whose mouth is the fire that is not quenched, the great god who is seated (13) in the fire, he who is in the midst of the fire which is in the lake of heaven, in whose hand is the greatness and the power of god; reveal thyself to me (14) here to-day in the fashion of thy revelation to Moses which thou didst make upon the mountain, before whom thou thyself didst create darkness and light, (15)—*insertion*—I pray thee that thou reveal thyself to me here to-night and speak with me and give me answer in truth without falsehood; for I will glorify thee (16) in Abydos, I will glorify thee in heaven before Phre, I will glorify thee before the Moon, I will glorify thee (17) before him who is upon the throne, who is not destroyed, he (= thou) of the great glory, Peteri (*bis*), Pater, Enphe (*bis*), (18) O god who is above heaven, in whose hand is the beautiful staff, who created deity, deity not having created him. Come down ⟨in⟩ to me (19) into the midst of this flame that is here before thee, thou of Boel (*bis*), and let me see the business that I ask about (20) to-night truly without falsehood. Let it be seen (?), let it be heard (?), O great god Sisihoout, otherwise said Armioouth, come (21) in before me and give me answer to that which

---

l. 15. The pointer at the beginning of the line refers to the similar sign at the beginning of ll. 33–4, which offer a variant version of l. 15. One may conjecture that the pointer represents the Eg. *dg*', Copt. ⲧⲱϭ : ⲧⲱϫ, 'plant,' 'insert,' 'join.'

l. 17. *thm*, a mistake or metathesis for *htm*; cf. 7/12, 17/5, 30.

petery, &c. See vol. ii, Mythological Index.

22. n ʿtwgy (ⲛⲕⲁⲃⲁⲱⲛ) ghʿbʿh-ʿo ʾm n-y a ẖn my wn yr·t a bl n py grḥ ẖr t mn t mt·t

23. nt e-y šn ẖrr-s n mt·t mʿ·t n wš n mt·t n ʿze a . . . ẖrw (?) n p leʾsphwt nb-lot . . lylʾs sp VII nte-k str n-k

24. n wš n sze p kys nt e·ʾr-k ty-s a yr·t-k e·ʾr-k ʾnnʿy a šn n p ẖbs n šn nb n ẖbs ẖr ʾny-k hyn·w ḥrre n *ⲃⲟⲩⲗ*

25. n *ⲉⲃⲱⲕ* ẖr gm-k-ysw n p mʿ n p s-qlm ke-z p s-trmws e·ʾr-k ʾny·t-w e-w knn e·ʾr-k ty-sw

26. e wʿ lq n yl e·ʾr-k ʿm r-f m šs sp-sn šʿ hw XX n wʿ mʿ e-f hep e-f n kke bn-s hw XX e·ʾr-k

27. ʾny·t-f a ḥry nte-k wn ar-f ẖr gm-k hyn·w ẖry·w ẖn-f erme wʿ mz e·ʾr-k ẖʿ-f šʿ hw XL nte-k ʾny·t-f a ḥry

28. nte-k wn ar-f ẖr gm-k-f e·ḥr-f ʾr snf e·ʾre ẖr ʾr-k ty-f a wʿ nk n yl nte-k t p nk n yl a ẖn wʿ nk

29. n blz n wʿ mʿ e-f hep n nw nb e·ʾr-k wẖ a ʾr . . . . . n p ẖbs nʾm-f n nw nb e·ʾr-k mḥ yr·t-k n py

30. snf nt ḥry eʾr-k ʾnnʿy a ẖn a ʿš sẖ a p ẖbs ẖr nw-k a wʿ sšt n ntr e-f ʿḥ n p bl n p ẖbs nte-f sze

31. wbe-k ẖr p šn nt e·ʾr-k wẖ-f nge nte-k str ẖr ʾw-f n-k a ʾr-f tm ʾy n-k e·ʾr-k nhs e·ʾr-k ʿš pe-f thm

---

l. 22. Atugi with gloss Gabaon: cf. 7/17.

l. 24. Lines 24–30 are repeated in 27/24–29.

l. 25. ⲃⲟⲩⲗ *n* ⲉⲃⲱⲕ = ⲃⲁⲗⲁⲃⲱⲕ, 'raven's eye,' the Greek bean.

gm-k-ysw, an extraordinary form; but, it is to be feared, no guide to the real pronunciation, which was probably *gemyoks* or *gemyoksu*; the written *y* is thus superfluous, cf. 3/9 note, or at least misplaced.

s-qlm, see note in glossary. 'The place of the garland-seller': does this mean his shop or his garden?

ty-sw: the regular form in this papyrus, as it were, *ⲧⲏⲓⲥⲟⲩ. In *gm-k-ysw*, above, the *sw* = Eg. *st*, plur. of the absolute object-pronoun. Here, after the infinitive, it is abnormal, the *s* being inserted before the proper suffix *-w* on false analogy. In Coptic (St., § 342, p. 169, and Piehl, A. Z., 95. 42) the only clear instance of this false form seems to be Sah. ⲥϩⲁⲓⲥⲟⲩ. The similar ⲧⲉⲛⲛⲟⲟⲩⲥⲉ, ⲧⲉⲛⲛⲟⲟⲩⲥⲟⲩ, &c., are also etymologically wrong, but they seem to be helped by the causative with *stm-f*: see Griff., High Priests, p. 85.

l. 26. *yl*: ⲓⲁⲗ : ⲉⲓⲁⲗ probably to be connected with ὕαλος.

I shall ask about, truly without falsehood. O great god that is on the mountain (22) of Atuki (of Gabaon), Khabaho, Takrtat, come in to me, let my eyes be opened to-night for any given thing (23) that I shall ask about, truly without falsehood . . . the voice (?) of the Leasphot, Neblot . . . lilas.' Seven times: and you lie down (24) without speaking.

The ointment which you put on your eyes when you are about to inquire of the lamp in any lamp-divination: you take some flowers (25) of the Greek bean; you find them in the place of the garland-seller, otherwise said of the lupin-seller; you take them fresh and put them (26) in a *lok*-vessel of glass and stop its mouth very well for twenty days in a secret dark place. After twenty days, if you (27) take it out and open it, you find a pair (?) of testicles in it with a phallus. You leave it for forty days and when you take it out (28) and open it, you find that it has become bloody; then you put it on a glass thing and put the glass thing into a pottery thing (29) in a place hidden at all times. When you desire to make inquiry of the lamp with it at any time if you fill your eyes with this (30) blood aforesaid, and if you go in to pronounce a spell over the lamp you see a figure of a god standing behind (?) the lamp, and he speaks (31) with you concerning the question which you wish; or you lie down and he comes to you. If he does not come to

---

ʿm. This group cannot be read *tm*, ⲧⲱⲙ. It must be connected with **ⲟⲙⲉ**, 'clay.'

l. 27. *ḥyn·w*, 'some,' here and elsewhere suggests the meaning of 'a pair' (Hess, Setne, p. 30).

l. 28. **ⲉ(ϩ)ⲁϥⲣ̄ⲥⲛⲟϥ**, see the chapter on Grammar.

e·ʾre: probably the Eg. emphasizing particle 𓇋𓂋, cf. 7/1.

The meaning of *ḫr ʾr-k*, **ϣⲁⲕ**, here is not merely consuetudinal but injunctional, equivalent to the old *sdmḫrf*, as used e.g. in Pap. Ebers (Erman, Grammar, 2nd ed. § 221).

32. e·ʾre ḫr ʾr-k str ḥr qme wt e·ʾr-k wʿb a s-ḥm·t e zz-k st a rs e ḥr-k st a mḫty [e] ḥr-f n p ḫbs st a mḫty ḥ-f

33. tg(?) a ḫry te-y tbḥ nʾm-k nte-k wnḥ-k ar-y ty n py grḥ nte-k sze erme-y nte-k z n-y wḥ n mt·t mʿ·t ḫr t mn t mt·t

34. nt e-y šn nʾm-k e-tbe·t[-s ?]

Col. VI.

1. wʿ šn n p ḫbs ḫr še-k a wʿ·t ry·t n kke e-s wʿb ʾt wyn nte-k šte wʿ qel nmy ḥr wʿ·t zʿe·t

2. ybt nte-k ʾny wʿ ḫbs ḥt e bnp-w t prš mw n qme ar-f e pe-f sʿl wʿb nte-k mḥ-f n nḥe n mʿ·t e-f wʿb n whe

3. nte-k ʿš n sḫ·w n tʾw Rʿ tp twe m ḫʿ-f nte-k ʾny p ḫbs wbe p rʿ e-f mḥ nte-k ʿš n sḫ·w nt ḫry ar-f n sp IV

4. nte-k θy·t-f a ḫn a t ry·t e·ʾr-k wʿb erme p ʿlw nte-k ʿš n sḫ·w a p ʿlw e·bnn-f nw m-s p ḫbs ʿn e yr·t-f

5. ḫtm šʿ sp VII e·ʾr-k t ʾlbwnt a p ʿḫ e-f wʿb e·ʾr-k t·t n pe-k tbʿ a zz-f n p ʿlw e yr·t-f ḫtm

6. e·ʾr-k wḥ e·ʾr-k t ʾr-f wn yr·t-f a ḥr p ḫbs ḫr nw-f a t ḫyb·t n p ntr n p qte n p ḫbs nte-f šn n-k

7. a p nt e·ʾr-k wḫ-f e·ʾre ḫr ʾr-k-f n mre·t n wʿ mʿ e mn-te-f wyn e-f ḫp e·ʾr-k šn ḫr ʾyḫ sšre wʿ sʿl n ht

8. n zy p nt e·ʾr-k ty-f a p ḫbs nte-k mḥ-f n syr e-f wʿb e-f ḫp e ge ʿš-sḫne pe sʿl e-f wʿb ḥr nḥe n mʿ·t e-f wʿb

9. p nt e·ʾr-k ty-f a p ḫbs e-f ḫp e·ʾr-k a ʾr-f a ʾny s-ḥm·t n hwt skne n wrt p nt e·ʾr-k ty-f a p ḫbs e·ʾre ḫr wḥ-k p ḫbs

---

l. 34. *e-tbe·t-s* must be the reading.

Col. VI.

l. 1. A niche in a wall with special orientation for magic utensils, &c., occurs in the nineteenth dynasty; see Naville, Quatre stèles.

l. 3. *tʾw Rʿ*, &c. Perhaps the title of some specific religious work, like the hymns to the rising sun prefixed to the New-Kingdom Books of the Dead: or an invocation in an earlier part of the papyrus now lost.

l. 7. *ʾyḫ sšre.* The meaning is not quite clear. In II Kham. ii. 26

you, you rise and pronounce his compulsion. (32) You must lie down on green reeds, being pure from a woman, your head being turned to the south and your face being turned to the north and the face of the lamp being turned northwards likewise.

(33) *insert above*—'I pray thee to reveal thyself to me here to-night and speak with me and give me answer truly concerning the given matter which I ask thee about.'

Col. VI.

(1) An inquiry of the lamp. You go to a clean dark cell without light and you dig a new hole in an east wall (2) and you take a white lamp in which no minium or gum water has been put, its wick being clean, and you fill it with clean genuine Oasis oil, (3) and you recite the spells of praising Ra at dawn in his rising and you bring the lamp when lighted opposite the sun and recite to it the spells as below four times, (4) and you take it into the cell, you being pure, and the boy also, and you pronounce the spells to the boy, he not looking at the lamp, his eyes being (5) closed, seven times. You put pure frankincense on the brazier. You put your finger on the boy's head, his eyes being closed. (6) When you have finished you make him open his eyes towards the lamp; then he sees the shadow of the god about the lamp, and he inquires for you (7) concerning that which you desire. You must do it at midday in a place without light. If it be that you are inquiring for a spirit damned, a wick of sail-cloth (?) (8) is what you put in the lamp and you fill it with clean butter. If it is some other business, a clean wick with pure genuine oil (9) is that which you put in the lamp; if you will do it to bring

---

there is mentioned a book for *sḫr ʾḫy*, 'overthrowing (or laying) demons'; cf. note 3/25.

l. 9. *skne n wrt*, ροδινον ελαιον, Diosc. i. 53.

10. ḥr wꜥ·t tbe·t nmy nte p ꜥlw ḥms ḥ-f ḫr ke tbe·t e yr·t-f ḥtm e·ʾr-k ꜥš a ḫry ḫn zz-f šꜥ sp IV

11. n sḫ·w nt e·ʾr-k ꜥš-w a p sꜥl a p ḥbs a t ḥꜥ·t e b-ʾr te-k ꜥš a p ꜥlw z-mt·t ꜥn nte-k p sꜥl wꜥt ꜥo n t mnḫ·t n Tḥwt

12. ʾn nte-k p ḥbs n š-stn n Wsr p ḥsy ntr n sšne n t·t ʾS·t n msne n t·t Nb·t-ḥ·t

13. ʾn nte-k p ḫrt tp a·ʾr-w n Wsr ḫnt ʾmnt ʾn nte-k p snb ꜥo a·fy ʾNp t·t-f erme-f a t ḫe·t n Wsr p ntr wr

14. a·ʾr-y ʾny nʾm-k n p-hw ʾy p sꜥl a t nw p ꜥlw a ḫn-k nte-k ʾr wḥ a mt·t nb nt e-y šn ḫrr-w ty n p-hw ʾn

15. tm ʾr·y-s p nt e·ʾr-k ʾr-f ʾy p sꜥl a·ʾr-y t nʾm-k a t gyz·t n t ʾḥ·t kme·t a·ʾr-y t mḥ nʾm-k ḫn t gyz·t

16. n t ʾḥ·t s-ḥm·t snf n p ḥsy p nt e-y t nʾm-f m-s-k ḫr nḥe t kyz n ʾNp t nt wḥ ar-k n sḫ·w

17. n p wr ḥyq n nt e-y ꜥš n-k nʾm-w nte-k ʾny n-y p ntr nte p wḥ-sḥne n t·t-f n p-hw nte-f z n-y wḥ a mt·t nb nt e-y šn

18. ḫrr-w ty n p-hw n mt·t mꜥ·t n wš n mt·t n ꜥze ʾy Nw·t mw·t mw hy ʾP·t mw·t st·t

---

l. 12. *p ḥsy*, cf. l. 16, and above, note to 3/31. 'Approved,' 'praised' would be a rather unexpected term to apply to Osiris himself, though it could be explained as equivalent to *mʾꜥ ḫrw* and 'deified.' The sense 'drowned' is quite applicable, as Osiris' body was at least sunk in the waters, cf. the text of Ptah published by BREASTED, A. Z., 1901, Pl. II, ll. 19, 62; and this sense is implied in Brit. Mus. Pap. XLVI. 259–63 *οστα Εσιηους . . . . τον Εσιη* (ϩⲁⲥⲓⲉ) *τον ενεχθεντα εν τω ρευματι του ποταμου* for three days and three nights. Plutarch's account, De Iside et Osiride, cap. 13 et seqq., hardly needs quotation.

sšne, &c. Cf. similar passage in Pap. Boul. I. Pl. 12, l. 1.

t·t ʾS·t . . . t·t Nb·t-ḥ·t. In both cases the strong *t* is written at the end of the word for 'hand.' Presumably it is an old dual form.

l. 13. *snb a·fy*, &c., the linen used by Anubis in wrapping the mummy of Osiris.

l. 14. *a·ʾr-y ʾny*, ⲁⲓⲉⲓⲛⲉ, rather than past relative, which would have taken *nʾm-f* instead of *nʾm-k*; so also in l. 15, &c.

a t. This is hardly an imperative *a·t.*

a woman to a man, ointment of roses is that which you put in the lamp. You must lay the lamp (10) on a new brick and the boy also must sit on another brick with his eyes closed. You cry down into his head four times. (11) The spells which you recite ⟨to the lamp⟩ to the wick previously before you recite to the boy: formula: 'Art thou the unique great wick of the linen of Thoth? (12) Art thou the byssus robe of Osiris, the divine Drowned, woven by the hand of Isis, spun by the hand of Nephthys? (13) Art thou the original band that was made for Osiris Khentamente? Art thou the great bandage with which Anubis put forth his hand to the body of Osiris the mighty god? (14) I have brought thee to-day—ho! thou wick—to cause the boy to look into thee, that thou mayest make reply to every matter concerning which I ask here to-day. (15) Is it that you will (?) not do it? O wick, I have put thee in the hand of the black cow, I have lighted thee in the hand (16) of the female cow. Blood of the Drowned one is that which I put to thee for oil; the hand of Anubis is that which is laid on thee. The spells (17) of the great Sorcerer are those which I recite to thee. Do thou bring me the god in whose hand is the command to-day and let him give me answer as to everything about which (18) I inquire here to-day truly without falsehood. Ho! Nut, mother of water, ho! Apet, mother of fire,

---

l. 15. ⲁⲛ *ⲧⲙⲁⲓⲥ, lit. 'Is not-doing-it that which you will (?) do?' Cf. l. 37.

'ḥ·t kme·t, black animals are generally prescribed in both Greek and demotic magic. Cf. B. M. Gk. Pap. CXXI. l. 301, &c., &c.

l. 16. *t 'ḥ·t s-ḥm·t*, 'the female cow,' seems curious, but is quite correct, being due to the fact that, except for the gender of the article, there is no distinction in sound between the words for 'ox' and 'cow.' Cf. 7/1, 2.

l. 17. *p wḥ-sḥne*. The 365 gods are mentioned V. 33/6. Probably one of these presided over the course of each day.

l. 18. Nut, goddess of the sky, wife of Geb and mother of Osiris; Apt, probably the birth-goddess, worshipped in a small temple at Karnak, in

19. ʾw(?)n-y Nw·t mw·t mw ʾm·t ʾP·t mw·t st·t ʾw(?)n-y yʿh-ʿo e·ʾr-k zt-f e·ʾr-k sq n ẖrw-k m šs sp-sn

20. e·ʾr-k z ʿn eseks p-ʿo-e e-f ẖtn(?) ke-z ẖt-ʾN sp VII e-f ẖp e . . . . . pe ny n nt e·ʾr-k ʿš-w

21. wʿt-w a p ẖbs nte-k str n-k n wš n sze ʾnn-e ʿw n ḥt ẖp e·ʾr-k nhe e·ʾr-k ʿš

22. pe-f thm nte pe-f ḥtr pe z-mt·t ʾnk p ḥr n sr*í*w ḥwnw rn-y a·ʾr-w ms·t ẖr p ʾšte šps

23. n ʾBt ʾnk p by n p sr wr nt m ʾBt ank p sʾwte n t ẖe·t ʿo·t nt m ww-pq

24. ank p nte yr·t-f n yr·t n ʿẖm e-f rs a Wsr n grḥ ank tp tw-f ḥr ẖs·t n ʾBt

25. ank nt rs a t ẖe·t ʿo·t nt m tt ʾnk nt rs n . . . . n sẖ·w nt e·ʾr-k sẖ-w a p ẖbs ⲃⲁⲭⲩⲭⲥⲓⲭⲩⲭ

26. nt *í*w rn-f ḥep ẖn ḥt-y by by·w rn-f z-mt·t sp VII e-f ẖp e . . . . . pe

27. ny wʿet-w n nt e·ʾr-k ʿš-w e-f ẖp e šn n p ʿlw p nt e·ʾr-k ʾr-f e·ʾr-k ʿš n·y nt ḥry a p ẖbs

28. e b-ʾr te-k ʿš a ḥry ẖn a (*sic*) zz-f n p ʿlw e·ʾr-k st-k e·ʾr-k ʿš py ke ʿš a p ẖbs ʿn z-mt·t ʾy Wsr p ẖbs

29. e-f t nw nʾ·w hw·w ḥr-w ʾw-f t nw nʾ·w ẖr-w

---

the inscriptions of which she is often identified with Nut. ROCHEMENTEIX, Œuvres, pp. 261, 302.

l. 20. *e-f ẖtn*, &c. The pronunciation of both groups was probably almost identical *ẖetôn*.

l. 23. *ww-pq*, a sacred place at Abydos, cf. BRUGSCH, Dict. Geog., 226.

l. 24. *ʿẖm*. Perhaps, according to its ancient significance, meaning one of the mummied hawk-figures placed watching at the corners of the coffin, but in Coptic the word ⲁϧⲱⲙ has acquired the meaning 'eagle.'

n grḥ: the gloss ⲙ over the *n* is strange, as the group evidently corresponds to Boh. ⲛϫⲱⲣϩ.

tp tw-f. The old title of Anubis.

'desert,' probably in the sense of 'necropolis.'

l. 25. The name written with three hieratic signs , cf. 11/9, 16, is quite uncertain. The first sign probably reads *ʾẖ*, 'spirit,' but might read *wyn*, 'light,' *wbn*, 'shine' or 'rise,' or possibly *šw*, 'light,' or the god 'Shu.' The scarab may read *ẖpr*, 'scarab,' 'become,' the god Khepera, but hardly *t*, 'land': and the last sign *wr*, 'great,' *ʿo*, 'great,' *sr*,

(19) come unto me, Nut, mother of water, come Apet, mother of fire, come unto me Yaho.' You say it drawling (?) with your voice exceedingly. You say again: 'Esex, Poe, Ef-khe-ton,' otherwise said, 'Khet-on,' seven times. If it is a direct (?) inquiry, these alone are the things that you recite (21) to the lamp, and you lie down without speaking. But if obduracy take place, you rise, you recite (22) his summons, which is his compulsion. Formula: 'I am the Ram's face, Youth is my name; I was born under the venerable persea (23) in Abydos, I am the soul of the great chief who is in Abydos; I am the guardian of the great corpse that is in U-pek; (24) I am he whose eyes are as the eyes of Akhom when he watcheth Osiris by night; I am Teptuf upon the desert of Abydos; (25) I am he that watcheth the great corpse which is in Busiris; I am he who watcheth for Light-scarab-noble (?).' (*In margin*) The spells that you write on the lamp, Bakhukhsikhukh (*and figures*) (26) 'whose name is hidden in my heart; Bibiou (Soul of souls) is his name.' Formula, seven times. If it is a direct (?) inquiry, (27) these things alone are what you recite. If it is an inquiry by the boy that you are about, you recite these aforesaid to the lamp (28) before calling down into the head of the boy, you turn round (?), you recite this other invocation to the lamp also. Formula: 'O Osiris, O lamp (29) that giveth vision

---

'magnate,' *ἰ'w*, 'old.' It is no doubt a solar name (here for Osiris ?), and it occurs in ch. 162 of the Book of the Dead, but unfortunately without variants (PLEYTE, Chap. Suppl., Pl. 21, 130)*.

l. 29. *hw·w*. This has evidently been written by mistake for *ḥry·w*, which has been inserted above. The mistake is important as indicating that the *r* of *hrw*, *hw*, 'day,' was retained in the plural (sing. ϩⲟⲟⲩ).

---

* Cf. perhaps the inscription on a hypocephalus at Cairo 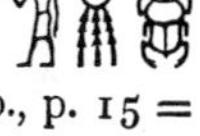 , DARESSY, Textes Mag., p. 56, and , ib., p. 15 =  METT., ST., l. 39.

θs-pḫr ʾy p ḫbs sp-sn ʾMn mne nʾm-k ʾy p ḫbs sp-sn te-y

30. ʿš n-k e·ʾr-k ʾnnʿ a ḥry ḫr zz p yʿm ʿo p yʿm n [ḫ]r p yʿm n Wsr ʿn e-y z

31. n-k ʾn e·ʾr-k ʾy hb-yt-k ʾy p ḫbs mtr ar-k n-t gm-k Wsr ḥr pe-f rms n zwf tḥn

32. e ʾS·t ne-zz-f e Nb·t-h·t ne-rt-f e n [ntr·w] ḥwt·w n ntr·w s-ḥm·tw n pe-f qte a·zy-s ʾS·t my z-w-s

33. n Wsr e-tbe n mt·tw nt e-y šn ḫrr-w a t ʾw p ntr nte p wḥ-sḥne n t·t-f nte-f z n-y wḥ a mt·t nb nt e-y šn ḫrr-w

34. ty n p-hw e ʾS·t z my ʿš-w n-y a wʿ ntr hb-y-s e n(?) šq-f a n mt·tw nt e-f a še nʾm-s nte-f mnq-s

35. šm-w ʾny-w n-s nte-k p ḫbs p-e·ʾny-w n-s p ḫyt n Sḫm·t te-k.t mw·t erme Ḥke pe-k yt

36. ḥwy ar-k bnn-k mḥ a Wsr erme ʾS·t bnn-k mḥ ʾNp e bnp-k z n-y wḥ a mt·t nb nt e-y šn

37. ḫrr-w ty n p-hw n mt·t mʿ·t n wš n z n-y mt·t n ʿze ʾn tm ʾry-s p nt e·ʾr-k a ʾr-f bn e-y a t n-k nḥe

Col. VII.

1. bn e-y a t n-k nḥe bn e-y a t n-k ʿt ʾy p ḫbs e·ʾry e-y a t n-k n t ḫe·t n t ʾḥ·t s-ḥm·t nte-y t·t snf

---

l. 31. *hb-yt-k,* note the final *stm-f,* especially common in the 1 pers. sing. Cf. l. 34.

n-t with *stm-f* = ⲛ̄ⲧⲉⲣⲉ, cf. I Kham. 5/35, II Kham. 6/3 (Griff., High Priests, p. 193).

rms, see Griff., High Priests, p. 100. Evidently the *πλοιον παπυρινον ο καλειται αιγυπτιστι ρωψ* of Leyd. Pap. U. col. 2, l. 6, 7; an *m* before *s* would naturally become *p* in the mouth of a Greek.

l. 32. *n ntr·w ḥwt·w . . . s-ḥm·tw,* O. C. Par. ⲛ̄ⲧⲉⲣ ϩⲥⲓⲙⲉ . . . ⲛⲧⲉⲣ ϩⲟⲟⲩⲛⲧ A. Z., 1900, p. 88. Cf. the same expression in the Hittite treaty, L. D. III. 146, ll. 26, 30.

l. 34. *e n*(?) *šq-f.* Perhaps an adjectival verb of the form ⲛⲁⲛⲟⲩϥ 'he being clever' (or discreet, or swift, &c.).

l. 35. *p ḫyt n . . . ḥwy* seems to be equivalent to *ἐξορκίζω σε κατα* . . . .

Ḥke, cf. Lanzone, Diz. Mit., 851, 859. As a form of the god Shu

of the things ⟨of days⟩ above, that giveth vision of the things below and vice versa; O lamp (*bis*), Amen is moored in thee; O lamp (*bis*) I (30) invoke thee, thou goest up to the shore of the great sea, the sea of Syria, the sea of Osiris. Do I speak (31) to thee? Dost thou come that I may send thee? Ho, lamp, witness (?) to thyself, since thou hast found Osiris upon his boat of papyrus and *teḥen*, (32) Isis being at his head, Nephthys at his feet, and the male and female gods about him. Speak, Isis, let it be told (33) to Osiris concerning the things which I ask about, to cause the god to come in whose hand is the command, and give me answer to everything about which I shall inquire (34) here to-day. When Isis said "Let a god be summoned to me that I may send him, he being discreet (?) as to the business on which he will go and he accomplish it," (35) they went and they brought to her; thou art the lamp that was brought to her. The fury of Sekhmet thy mother and of Heke thy father is (36) cast at thee, thou shalt not be lighted for Osiris and Isis, thou shalt not be lighted for Anubis until thou hast given me an answer to everything which I ask (37) about here to-day truly without telling me falsehood. If thou wilt not do it, I will not give thee oil.

Col. VII.

(1) 'I will not give thee oil, I will not give thee fat, O lamp; verily I will give thee the body of the female

---

he would be connected with the lion-headed goddess Tefnut, here perhaps assimilated to the lion-goddess Sochmet.

l. 37. *bn e-y a* (sic) *t*. The *a* is false with neg. fut., but occurs commonly in this papyrus. See 7/1, &c.

Col. VII.

l. 1. *e·ʾry* with gloss ⲉⲣⲉ, apparently = Eg. 𓇋𓂋, as *eʾre* in 5/28: here 'verily' or 'but.'

2. n p ʾḥ ḥwt m-s-k nte-y t t·t-k n p ʾswe(?) n ḫft Ḥr a·wn n-y ʾy na t ty·t t tb·t n ḫl nt n t·t-y

3. šp·t a ḥr-tn ʾy n by·w ʾqr·w(?) na bywkm t tyb·t n ʿnte nt ḫr qh IV ʾy p ʾʾe nt e-w

4. z n-f ʾNp n rn nt ḥtp ḥr t tybe·t n ḫl e rt-f smn·t ḥr t tybe·t n ʿnte my ʾw n-y

5. p kys m-s p šre ḫbs nte-f z n-y wḥ ḫr mt·t nb nt e-y šn ḫrr-w ty n p-hw n mt·t mʿ·t e mn mt·t n ʿze nʾm-w

6. y-ʿo tʿbʿ-ʿo swgʿmʿmw ʿkhʿkhʿ·nbw sʿnʿwʿny etsie qm-t

7. geth-ʿo-s bʿsʿe·th-ʿo-ry thmylʿ·ʿkh·khw a·ʾry n-y wḥ a mt·t nb nt e-y šn ḫrr-w ty n p-hw sp VII

8. n sḫ·w n p ʿlw b-ʿo-el b-ʿo-el sp-sn y·y sp-sn ʿ·ʿ sp-sn tt tt sp-sn p nt t wyn m šs sp-sn p ḫber n t st·t

9. p nte t st·t n r-f nte b·ʾr-s ʿḫm p ntr ʿo nt ḥms ḫn t st·t p nt n t mt·t n t st·t p nt n p šy n t p·t

10. nte p ʿw erme p nʿš n p ntr n t·t-f wnḥ-k a py ʿlw nt ḫr pe hne n p-hw nte-f z n-y wḥ n mt·t

11. mʿ·t n wš n mt·t n ʿze e-y a ty ʿy-k n ʾBt e-y a šʿšʿ-k n t p·t ne-ḥr p rʿ e-y a šʿšʿ-k

12. ne-ḥr ʿḥ e-y a šʿšʿ-k n p t e-y a šʿšʿ-k ne-ḥr p nt ḥr p bḥt nte b·ʾr-f htm pe p šʿšʿ

13. ʿo petery petery pʿter enphe enphe p ntr nt n t ry·t ḥry·t n t p·t nte p šbt nt (ne)-

---

l. 2. Referring to the contest between Horus and Set when Horus injured the testicles of Set, and Set, at the same time, put out the eye of Horus. The eye of Horus symbolizes light—hence the threat to the lamp. But the reading and meaning are uncertain. Cf. note to 1/3.

t tb·t n ḫl seems to be in apposition to *ty·t*; a similar construction in l. 3.

l. 3. *ʾqr.* The double figure in the underworld formed of the foreparts of two lions or of a lion and a bull. Lanzone, Diz. Mit., p. 5.

bywkm seems to be the name of the Arabian desert at the latitude of El Kab, according to Brugsch, D. Geogr., 211, 1154, where the lion-

cow and put blood (2) of the male bull into (?) thee and put thy hand to the testicles (?) of the enemy of Horus. Open to me, O ye of the underworld, the box of myrrh that is in my hand; (3) receive me before you, O ye souls of Aker belonging to Bi-wekem, the box of frankincense that hath four corners. O dog, which is (4) called Anubis by name, who resteth on the box of myrrh, whose feet are set on the box of frankincense, let there come to me (5) the ointment for the son of the lamp that he (?) may give me answer as to everything about which I ask here to-day, truly without falsehood therein. (6) Io, Tabao, Soukhamamou, Akhakhanbou, Sanauani, Ethie, Komto, (7) Kethos, Basaethori, Thmila, Akhkhou, give me answer as to everything about which I ask here to-day.' Seven times. (8) The spells of the boy: 'Boel, Boel (*bis*), Ii (*bis*), Aa (*bis*), Tattat (*bis*), he that giveth light exceedingly, the companion of the flame, (9) he in whose mouth is the fire that is not quenched, the great god that sitteth in the fire, he that is in the midst of the fire, he that is in the lake of heaven, (10) in whose hand is the greatness and might of God, reveal thyself to this boy who hath my vessel to-day, and let him give me answer truly (11) without falsehood. I will glorify thee in Abydos, I will glorify thee in heaven before Phre, I will glorify thee (12) before the moon, I will glorify thee on earth, I will glorify thee before him who is upon the throne, who is not destroyed, he of the great glory, (13) Peteri, Peteri, Pater, Enphe, Enphe, the god who is above heaven, in

---

pair Shu and Tefnut were worshipped. Possibly the latter were identified with Aker.

The animal of Anubis was strictly a fox according to its shape, but coloured black.

l. 5. *p šre ḫ̮bs*. Is this an expression for the wick, or for the boy-medium, or for the god?

l. 8. Lines 8–18, cf. 5/12–22.

14. ʿne-f n t·t-f ʾr t ḫp ntr e bnp ntr t ḫp-f ʾm a ḫn n t mt·t n ty st·t nt ty ḥ·t-k pa bwel (ⲁⲛⲓⲏⲗ)

15. nte-k t { m’-y p ʿš-sḫne nt e-y šn ḫrr-f ty n p-hw
16. { p zr n n bel·w n p ʿlw nt ḫr pe hne a t

my mʾ-s my stm-s p ntr ʿo }
mʾ-f-s erme msz-f a t stm-f p ntr ʿo } s-ʾy-s-ʾy-ḥwt sp-sn

17. (ⲁⲭⲣⲉⲙⲙⲧⲱ) ʾm a ḫn { ḫr zz-y n p-hw nte-k t wn
18. { n t mt·t n ty st·t

yr·t a bl n mt·t nb nt e-y šll ḫrr-w ty n p-hw } p ntr ʿo nt

ḥr p tw n gʾbʾ·wn ghʿbʿh-ʿo (ⲧⲁⲕⲁⲣⲧⲁⲧ) e·ʾr-k ʿš ny

19. šʿ nte p wyn ḫp a·ʾre p wyn ḫp e·ʾr-k st e·ʾr-k ʿš ty ḫ·t(?) sḫ n wḥm ʿn tey-s t ḫ·t n p thm

20. ḥ-s nt e·ʾr-k ʿš-s ʾy a·z(?) n-y sp-sn ths ten-ʿo-r p yt n nḫe z·t p ntr nt ḥr p t tre-f sʿlkm-ʿo

21. bʿlkm-ʿo brʿk nephr-ʿo·b-ʿn-p-rʿ bryʿs sʿry-ntr·w melykhryphs

22. lʿrnknʿnes herephes mephr-ʿo·bryʿs phrgʿ phekse ntsywpšyʿ

23. mʿrmʿreke·t lʿ-ʿo-re·grepšye my nw-y a p wḥ n p šn nt e-y ty e-tbe·t-f my ʾr-w n-y wḥ

24. a mt·t nb nt e-y šn ḫrr-w ty n p-hw n mt·t mʿ·t n wš n mt·t n ʿze ʾy ʾtʿel ʾpthe gh-ʿo·gh-ʿo·m-ʿo-le

25. hesen·myngʿ·nt-ʿo-n ʿo-rth-ʿo·bʿwb-ʿo n-ʿo-ere sere·sere sn-gʿthʿrʿ

26. eresgšyngʿl sʿkgyste n-t-te·gʿgyste ʿkrwr-ʿo·b-ʿo-re g-ʿo-ntere

---

ll. 15, 17. These interlineations are words to be substituted in the case of no medium being employed.

l. 19. *ty k·t* was first written before *sḫ*, and then *ḫ* written upon the *k*: see the Glossary.

l. 20. *ʾy*: after this word the name of the deity invoked would be expected: a vertical line following may indicate an omission. *z n-y sp-sn* would seem to be an imperative with emphasis.

l. 22. *ntsywpšyʿ*. *nt* represents δ and *ts* θ, so *nts* probably represents an aspirated *d*, i.e. *dh*, which is transcribed in the Greek by Δ alone; but *ts* also represents Δ in 2/26.

l. 25. Hesenmigadon, &c. A similar string of names occurs in Brit.

whose hand is the beautiful staff, (14) who created deity, deity not having created him, come into the midst of this fire that is here before thee, he of Boel, Aniel

(15) { cause me to see the business about
(16) and do thou { give strength to the eyes of the boy

{ which I am inquiring here to-day, let it be seen, let
{ who has my vessel, to cause him to see it, and to his

{ it be heard } O great god Sisihout,
{ ears to cause him to hear it, }

(17) { before me and cause my eyes
(18) Akhremto, come in { into the midst of this flame,

(17) to be opened to everything for which I pray here to-day, (18) O great god that is upon the hill of ⟨Atugi⟩ Gabaon, Khabaho, Takrtat.' You recite this (19) until the light appear. When the light appears, you turn round (?), you recite this spell-copy a second time again. Behold the spell-copy also (?) of the summons (20) that you recite: 'Ho! speak to me (*bis*) Thes, Tenor, the father of eternity without end, the god who is over the whole earth, Salkmo, (21) Balkmo, Brak, Nephro, Bampre, Brias, Sarinter, Melikhriphs, (22) Largnanes, Herephes, Mephrobrias, Pherka, Phexe, Diouphia, (23) Marmareke, Laore-Krephie, may I see the answer to the inquiry on account of which I am here, may answer be made to me (24) to everything about which I ask here to-day, truly without falsehood. Ho! Adael, Aphthe, Khokhomole, (25) Hesenmigadon, Orthobaubo, Noere, Sere, Sere, Sere, San-kathara, (26) Ereskhigal, Saggiste, Dodeka-

---

Mus. Gr. Pap. No. XLVI. l. 424, et seq.; WESSELY, Ephes. Gram., 36, 244–5, 341, 377.

l. 26. Ereshkigal is the Sumerian goddess of the Underworld, cf. LEGGE, P. S. B. A., xxii. 121, lit. 'mistress of the Great Land,' i. e. the infernal regions; see the myth in BUDGE and BEZOLD, Tel-el-amarna Tablets, No. 82, p. 140; the name is found also in an Assyrian text in R. C. THOMPSON, Reports of the Magicians and Astrologers, No. 267 (from

27. e·ʾr-k t ʾr-f wn yr·t-f nte-f nw m-s p ḫbs nte-k šn·t-f a p nt e·ʾr-k wḫ-f a·ʾre ʿw n ḥt ḫp e bnp-f nw a p ntr e.ʾr-k st-k

28. e·ʾr-k ʿš pe-f ḥtr z-mt·t semeʿ·gʿn-tw gen-tw g-ʿo-n-tw geryn-tw ntʿreng-ʿo lekʿwks

29. ʾm n-y gʿnʿb a·ʾry kʿt-ʿy bʿrykʿt-ʿy ʾtn ʿḥ n n ntr-w ʾtn stm ḫrw-y my z-w n-y wḥ

30. a mt·t nb nt e-y šn ḫrr-w ty n p-hw ʾy p ste nsʿlʿbʿḥ-ʿo nʿsyrʿ hʿke twn-f p my sr*i*w

31. my nw-y a p wyn n p-hw erme n ntr·w nte-w z n-y wḥ a mt·t nb nt e-y šn ḫrr-w ty n p-hw n mt·t mʿ·t nʿ·nʿ·nʿ·nʿ rn-k

32. nʿnʿ pe-k rn n mte e·ʾr-k ʿš šmšeke n ḫrw-k e-f ʿy e·ʾr-k ʿš z ʾm n-y yʿh-ʿo yʿ-ʾw

33. yʿh-ʿo ʿwḥ-ʿo yʿh-ʿo hʾy k hw qʾ nʿ-šbt ʾr-py-hpe ʿblʿ-bl-n-bk

34. ḥr n bk ny-ʿbyt thʿtlʿt my-ʾry-bl

Col. VIII.

1. a [ʾre p ntr (?)] ʾsq a tm ʾy a(?) ḫn e·ʾr-k ʿš

2. my-ʾry-bl·qmlʿ·kykḥ p-yt-yt·w n n ntr·w pḫr wʿ·t yr·t rym k·t sby yʿḥ sp-ṣn sp-sn ḥʿ·ḥʿ·he

3. st·st·st·st yḥʾ yʿh-ʿo ḥḥ my ʾw n-y p ntr nte p wḥ-sḥne n p-hw n t·t-f nte-f z n-y wḥ a mt·t nb

4. nt e-y šn ḫrr-w ty n p-hw e·ʾr-k z pf-ntr(?) n r-k tne sp nb n e·ʾr-k ʿš te-y ḥwy ḫyt ar-k n p nt ḫt nʾm-k n p nt ʿme nʾm-k

---

information kindly supplied by Mr. Thompson and Mr. Hall, of the British Museum).

l. 28. The names in this line are found in Pap. XLVI above, l. 428, and also on a Gnostic gem described by Goodwin, Cambridge Essays, 1853, p. 54.

l. 30. *twn-f*, 'raise him up!' or with reflexive masc. suffix 'arise!' instead of fem. as in Coptic τοϒнοс, 'arise!'

Col. VIII.

l. 1. The short heading seems only intended to remind the reader of the subject in hand (see 6/27), and is not a new heading.

kiste, Akrourobore, Kodere.' (27) You make him open his eyes and look at the lamp, and ask him as to that which you wish. If obstinacy appear, he not having seen the god, you turn round (?), (28) you pronounce his compulsion. Formula: 'Semea-kanteu, Kenteu, Konteu, Kerideu, Darenko, Lekaux, (29) come to me, Kanab, Ari-katei, Bari-katei, disk, moon of the gods, disk, hear my voice, let answer be given me (30) as to everything about which I ask here to-day. O perfume of Zalabaho, Nasira, Hake, arise (?) O Lion-ram, (31) let me see the light to-day, and the gods; and let them give me answer as to everything about which I ask here to-day truly. Na, Na, Na, Na, is thy name, (32) Na, Na, is thy true name.' You utter a whisper (?) with your voice loudly; you recite saying, 'Come to me Iaho, Iaeu, (33) Iaho, Auho, Iaho, Hai, Ko, Hoou, Ko, Nashbot, Arpi-Hap (?), Abla, Balbok, (34) Honbek (Hawk-face), Ni, Abit, Thatlat, Maribal.'

COL. VIII.

(1) If [the god (?)] delay so as not to come in, you cry: (2) 'Maribal, Kmla, Kikh, Father of the fathers of the gods, go round (?), one Eye weeps, the other laughs. Ioh (*bis*, *bis*), Ha, Ha, He, (3) St, St, St, St, Ihe, Iaho, seek (?); let there come to me the god in whose hand is the command to-day, and let him give me reply to everything (4) about which I ask here to-day.' You say, 'Pef-nuti (?)' with your mouth each

---

l. 2. This continues from 6/34, which is short because of meeting the ruling: v. the facsimile.

my 'r-y bl is repeated from the end of 6/34. Such repetition is usual where a page ends in the middle of a paragraph (e.g. in Cols. II–III, VI–VII), but there are exceptions as in Cols. IX–X. The sign over *bl* is hieratic for [hieroglyph] (=*bl*), as in 11/12.

l. 4. *pf-ntr*(?): possibly an archaic expression, 'that god,' but this and

5. my ʾre p kke prze a p wyn ne-ḥr-y ʾy p ntr ḥw-ḥs rʿ·t ḫtm sy sp-sn ʾw ḥw ʾw ḥ·t b-ʾr-y

6. ghʾ ʾt rʿ·t šfe bybyw yʿh-ʿo ʿryʿḥʿ sp-sn a·ʾry n-s e-w a st ḥr bks gs·gs·gs·gs

7. yʿnyʿn e·ʾr-n e-y bs ks·ks·ks·ks my ʾw n-y p ntr nte p wḥ-sḥne n t·t-f nte-f z n-y wḥ a mt·t nb nt e-y

8. šn ḫrr-w ty n p-hw ʾm a ḫn pyʾ-t·w ḫy-tre·t ʾy ḫp ḫpe ḫp ʿbrʿ-ḥmė p zf n t yr·t n t wz

9. qmr·qmr·qmr·qmr qm-r a·t ḫp qm·qm wr wt š . . knwš pe-k rn n mte my z-w n-y wḥ

10. a mt·t nb nt e-y šn ḫrr-w ty n p-hw ʾm n-y bʿkʿksykhekh a·zy n-y wḥ a mt·t nb nt e-y šn ḫrr-w ty n p-hw n mt·t mʿ·t

11. n wš n z n-y mt·t n ʿze z-mt·t sp VII

12. wʿ . . . . a ḫrw pe-sḫ p wʿb n ks e-f z nʾm-f z e-f znt n sp IX

13. ank r-mšw šw r-mšw p šre n ta p šw n mw·t-f ta p šw e-f ḫp

14. e t mn t mt·t ne ḫp mpr ʾy n-y n pe-k ḥr n pḫe·t e·ʾr-k a ʾy n-y n pe-k ḫbr n wʿb

15. n pe-k sšt n rm ḥ·t-ntr e-f ḫp e bn-e-s a ḫp e·ʾr-k ʾy n-y n pe-k smte n gʿlʿšyre

16. z ʾnk r-mšw šw r-mšw p šre n ta p šw n mw·t-f ta p šw a ḥr

---

other expressions that seem to have a meaning, such as 'do for her' *arainas*, 'they shall return' *euesôl*, in l. 6, are likely to be only gibberish ejaculations; cf. δωδεκακιστη in Greek magic.

ne'r-k = conjunctive ⲛⲧ̄, usually written *nte-k* as Boh. ⲛⲧⲉⲕ.

l. 8. *wz*. The 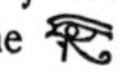 eye is named ους (cf. gen. ουατ-ος), ουατιον B. M. Pap. XLVI. 75 and 92, pointing to the pronunciation ⲟⲩⲁϫⲉ, ⲟⲩⲟϫⲉ (?), cf. ταουατις, 'she of the sacred eye,' in Spiegelb., Eigenn., p. 51*.

l. 12. *pe-sḫ*. There is no determinative to prove that this is a proper name. The previous sign instead of *ḫrw*, 'voice,' might be read as 'foreigner,' or 'Greek,' cf. 4/7, V. 3/12.

time, and you cry, 'I cast fury at thee of him who cutteth thee, of him who devoureth thee. (5) Let the darkness separate from the light before me. Ho! god, Hu-hos, Ri-khètem, Si (*bis*), Aho (?), Ah, Mai (?) ("I do not"?), (6) Kha, Ait, Ri-shfe, Bibiu, Iaho, Ariaha (*bis*), Arainas ("do for her"), Euesetho ("they will turn the face"), Bekes, Gs, Gs, Gs, Gs, (7) Ianian, Eren, Eibs, Ks, Ks, Ks, Ks, let the god come to me in whose hand is the command and give me answer as to everything about which I (8) inquire here to-day. Come in, Piatoou, Khitore; ho! Shop, Shope, Shop, Abraham, the apple (?) of the Eye of the Uzat, (9) Kmr, Kmr, Kmr, Kmr, Kmro, so as to create, Kom, Kom-wer-wot, Sheknush (?) is thy real name, let answer be told to me (10) as to everything about which I ask here to-day. Come to me Bakaxikhekh, tell me answer to everything which I ask about here to-day truly (11) without telling me falsehood.' Formula. Seven times.

(12) A direct (?) inquiry by (?) the voice of Pasash (?) the priest of Kes; he (the informant) tells it, saying it is tested, nine times: (13) 'I am Ramshau, Shau, Ramshau son of Tapshau, of his mother Tapshau, if it be that (14) any given thing shall happen, do not come to me with thy face of Pekhe; thou shalt come to me in thy form of a priest, (15) in thy figure of a servant of the temple. (But) if it shall not come to pass, thou (shalt) come to me in thy form of a Kalashire, (16) for I am Ramshau, Shau, Ramshau, the son of Tapshau, of his

---

Ks may be Cusae, or Cynopolis (El Qais), or some other town in Middle Egypt.

'Nine times tried' seems proverbial, cf. 14/31; and for the whole sentence, 29/1.

l. 14. *Pḫe·t*, a feline goddess worshipped at Speos Artemidos near Beni-Hasan in Middle Egypt. LANZONE, Diz. Mit., 234.

l. 15. *gꜥlꜥšyre*, see the Glossary.

17. p ḫpš n p mḥ III n p wrš e wn wʿ yb n mzwl ḥt n ḫlpe III e wn mḥ-n-tp III

18. n bʿnyp tks nʾm-f nte-k ʿš n·y ar-f n sp VII nte-k ḫʿ·f ne-zz-k ḫr nw-f n-k nte-f sze erme-k

Col. IX.

1. p šn-hne n Ḫns . . . ḥr-k Ḫns m ws·t nfr ḥtp p syf šps ʾr pyr n p sšn Ḥr nb nw wʿ pw . . .

2. ʾy ḥt nb ḥt ʾy šn-ty·t nb šn-ty·t nb ʾtn p ntr ʿo p k wt p šre n p ʾkš ʾm n-y p syf šps p ntr ʿo nt [ḫn]

3. p ʾtn nte ḥn-w . . . p-ʿo-m-ʿo nt e-w z n-f p k sp-sn wr p ntr ʿo nt ḫn t wz·t ʾr pyr a bl ḫn p IV [ḫn]

4. n z·t p tbe n n ef·w nt e b ʾr-rḫ-w rn-f b ʾr-rḫ-w ky-f b rḫ-w smte-f te-y ʾr-rḫ⟨-w⟩ rn-k te-y ʾr-rḫ⟨-w⟩ ky-k te-y [ʾr-rḫ⟨-w⟩]

5. smte-k ʿo rn-k ʾw rn-k ʾḫ rn-yk ʾmn rn-k wr ntr·w rn-yk ʾmn rn-f a ntr·w nb rn-yk ʿo·m

6. wr ʿm rn-k ntr·w nb rn-yk srpt-my-sr rn-yk l-ʿo-w ʾy nb t·w sp-sn rn-yk ʾmʿḫr n p·t rn-k sšn n syw . . .

---

l. 17. τριταιας ουσης της σεληνης Pap. Bibl. Nat. l. 170.

yb, lit. 'tooth.' Cf. Lat. 'spica allii.'

Col. IX.

l. 1. *Ḫns-m-ws·t-nfr-ḥtp*, the title of the principal form of Khons at Thebes, see the Bekhten stela. Khons was a moon-god, son of Amen and Mut. He is here identified with Horus and other gods.

For Horus rising from the lotus-flower see Lanzone, Diz. Mit., ccxiv.

'Lord of time,' as the moon regulating seasons.

l. 2. *ḥt*, 'silver,' the moon-colour.

šn-ty·t, 'circuit of the underworld (?).'

p k wt, cf. his title 'ein feuriger Stier' in an inscription translated by Brugsch, Religion, p. 360; *wt* is evidently the Eg. *wʾz*.

p ʾkš, the Ethiopian, i. e. Amen, who at this time was popularly considered as, above all, the god of Meroe: see V. 20/1 and note.

l. 3. *nte ḥn-w* . . . Cf. ϩⲛⲉ- ϩⲛⲁ= and below l. 10, and with the idea cf. Khons' title *nb ʾw·t ib*, 'lord of joy.'

p IV ḫn n z·t, cf. l. 13 with gloss. ϩⲛⲁⲉ. *ḫn* is a vessel below 12/29. Here it may be a 'space' referring to the 'four quarters.' *z·t* may perhaps refer to 'space,' not time. One may also suggest the meaning of 'four boundaries' or 'four seasons,' and in l. 8 *ḫn* seems to mean

mother Tapshau.' [Say it] opposite (17) the Shoulder constellation on the third day of the month, there being a clove of three-lobed white garlic and there being three needles (18) of iron piercing it, and recite this to it seven times; and put it at thy head. Then he attends to you and speaks with you.

Col. IX.

(1) The vessel-inquiry of Chons. '[Homage ?] to thee, Chons-in-Thebes-Nefer-hotep, the noble child that came forth from the lotus, Horus, lord of time (?), one he is . . . (2) Ho! silver, lord of silver, Shentei, lord of Shentei, lord of the disk, the great god, the vigorous bull, the Son of the Ethiopian, come to me, noble child, the great god that is in (3) the disk, who pleaseth men (?), Pomo, who is called the mighty bull (*bis*), the great god that is in the *Uzat*, that came forth from the four [boundaries ?] (4) of eternity, the punisher of the flesh (?), whose name is not known, nor his nature, nor his likeness (?). I know thy name, I know thy nature, I [know] (5) thy likeness. Great is thy name, Heir is thy name, Excellent is thy name, Hidden is thy name. Mighty one of the gods is thy name, "He whose name is hidden from all the gods" is thy name, Om, (6) Mighty Am is thy name, "All the gods" is thy name, Lotus-lion-ram is thy name, "Loou comes, lord of the lands" (*bis*) is thy name, Amakhr of heaven is thy name, "Lotus-flower of stars (?)

---

a 'cycle.' Cf. *τα τεσσαρα μερη του ουρανου και τα τεσσαρα θεμελια της γης*, B. M. Pap. CXXI. 552.

l. 4. *p tbe*, cf. note on Petbe in P. S. B. A. xxii. 162.

te-y ʾr-rḫw: the written *w* seems meaningless, for *rḫ* is not here in *stm-f* dependent on *te-y*. The latter is the pron. 1st sing. ϯ followed by inf. or pseudo-part. For *ʾr-rḫ* see Griffith, High Priests, p. 106.

l. 5. *ʾḫ* with gloss ⲁϧ and therefore not 'spirit,' which would be ⲓϧ. Perhaps it is the adjective 'beneficial.'

'He whose name is hidden from all the gods,' a phrase current in the New Kingdom for Amenra.

7. ꜣy ꜣy-y-ꜥo ne-ꜣy-ꜥo rn-yk pe-k sšt mẖrr n ḥr n sre e st-f n bk e bs II ẖrr-f pe-k [ḥfe ḥfe]

8. n z·t pe-k ḥn n wrš pe-k ẖ n ẖ n elle ꜣšt pe-k sym n sym n ꜣMn pe-k ꜣrw n t p·t byn pe-k rym n [p mty ?]

9. lbs km st smn·t ḥr p t yb rn-k n te-k·t ẖe·t n p yꜥm pe-k sšt n ꜣny a·pyr-k nꜣm-f . . .

10. t p·t te-k·t qnḥ·t p t te-k·t hyw·t wn-ne p ḥny a mḥt nꜣm-k ty n p-hw z ꜣnk ẖꜥ(?) mne nw . . . y

11. ꜣꜣe e bnp-y ꜣr-f ẖr ꜣsq e bnp-y gm rn-yk p ntr ꜥo nte (ne-)ꜥy rn-f p ḥry ẖte·t n t p·t a·ꜣr-y ꜣr-f ꜣr [p ḥkr ?]

12. n p t p ꜣyb n p mw nte-k nẖt nte-k t wz-y nte-k t n-y ḥs·t mr·t šfe·t a ḥr rm nb z ꜣnk pe p k . . .

13. p ntr ꜥo nt ẖn t wz·t ꜣr pyr a bl ẖn p IV ḥn n z·t ꜣnk ḥwne p rn ꜥo nt n t p·t nt e-w z n-f . . .

14. ꜣm-ph-ꜥo-w sp-sn n mꜥ·t sp-sn ḥs-f a ꜣBt Rꜥ Ḥr ḥnn(?) pe pe rn ḥry ntr·w rn-t n mte nẖt my wz-y my ẖpe pe hne . . .

15. a·wn n-y n ꜥrq-ḥḥ a ḥr ntr nb rm nb ꜣr pyr

---

l. 7. The figure described may be compared with the ram-headed scarabs having hawk's wings which are common on late coffins, on the breast of the figure upon the inner coffins. What *bs* is is not evident. These scarabs often hold two Shen rings, or two sceptres with Maat feathers on the end.

pe-k [*ḥfe ḥfe*] *n z·t*. There seems to be space in the lacuna for the whole groups spelled out, as in l. 20. The extent of the lacuna, about 2 cm., can be judged by l. 12, where *k*[*wr*] has to be read. For the *ḥf n z·t*, cf. I Kham. iii. 31; GRIFF., High Priests, p. 22; and *τον αειζωον οφιν* Pap. Bibl. Nat. 1323.

l. 8. *ꜣšt*. The identity of this fruit-tree is very uncertain, v. LORET, Flore Phar., 2nd ed. p. 102.

rym n [*p mty* ?]. Cf. I Kham. iii. 13, but the precise wording required is quite uncertain.

l. 9. *lbs*. There is a fish called *λεβιας*; and there is the modern لبيس. On the latter Mr. G. A. BOULENGER kindly furnishes a note, 'the lebis is the Arabic name of Labeo Niloticus, a fish allied to and not unlike our carp. Like the latter, without being absolutely black, it may be of a very dark olive brown above.'

yb probably has a definite meaning, but as yet it is obscure.

l. 10. *e ḥn-y*. This reading is possible, see the facsimile.

(7) cometh," Ei-io Ne-ei-o is thy name. Thy form is a scarab with the face of a ram; its tail a hawk's, it wearing (?) two panther-skins (?). Thy [serpent is a serpent ?] (8) of eternity, thine orbit (?) a lunar month, thy tree a vine-tree and persea (?), thy herb the herb of Amen, thy fowl of heaven a heron, thy fish of [the deep (?)] (9) a black *lebes.* They are established on earth. Yb is thy name in thy body in (?) the sea, thy figure of stone in which thou camest forth is a . . .; (10) heaven is thy shrine, the Earth thy fore-court; it was my will (?) to seize thee here to-day, for I am one shining, enduring: my . . . (11) faileth (?) if I have not done it through (?) the delay, I not having discovered thy name, O great god whose name is great, the lord of the threshing-floor (?) of heaven. (But) I have done it, [enduring ?] hunger (12) for bread, and thirst for water; and do thou rescue (?) me and make me prosper and give me praise, love, and reverence before every man. For I am (?) the [mighty] bull, (13) the great god that is in the *Uzat*, that came forth from the four regions (?) of space (?). I am *Hune* (youth), the great name that is in heaven, whom they call . . . (14) Amphoou (*bis*), "True" (*bis*), "He is praised to (?) Abydos," "Ra," "Horus the boy" is my name, "Chief of the gods" is my correct name, preserve me, make me to prosper, make my vessel to become [successful ?]. (15) Open to

---

l. 11. *a·ʾr-y.* The translation is uncertain owing to the lacuna.

l. 12. *ʾnk pe p k* might mean 'I am he of the [mighty] bull'; if not, the magician identifies himself with Khons, see l. 3.

l. 14. *ḥs-f a ʾBt.* The *a* as a separate letter seems certain, v. the facs. The gloss *hsef* has the appearance of a construct form, but it may well be for *hsaf.* Even so it is difficult to find a meaning for the phrase.

The reading of the group following *Rʿ-Ḥr* is not certain. The signs are 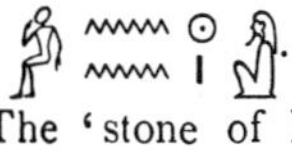.

l. 15. The 'stone of Ptah' is not otherwise known. For Ptah as a creator see BRUGSCH, Religion, p. 110; BREASTED, A. Z., 1901, 51.

a bl ḫn p ʾny n Ptḥ z ank p ḥf ʾr pyr n p nwn ʾnk . . .

16. bre n ʾkš ʿnḫ n ḥf n nb n mʿ·t a·ʾre ʾbye n sp·t p nt e-y a z·t-f ḫr ḫpe-f twn hy . . .

17. apḥte z ʾnk ʾNp p sst (*sic*) nḫne ʾnk ʾS·t e-y a mr-f ank Wsr e-y a mr-f ank ʾNp [e-y a mr]-f e·ʾr-k a nḥm-t a . . . nb

18. s·t thth nb lsmtnwt lsmʿtot nḫt my wz-y my n-y ḥs·t mr·t šfe·t ḫn pe hne . . .

19. pe swt ty n p-hw ʾm-t n-y ʾS·t t nb ḥyq t wr ḥyq n n ntr·w tre·w Ḥr ḥ·t ʾS·t m-s-y Nb·t-ḥ·t n te grpe

20. wʿ ḥf n šre ʾTm p nt . . . n ʿre·t a zz-y ze p nt e-f a myšt e-f a myš stn Mnt ty n p-hw(?) n wʿ(?) . . .

21. a my-ḥs apḥte a t še a wʿ my n šr my-ḥs a bl e-f qby a·ʾn·t-w n-y sp-sn n by n ntr n by

22. n rm n by n t ty·t n by n t ʾḫy·t n ʾyḫ·w n n·mw·t-w nte-w ⟨my ʾr-w⟩ z n-y n t mʿ·t n p-hw a p nt e-y šn m-s-f z ʾ[nk]

The snake as word-sign has six loops here and in 21/4, four loops in l. 16. This agrees with the snake determinative of *šʿy* which has usually four loops, once (19/12) six loops, and twice (3/3, 5/9) two loops, and Shoi is said to be 'in Nun' 2/5. It is thus the snake of Shay. But the sign, meaning distinctly a (sacred) snake, cannot read *šʿy*, which always means distinctly a divinity. *Ḥfe* is perhaps the most probable reading, see esp. 21/4; the det. of that word in 9/20 has only two loops, but in Louvre dem. Mag. iii. 9 five or six loops. *Syt* 14/3, V. 27/1 has four loops, but the head seems to be raised high; *syt* is derived from Eg. *sʾ-tʾ* which is represented by  in late texts, Br., Dict. Geogr., 762.

l. 16. *bre*: cf. ⲃⲱⲱⲣⲉ, 'intumescere,' ⲃⲟⲣⲉ, 'fastuose se gerere,' or better ⲃⲉⲣⲓ, 'juvenis.'

ʿnḫ is evidently the serpent word met with in 1/3. Possibly both *bre* and *ʿnḫ* are adjectives, and the construction may resemble the familiar Coptic construction with adjectives, St., § 187.

t-wn, apparently an unetymological spelling for ⲡⲧⲟⲩⲛⲟⲩ: cf. 18/21.

l. 17. *sst*, error for *snt*: cf. 18/22.

l. 20. *wʿ ḥf n šre ʾTm*. Atum being a form of Ra, this may refer to the

me Arkhah before every god and every man that hath come forth from the stone of Ptah. For I am the serpent that came forth from Nun, I am a (16) proud (?) Ethiopian, a rearing serpent of real gold, there being honey in my (?) lips; that which I shall say cometh to pass at once. Ho! . . . (17) mighty one, for I am Anubis, the baby creature (?); I am Isis and I will bind him, I am Osiris and I will bind him, I am Anubis [and I will bind] him. Thou wilt save me from every . . . (18) and every place of confusion (?). Lasmatnout, Lesmatot, protect me, heal me, give me love, praise and reverence in my vessel (19), my bandage (?) here to-day. Come to me, Isis, mistress of magic, the great sorceress of all the gods. Horus is before me, Isis behind me, Nephthys as my diadem, (20) a snake of the son(s) of Atum is that which . . . a uraeus-diadem at my head; for he that shall strike (?) me (?) shall strike (?) King Mont here to-day . . . (21) Mihos, mighty one shall send out a lion of the sons of Mihos under compulsion to fetch them to me (*bis*) the souls of god, the souls (22) of man, the souls of the Underworld, the souls of the horizon, the spirits, the dead, so that they tell me the truth to-day concerning that

---

poisonous serpent formed by Isis from the spittle of Ra, to bite him and make him reveal his secret name (texts of New Kingdom). With the construction compare l. 21 *wᶜ my n šr my-hs*, 10/13 *tbe·t III n tbe·t nmy*, and 10/10 *šᶜ n ʾny*.

l. 21. *My-ḥs*, a lion-god, son of Bubastis. For the pronunciation of the name see Spiegelberg, Eigennamen, p. 4*.

t še a: the *a* is quite certain, but is very puzzling.

a·ʾn·t-w n-y sp-sn. This should be an imperative: see also the parallel l. 35. Possibly *sp-sn* is falsely written here.

n by, gloss. ⲛⲃⲁⲓ. The plural sign is often omitted with *by*, and here we see the reason, viz. that the plural had no special form.

l. 22. *n·mw·t-w*, cf. l. 25. The prefixed *n* seems to represent a reduplication of the initial *m*, *n* being regularly assimilated to a following *m*.

Here we have νεκυες και οι δαιμονες of Pap. Bibl. Nat. 1453.

23. Ḥr s ʾS·t e-f ʾnnʿ a mr n ʿrq-ḥḥ a hwy qs·t a ḥr n s·w a t mnḫ·t n p ḥsy

24. p ḥsy nfr n n ḥsy·w e·ʾr-k nhs e·ʾr-k a rpy ḥr r n r·w n pe hne pe swt pe zʿl mt·t . . .

25. nhs nʾm-w n-y [n] ʾyh·w n mt·w nhs pe-w by pe-w sšt n n r·w n pe hne nhs-w nʾm-w n-y . . .

26. erme n mt·w nhs nʾm-w n-y sp-sn nhse(?) pe-w by erme pe-w sšt p ḫyt n py-s s wnte ta ʿrb . . .

27. nhs nʾm-w n-y sp-sn [n wn]te-w n ne-w s·t tbe my ʾr-w sze n r-w my ʾr-w mt·t n spe-w my ʾr-w z p-e·z-y [a p nt]

28. e-y šn ḫrr-f ty n p-hw my ʾr-w mt·t n . . . my ʾre mt·t mʿ·t ḫp n-y mpr t ḥr ḫr ḥr rn ḫr rn n mʿ·t sp-sn(?) [e mn]

29. mt·t n ʿze nʾm-w(?) [ʾy] p mḫrr n ḫstb n mʿ·t nt ḥms ḥr zz p šy n p pr-ʿo Wsr wn-nfr . . .

30. mḥ r-k n mw n(?) . . . kš-f a zz-y erme p nt ne-t·t my wz-y my wz-f θs-pḫr šʿ nte p-e·z[-y ḫp m]y ʾre

31. p-e·z-y ḫp z e·ʾre tm te(?) p-e·z-y ḫp e-y a t qte t st·t n p qte n ty sewe šʿ nte p-e·z-y ḫp z . . .

32. a p t stm-w n-y . . . z-w n-y nte-k nym sp-sn ʾnk ʾTm n p wtn n p rʿ ank ʿryʿttw t št-ʿo·t n(?) . . .

---

l. 23. *a mr·t* in the Khamuas stories means 'on board ship' (High Priests, p. 98), but **ⲉⲙⲏⲣ** in Coptic is 'across,' 'to the other side,' 'beyond.' *a mr n* may be 'beyond' as a preposition; the same word is used in 15/12 in the same connexion (with the tomb of Osiris at Abydos).

l. 24. *e·ʾr-k.* The gloss is certainly **ⲉⲧ**, and must be a correction.

swt is difficult to understand. The idea must be founded on the use of knots in magic, Lat. 'ligatura.'

zʿl-mt·t probably = 'word-seeking,' from Eg. *zʿr*, preserved also in **ϫⲏⲣ**, &c. Were all these used at once, or were they alternatives?

l. 26. *wnte*: cf. Lanz., Diz. Mit., 165, or better Brugsch, Wtb. Suppl., 322. It would be possible to read *ḥwnte*. From the next line the *wnte* would seem to be souls in torment or else punishing demons.

l. 27. *spe-w*, see Glossary, s.v. *spt*.

after which I am inquiring: for I am (23) Horus son of Isis who goeth on board at Arkhah to put wrappings on the amulets, to put linen on the Drowned one, (24) the fair Drowned one of the drowned (?). They shall rise, they shall flourish at the mouths of my vessel, my bandage (?), my word-seeking (?). (25) Arouse them for me (*bis*), the spirits, the dead; rouse their souls and forms at (?) the mouths of my vessel; rouse them for me (26) with the dead; rouse [them] for me (*bis*); rouse their souls and their forms. The fury of Pessiwont ("Her (whose) son is Wont"), the daughter of Ar . . . (27) rouse them for me (*bis*), the Unti from their places of punishment, let them talk with their mouths, let them speak with their lips, let them say that which I have said, [about that which] (28) I am asking them here to-day; let them speak before (?) me, let truth happen to me; do not substitute a face for a face, a name for a true (*bis*) name [without] (29) falsehood in it. [Ho ?] scarab of true lapislazuli that sitteth at the pool of Pharaoh Osiris Unnefer! (30) fill thy mouth with the water of [the pool ?], pour it on my head together with him who is at my hand; make me prosper, make him prosper, and conversely, until my words [happen ?], let (31) that which I say come to pass; for if that which I have said do not come to pass, I will cause fire to go round about this *Seoue* until that which I have said do come to pass; for [they came] (32) to the earth, they listened to me . . . they said to me, "Who art thou?" (*bis*), I am Atum in the sun-boat of Phre;

l. 28. *n ḥr*(?) *t-y*(?). Perhaps a very incorrect writing for *n ḥ·t-y*, 'before me.'

l. 29. *p šy*. Perhaps the 'lake of U-Peke' in 12/17.

l. 31. *e·'re tm te*, **ерет̄ϫ̄-**, but the *te* is inexplicable.

sewe. This seems a threat to burn the bandages or even the mummy of Osiris.

l. 32. *št-'o·t*, probably the chest, Eg. *šty·t*, of Osiris, Br., Wtb., 1410.

33. a·e-y kšp a bl ḥ‘[·t-k?] a nw m-s Wsr p ʾkš e-f ʾn·ʾw a ẖn a zz-y e wn šr ʾNp II ḥ·t-f šr Wpy [II m-s-f]

34. šr rr·t II mne [nʾm-]f z-w n-y nte-k nym sp-sn ank w‘ n py bk II nt rsy a ʾS·t erme Wsr t grp·t t . . .

35. erme py-s ‘w . . . a·ʾny·t-w n-y sp-sn n by n ntr n by n rm by n t ty·t n by n t ʾẖy·t

Col. X.

1. n ʾyẖ·w n mt·w my ʾr-w z n-y t m‘·t n p-hw ẖr p nt e-y šn ẖrr-f z ʾnk ʾrtemy(?) . . . mw·t e-f ẖ‘ ḥr ybt

2. ʾm n-y a ẖn ʾNp n pe-k ḥr nfr a·ʾr-y ʾy a wšte-k . . . sp-sn ẖ·t sp-sn . . . [rs mḥ]t ʾmnt ybt

3. tw n ʾmnt nb my ʾr-w ẖp e-w šs sp-sn e-w smn·t e-w swtn e-w pẖr e ẖ p ẖyt [n p wr?] šfe z ʾnk

4. y‘e y‘-‘o y‘e‘ y‘-‘o s‘b‘-‘o-th ‘-t-ne z te-y ḥwy [ẖyt] ar-k tsye gl‘te

5. ʾrkhe y-‘o-‘ ph‘lekmy y‘-‘o m‘kh‘h‘y yee kh-‘o . . . n kh-‘o-khrekhy ee-‘o-th

6. s‘rby‘qw ygr‘ pšybyeg m-‘o-mw mwnekh stsyth-‘o s-‘o-th-‘o-n n‘-‘o-n kh‘rm‘y

7. p ẖyt n ny ntr·w tre-w a·z-y rn-w ty n p-hw nhs nʾm-w n-y sp-sn n ḥsy·w n mt·w ‘nẖe(?) pe-tn by pe-tn sšt n-y

8. a n r·w n pe ẖbs pe swt pe z‘i‘ mt·t my ʾr-f n-y wḥ ẖr mt·t nb nt e-y šn [ẖrr-w] ty n p-hw n mt·t m‘·t sp-sn e mn mt·t

---

l. 33. 'The Ethiopian,' a curious epithet of Osiris. But he was worshipped in Ethiopia, Hdt. ii. 99, as well as at Philae, and he was dark-coloured, Plut., Is. et Os., c. 22. 33.

Ophois, Eg. *wp-w'·wt*, a jackal god.

l. 34. *Rr·t*, the name of the sow, **pıp**, and of the hippopotamus goddess, but here perhaps a snake goddess. The det. has only two loops.

grp·t. The det. is the uraeus, as in *‘re·t*, l. 20. In 20/6 it seems to be simply a two-looped snake.

Col. X.

l. 1. Possibly the meaning is 'Artemi in the mother's womb.'

I am Ariotatu, the *Shto* of . . . (33) I looked out before . . . to observe Osiris the Ethiopian, he came into my head, there being two sons of Anubis in front of him, [two] sons of Ophois behind him, (34) two sons of Rere mooring him. They said to me "Who art thou?" (*bis*). I am one of those two hawks that watch over Isis and Osiris, the diadem, the . . . (35) with its glory (?) . . . , bring them to me (*bis*), the souls of god, the souls of man, the souls of the Underworld, the souls of the horizon,

Col. X.

'(1) the spirits, the dead; let them tell me the truth to-day in that about which I shall ask: for I am Artemi . . . se(?)-mau, rising in the East. (2) Come in to me, Anubis with thy fair face, I have come to pray to thee. Woe (?) (*bis*), fire (*bis*), [South, North,] West, East, (3) every breeze of Amenti, let them come into being, proved (*bis*), established, correct, enchanted, like the fury [of the great one] of reverence; for I am (4) Iae, Iao, Iaea, Iao, Sabaoth, Atone; for I cast fury at thee, Thiai, Klatai, (5) Arkhe, Ioa, Phalekmi, Iao, Makhahai, Iee, Kho..n, Khokhrekhi, Aaioth, (6) Sarbiakou, Ikra, Phibiek, Momou, Mounaikh, Stitho, Sothon, Naon, Kharmai, (7) the fury of all these gods, whose names I have uttered here to-day, rouse them for me (*bis*), the drowned (?), the dead; let your (plur.) soul and your (plur.) form live for me (8) at the mouths of my lamp,

---

l. 2. *wšt*, 'salute with reverence' is the real meaning, not altogether lost in Coptic.

l. 4. *te-y ḥwy ẖyt ar-k* clearly corresponds to ἐξορκίζω σε.

tsye, gloss ⲑⲓⲁⲓ. ⲁⲓ is here probably = short ⲉ.

l. 7. *n ḥsy·w* opposed to *n mt·w*. In the Rhind. bil. *'ẖ ḥsy·w*, 'approved spirits,' often, vii. 10, xiii. 9, xvii. 2. So perhaps here 'approved,' not 'drowned.'

'nẖe, again with a meaning allied to that in 1/1

l. 8. *ẖbs*. Hitherto it has been the *hin*, 'vessel,' not the lamp.

9. n ʿze ḫn-w ys sp-sn tkr sp-sn pe-f swḥ-ʾyḫ ḫr še-k a wʿ pr n kke e [ḥr]-f wn a pr-rs nge pr-ybt

10. n wʿ mʿ e-f wʿb e·ʾr-k prḫ-f n šʿ e-f wʿb n ʾny n p yʿr-ʿo e·ʾr-k ʾny wʿ z n ḥmt e-f wʿb nge

11. wʿ hne n blz nmy nte-k t wʿ lq n mw n str nge mw e-f wʿb a p z ḥnʿ wʿ lq n nḥe n mʿ·t

12. e-f wʿb nge nḥe wʿet-f n wš n t mw ar-f nte-k t wʿ ʾny n qs-ʿnḫ(?) a ḫn p hne ḫr nḥe nte-k t wʿ ḥt

13. n pr-nfr n p ʾytn n p hne nte-k t qte tbe·t III n p qte n p hne n tbe·t nmy

14. nte-k ḫʿ t VII e-w wʿb ḥr n tbe·tw nt qte a p hne nte-k ʾny wʿ ḫm-ḫl e-f wʿb e-f znt

15. n ne-f msz·w a t ḥ·t z e-f [ʾr] šw n še ḫr p hne e·ʾr-k t ḥms-f ḥr [wʿ·t tbe·t] nmy nte-k ḥms ḥ-k

16. ḥr ke tbe·t e·ʾr-k wḥ pe-f [ḥr?] ke-z ʾ·t-f nte-k t t·t-k a r yr·t-f [e yr·t-f] ḫtm e·ʾr-k ʿš a ḫry

17. ḫn t mt·t n zz-f n sp VII [e·ʾr-k] wḥ e·ʾr-k fy t·t-k ḥr r yr·t-f e·ʾr-k . . . . p hne e·ʾr-k t t·t-k

18. a ne-f msz·w e·ʾr-k mḥt nʾm-w n t·t-k ḥ-k e·ʾr-k šn n p ḫm-ḫl z ʿn aeʾr-k [nw a p ntr? ʿo?] e-f z te-y nw a wʿ·t

19. kmeme·t e·ʾr-k z n-f ze a·z-ys z te-y nw a pe-k ḥr nfr e·ʾr-k . . . . . p ntr ʿo ʾNp

---

l. 9. *ys sp-sn tkr sp-sn* = ηδη ηδη ταχυ ταχυ of the Greek papyri.

l. 11. *lq* = **ⲗⲟϭ** : **ⲗⲟⲕ**, translating κοτυλη, which in the LXX. translates the Hebrew *log*. Whatever was the precise measure intended by the **ⲗⲟⲕ**, it seems to have taken the place of the Egyptian *hin* (less than a pint).

mw n str : apparently water allowed to stand for the night.

l. 12. *ḥt n pr-nfr*. The Good House is the place of embalming, GRIFF., High Priests, p. 25; but the presence of a plant det. no doubt indicates that it is a plant-name here. *Ḥt* might then be εγκαρδιον, as a botanical term 'core.' More probably the whole expression 'heart of the Good House' is to be taken as the name of a symbolical plant, such as the 'resurrection' plant, *Anastatica hierochuntina*, or something similar. Cf. the story of the flower enclosing the heart of Bata put in a cup of

my bandage (?), my word-seeking (?). Let him make me answer to every word [about] which I am asking here to-day in truth (*bis*) without (9) falsehood therein. Hasten (*bis*), quickly (*bis*).' Its spirit-gathering: You go to a dark chamber with its [face] open to the South or East (10) in a clean place; you sprinkle it with clean sand brought from the great river; you take a clean bronze cup or (11) a new vessel of pottery and put a *lok*-measure of water that has settled (?) or of pure water into the [cup] and a *lok*-measure of real oil (12) pure, or oil alone without putting water into it, and put a stone of *qs-ankh* in the vessel containing oil, and put a 'heart- (13) of-the-good-house' (plant ?) in the bottom of the vessel, and put three bricks round about the vessel, of new bricks, (14) and place seven clean loaves on the bricks that are round the vessel and bring a pure child that has been tested (15) in his ears before, that is, is profitable in proceeding with the vessel. You make him sit on a new [brick] and you also sit (16) on another brick, you being at (?) his face, otherwise said, his back, and you put your hand before [his] eyes, [his eyes being] closed and call down (17) into the middle of his head seven times. When you have finished, you take your hand from before his eyes, you [make him bend over] the vessel; you put your hand (18) to his ears, you take hold of them with your hand also, you ask the child saying, 'Do you [? see . . .]?' If he says, 'I see a (19) darkness,' you say to him 'Speak, saying, "I see thy beautiful face, and do thou [hear my salutation ?], O great god Anubis!"'

---

water to revive, in the story of the Two Brothers. *qs-ʿnḫ* might similarly be 'quicklime.'

l. 19. *wšte* is probably to be restored at the end of the gap, as in ll. 2, 26. The translation may be 'and do thou [pray to] the great god Anubis.'

20. e·ʾr-k wẖ a ʾr-f n hne wʿet-k e·ʾr-k mḥ yr·t-k n py kys e·ʾr-k [ḥms ẖr? p hne?] a ẖ p nt ḥry e yr·t-k

21. ẖtm e·ʾr-k ʿš p ʿš nt ḥry n sp VII e·ʾr-k wn yr·t-k e·ʾr-k šn·t-f a mt·t nb [nt e·ʾr-k wẖ-f? . . .] ẖr ʾr-k-f n θ n p hw

22. n mḥ IV n p wrš šʿ p hw n mḥ XV nte . . . pe e ʿḥ mḥ wz·t [šn hn]e wʿet a nw

23. a p wtn n p rʿ z-mt·t [a·]wn n-y t p·t t mw·t n n ntr·w my [nw-y a p wt]n n p rʿ e-f ẖty-ẖn[t]

24. ẖn-s z ʾnk Gb ʾrpe ntr·w šll p nt e-y ʾr nʾm-f mbḥ p rʿ pe y[t e-tbe] n mt·t·w ʾr še n t·t

25. ʾy ḥkne·t wr·t nb qnḥ·t tʾ-rʿ-št(?) a·wn n-y t nb ʾyẖ·[w a·wn] n-y t p·t ḥy[t]·t my

26. wšte-y n n wpt·w [z] ank Gb ʾrpe ntr·w ʾy p VII stn hy p [VII mnt] k syt nb šfe·t

27. sḥz t by nn(?) hy rw(?) mἰ rw(?) nn(?) k kke hy ẖnt-ybt·w

28. nwn wr ẖe hy by sre by ʾmnt·w hy [by by·w k] kke k k·w

---

l. 22. *ʿḥ mḥ wz·t*, i.e. at full moon.

šn hne wʿet = σκεψη δια λεκανης αυτοπτου, Pap. Bibl. Nat. l. 162; αυθοπτικη λεκανομαντεια, ib. l. 221; and αυτοπτ(ικος) λογος, B. M. Pap. XLVI. 53.

This passage to the end of the column is repeated in 27/1–12.

l. 23. *ẖty ẖn*[*t*]. The parallel 27/2 gives in hieratic *ẖt* followed by the nose *ẖnt* and the det. of a boat. *ẖt* means 'float down the river,' 'go north,' and *ẖnt*, 'sail up the river,' 'go south.' With this clue it is easy to read in Leemans' facsimile the verb *ẖty* in demotic, written as in the word *mẖty*, V. 1, with its proper det. of water, and following it the verb *ẖnt*, also in demotic, with its proper det. the boat. Thus, though Leemans' facsimile cannot be confirmed owing to the wear of the papyrus, it is clear that we have a compound expression *ẖty-ẖnt*, 'go down and up.' This is the proper order for the two verbs, as is shown by *ẖn m ẖd m ẖnt*, 'rowing to and fro,' in the Westcar Papyrus, V. 4. It of course refers to the sinking to the horizon and rising to the zenith of the sun-boat.

l. 24. *rpʿ ntr·w* is a very ancient title of Geb.

l. 25. *ḥkne·t*, cf. Lanzone, Diz. Mit., 855; Maspero, Rec. tr., i. 21.

l. 26. Whether the number 7 originally acquired its sacred character in Babylonia or not, it had that character in Egypt, cf. Brugsch, Thes.,

(20) If you wish to do it by vessel alone, you fill your eyes with this ointment, you sit (?) [over the vessel ?] as aforesaid, your eyes being (21) closed; you utter the above invocation seven times, you open your eyes, you ask him concerning everything [that you wish (?)]... you do it from the (22) fourth day of the lunar month until the fifteenth day, which is the half-month when the moon fills the *uzat*.

[A] vessel-[inquiry] alone in order to see (23) the bark of Phre. Formula: 'Open to me heaven, O mother of the gods! Let [me see the ba]rk of Phre descending and ascending (24) in it; for I am Geb, heir of the gods; prayer is what I make before Phre my father [on account of] the things which have proceeded from me. (25) O Heknet, great one, lady of the shrine, the Rishtret (?), Open to me, mistress of the spirits, [open] to me, primal heaven, let (26) me worship the Angels! [for] I am Geb, heir of the gods. Hail! ye seven Kings, ho! ye [seven Mônts], bull that engendereth, lord of strength (27) that lighteth the earth, soul of the abyss; ho! lion as lion of (?) the abyss, bull of the night, hail! thou that rulest the people of the East, (28) Noun, great one, lofty one, hail! soul of a ram, soul of the people of the West, hail! [soul of souls, bull] of the night,

117 seqq.; LEPS., Todtenb. Vorw., p. 6; Pap. Ebers LIV. 19 (eighteenth dynasty), the 7 Hathors (nineteenth dynasty, Pap. Orb. ix. 8; BR., Thes., 800) and the 42 assessors in the Book of the Dead, ch. 125. The occurrence of 7 spirits in the very ancient chapter 17 of the Book of the Dead is of special importance.

The 7 kings are not elsewhere mentioned. '4 Mônts in their cities' occurs in the text, 'Que mon nom fleurisse' (LIEBLEIN, x. 3, and parallel passages), and 7 is a number associated with Hermonthis, the city of Mônt (BRUGSCH, Relig., 164, 7 Hathors and 7 Horus, L. D., iv. 63 c).

l. 27. The reading of the name  is uncertain. *Rw*, an obscure lion-god (Hieroglyphs, pp. 17, 18).

29. s' nw·t a·wn n-y ank wb-t 'r pr n Gb ky [ank y·y·]y e·e·e [he·he·he]

30. h-ʿo h-ʿo h-ʿo ank e-nep-ʿo myryp-ʿo-rʿ mʿ·t(?) 'b thy[by-ʿo 'rw·]wy . . . [yʿh-ʿo]

31. z-mt snf n *ⲥⲙⲟⲩⲛⲉ* snf n *ⲕⲟⲩⲕⲟⲩⲡⲉⲧ* snf n *ⲉ[ⲙⲟⲩⲗϫ]* ʿnḫ-'m·w [snw-p·t]

32. ʿo-'mn qs(?)-ʿnḫ ḥstb n mʿ·t ḫl p-tgs-'S·t nt 'r m bnn·t [nte-k smt yr·t]-k n'm-f t·t(?) [rym ?]

33. n by-ʿo-n-p·t n wʿ ḫ n hr n 'ny nge ḫ n hbyn [nte-k mr-k] a pe-k qte [n wʿ·t]

34. pke n šr-bne·t ḥwt n [wʿ] mʿ e-f θse wbe p rʿ bn-s t . . . . . yr·t-k n . . . .

35. a ḫ p nt sḫ ar-f

Col. XI.

1. r n t ḥse·t 'm n-y p . . . . pe-k rn nfr Tḥwt ys sp-sn 'm n-y

2. my m'-y ḥr-k nfr ty n p-hw . . . . . . e-y n ky ʿʿn nte-k šme . . .

3. n ḥs 'e n pe-k ls n . . . . . . stm-]k ḫrw-y n p-hw nḥm-k-t mw 'ḫy nb t·w

4. r bn(?) nb hy p nte ḫbr-f n . . . . ḫbr-f ʿo št a·pry ntr ḫr wt·t-f

---

l. 29. 'Son of Nut' might be either Osiris or Set, probably here the former: 'soul (*b'*) of Nut' is a possible reading.

l. 30. Anepo may be 'great Anubis' or 'elder Anubis.'

The gloss ⲧⲟⲩ may be incomplete, in 27/9 it is ⲟⲩϫⲟⲩ: the hieratic probably reads 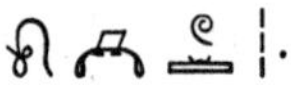.

l. 32. *p-tgs-'S·t*, pronounced perhaps *pteksese*. Cf. πιτταξις, the fruit of the κρανεια or cornel-tree.

l. 33. *ḫ n hr*, apparently the name of some object made of wood, lit. wood or stick of satisfaction, possibly the kohl-stick.

'ny, possibly Eg. *ʿnnw* (Eb.) = *ʿwn* = *wʿn*, 'juniper' (Loret, Fl. Phar., 2nd ed., p. 41), the αρκευθιτις of the Greek papyri. Its juice is used as a writing ink in Louvre dem. Mag. V. 20.

mr-k a pe-k qte, the restoration is from the parallel 27/11. The

bull (?) of bulls, (29) son of Nut, open to me, I am the Opener of earth, that came forth from Geb, hail! [I am I, I,] I, E, E, E, [He, He, He,] (30) Ho, Ho, Ho; I am Anepo, Miri-po-re, Maat (?) Ib, Thi[bio, Ar]oui, Ouoou, [Iaho.'] (31) Formula: blood of a *smun*-goose, blood of a hoopoe, blood of a n[ightjar], *ankh-amu* plant, [*senepe* plant], (32) 'Great-of-Amen' plant, *qes-ankh* stone, genuine lapis-lazuli, myrrh, 'footprint-of-Isis' plant, pound, make into a ball, [you paint] your [eyes] with it; put (?) a goat's-[tear] (33) in (?) a 'pleasure-wood' of *ani* or ebony wood, [you bind it (?)] around (?) you [with a] (34) strip of male-palm fibre in [an] elevated place opposite the sun after putting [the ointment as above on] your eyes ... (35) according to what is prescribed for it.

Col. XI.

1. A spell of giving favour: 'Come to me, O....... thy beautiful name. O Thoth, hasten (*bis*); come to me. (2) Let me see thy beautiful face here to-day....... [I stand (?)] being in the form of an ape; and do thou greet (?) me (3) with praise and adoration (?) with thy tongue of... [Come unto me] that thou mayest hearken to my voice to-day, and mayest save me from all things evil (4) and all slander (?). Ho! thou whose form is of .....his great and mysterious form, from whose be-

---

meaning 'to your side' is indicated by 21/12, *mr-k a pe-k ḥr* probably referring to a phylactery or knot tied at a particular plăce.

Col. XI.

l. 1. *t ḥse·t*, apparently not *t ḫp ḥse·t* as in l. 20. Cf. 12/21.

l. 2. *šme* (?), cf. *šm* 18/9, but with different det. One may perhaps conjecture *šm·t*, 'favour (?) me,' here; it is hardly ϣⲱⲙ, 'wash,' 'purify' (of clothes, Bsciai, Rec. trav., vii. 27).

l. 3. Cf. ll. 16–17, and Pleyte, Chap. Suppl., Pl. 128, *nḥm-k wì mꜥ ìḫ·t nb dw* (var. *ìḫ·t nb bìn dw*) *ḫpr m ꜥwy n rm·t ntr·w ìḫ·w mt·w*.

l. 4. *r bn* may mean 'evil spell.'

5. nt ḥtp a mt(?) n N ank . . . . n t sri͗·t(?) ᶜo·t nt e pyr Hᶜp(?)

6. ẖr-s(?) ank p ḥr n šfe·t ᶜo . . . . . . by m s·w-f ank syf šps

7. nt n pr rᶜ ank p nem šps nt m tpḥ·t . . . . . . [h]b n s·w n mᶜ·t nt ḥtp n ʾN

8. ank p nb ẖrwy ᶜo nb tm mʾ pḥt m . . . . [rn]-yt (?) ank sre s sre srpt-my-[sr] θs-pẖr

9. rn-yt ʾẖ-ẖpr-sr(?) rn-yt n mᶜ·t sp-sn my n-y ḥs mr·t [šfe·t ne-ḥr mn a·ms] mn n p-hw nte-f t n-y ʾẖy nb nfr

10. nte-f t n-y kew tfew nte-f ʾr mt·t nb nt e-y [a wẖ-s nte-k tm t ʾr-f(?)] the a·ʾr-y a ʾr n-y mt·t bn(?) nte-f z n-y mt·t

11. e mst-s m hw pn m grḥ pn m ʾbt pn m rnp·t tn m wne·t(?) . . . . . . e p rᶜ a sẖt ḥt-w nte-f knm

12. yr·t-w nte-f t ẖp p kke m ḥr-w z ank byrᶜy . . . [rᶜ]y ḥre-tn rᶜy ank s Sẖm·t

13. ank bygt k lt ank gᶜt s gᶜt nte . . . . . ty·t nte ḥtp a mt(?) m h·t-ᶜo·t m ʾN

14. ank s Ḥkne·t nb mke·t nt ᶜrf n ẖne·t . . . . . nte n nẖt·w ᶜo apḥt m sw-f

---

l. 5. *ḥtp a mt* (?), cf. l. 13. *mt* (?) is written differently from ⲙⲏⲧⲉ and may well be a masculine word, such as *mt*, 'depth.' It can hardly be ⲙⲏⲣ.

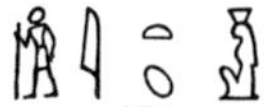 *sri͗·t* seems a possible reading.

pyr. The reading of the following words is uncertain. The construction with 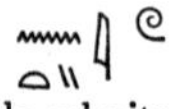 (ⲉⲧⲉ) suggests *nt e pyr Ḥp* (cf. V. 5/1) *ẖr-s*, and the facsimile admits of it.

l. 7. *pr rᶜ*, 'House of Re,' Heliopolis.

l. 8. *nb ẖrwy*. It seems as if the scribe had substituted 'hostility' for *ẖrwy*, 'testicles,' unless the words here are mere gibberish.

The tail of  *sr* is traceable in the gap after  in the Leiden facsimile.

l. 9. Cf. l. 17 for the restoration.

l. 11. *mst-s*, probably for *mst-y-s*, 'which I hate,' unless it be passive, 'which is hated.' Note the present sense of the *sḏm-f* in a relative clause, apparently confined in demotic to the verbs *mr*, 'love,' and *mst*, 'hate' (see chapter on Grammar).

getting came forth a god, (5) who resteth deep (?) in Thebes; I am ...... of the great Lady, under whom cometh forth the Nile, (6) I am the face of reverence great......... soul (?) in his protection; I am the noble child (7) who is in the House of Re: I am the noble dwarf who is in the cavern .... the ibis as a true protection, who resteth in On; (8) I am the master of the great foe, lord of the obstructor (?) of semen, mighty ...... my name (?) I am a ram, son of a ram, Sarpot Mui-Sro (and vice versa) (9) is my name, Light-scarab-noble (?) is my true name (*bis*); grant me praise and love [and reverence from N. son of] N. to-day, and let him give me all good things, (10) and let him give me nourishment and fat things, and let him do for me everything which I [wish for; and let him not] injure me so as to do me harm, nor let him say to me a thing (11) which (I) hate, to-day, to-night, this month, this year, [this] hour (?)... [But as for my enemies ?] the sun shall impede their hearts and blind (12) their eyes, and cause the darkness to be in their faces; for I am Birai ... rai, depart ye (?), Rai; I am the son of Sochmet, (13) I am Bikt, bull of Lat, I am Gat, son of Gat, whose ..... the Underworld, who rests deep (?) in the Great Residence in On, (14) I am son of Heknet, lady of the protecting bandage (?), who binds with thongs (?) .... [I am the ....] phallus (?) which the great and mighty Powers guard,

---

knm. Cf. Brit. Mus. Gr. Pap. XLVI, l. 488, and the early Christian curse invoking blindness (Crum, A. Z., 96. 85).

l. 12. ⲣⲁⲓ̈, with det. of hide, may be the name of the lion (?), but there is a tendency to write ⲁⲓ words with this det. Cf. ϩⲁⲉⲓ, 7/33.

ḥre-tn rʿy suggests a fanciful writing for 'be far from me (*a r-y*, ⲁⲣⲁⲓ̈).

'Son of Sochmet,' perhaps Nefertem or Mihos, both being lion gods.

l. 13. The 'Great Residence in On' is the name of the temple of the Sun at Heliopolis.

l. 14. *nḫt*. Cf. Rit. Pamonth, ii. 8, 'Hear ye, O divine powers of

15. nt ḥtp mw ḫn pr-wbst·t ank p ʿmʿm ntr nt . . . . . ḫn sḫym·t nb ʾy·t nb ʿot(?)

16. rn-yt ʾḫ-ḫpr-sr(?) rn-yt n mʿ·t sp-sn ʾy ny ntr·w tre-w [a·z-y rn-w(?)] ty n p-hw ʾm-n n·y stm-tn n e·z-y n p-hw

17. nḥm-tn[-t] m nene nb ze nb ʾḫy nb t nb m hw pn my n-y ḥs·t mr·t šf[e·t ne-ḥr] t mn p pr-ʿo erme pe-f mšʿ

18. p tw erme ne-f ʾw·w nte-f ʾr mt·t nb nt e-y a zt-w n-f erme(?) [rm nb nt e-w a·nw(?)] a·ʾr-y nt e-y a sze erme-w nt e-w a sze

19. erme-y ḫn ḥwt nb s-ḥm·t nb ḥm-ḫl nb ḫl-ʿo nb ḥr nb . . . . . [n p] t tre-f [nt e-w] a nw a·ʾr-y ḫn ny wne·tw n p-hw

20. nte-w ty ḫp te·t ḥse·t n ḥt-w n mt·t nb nt e-y a . . . . n mne erme n nt e-w a ʾy n-y e sḫr ḫfe(?) nb·w(?)

21. ys sp-sn tkr sp-sn e b-ʾr te-y zt-w nte-y whm zt·w . . . [ʾ]h *ⲉⲉⲛ* n mnḥ tbt(?) nte-k ty-f

22. a ḫn wʿ(?) sšn ke-z tšps tp nge nḥe n bq e-f . . . . n *ⲛⲉⲛⲉⲃⲉ* ar-f ḥr ʿnt tp ḥnʿ pr·w(?)

Bubastis, who have come out of your shrines,' and below, V. 33/5; I Kham. iv. 7; GRIFF., High Priests, p. 109.

l. 15. *ʿmʿm.* Cf. 13/11, 13, and in cipher ⲉⲙⲓⲙ 24/34, V. 32/2. This must be the shrew-mouse. Here it appears connected with Letopolis, where the shrew-mouse was sacred to the blind Horus (RENOUF, P. S. B. A., viii. 155). In 13/11 the animal is prescribed to produce blindness, and in 13/12 and 24/34 it produces death in a man, and in V. 32/2 erotic feeling in a woman. The *ʿmʿm*, with determinative of an animal, is prescribed in Pap. Eb. 91/10; and in Pap. Kah. 7/9 the remains of a determinative will suit very well the picture of a mouse. It is curious that the cipher writing yielding ⲉⲙⲓⲙ (which is certainly the same creature, cf. 13/19–21 with V. 32) makes its name almost identical with Sah. ⲁⲙⲏⲙ, which in Sap. 12/8 corresponds to σφῆκες of LXX. In Coptic, however, the shrew-mouse is ⲁⲗⲓⲗ : ⲁⲗⲓⲗⲓ (PEYR., Lex. and Gramm.). The μυγαλος (*sic*) is prescribed several times in Pap. Bibl. Nat. in ἀγωγαί.

Sḫym (ⲃⲟⲩ-ϣⲏⲙ) and *ʾy·t* are both names of Letopolis in the Delta. The last group in the line looks like *ʿḥ*, but is probably intended for *wʿḥ*.

l. 16. For the restoration cf. 10/7.

(15) which rests in Bubastis; I am the divine shrew-mouse which [resteth with-]in Skhym; lord of Ay, sole(?) lord ... (16) is my name Light-scarab-noble (?) is my true name (*bis*). Ho! all ye these gods, [whose names I have spoken] here to-day, come to me, that ye may hearken to that which I have said to-day (17) and rescue [me] from all weakness (?), every disgrace, everything, every evil (?) to-day; grant me praise, love [and reverence before] such an one, the King and his host, (18) the desert and its animals; let him do everything which I shall say to him together with [every man who shall see] me or to whom I shall speak or who shall speak (19) to me, among every man, every woman, every child, every old man, every person [or animal or thing (?) in the] whole land, [which] shall see me in these moments to-day, (20) and let them cause my praise to be in their hearts of everything which I shall [do] daily, together with those who shall come to me, to (?) overthrow every enemy (?), (21) hasten (*bis*) quickly (*bis*), before I say them or repeat them.' Over an ape of wax.

An oxyrhynchus (?) fish—you put it (22) in prime lily otherwise *teshops*-oil or moringa (?) oil which [has been ... and you put liquid ?] styrax to it, with prime frank-

---

l. 17. *šfe·t.* In the conspiracy against Rameses III (?) of the twentieth dyn., we hear of a spell to give *nrwy* and *šfe·t*, 'valour and respect.' Newberry, Amherst Pap. II, l. 2.

l. 20. The last words may perhaps be *ḫf nb* (?), 'every enemy,' *nb* being written over the line as a correction of the plural signs. 'Enemy' is written *ḫf* (without *t*) as in I Rhind dem. 2, 3. The passage is very obscure.

l. 21. *'h*, for a similar direction following the invocation, cf. V. 33/8. The fish is here masc., and therefore different from that in 12/31.

l. 22. *sšn*, 'lotus,' may be an error for *skn sšn*, 25/26, σουσινον, Diosc. i. 62, oil of lilies (κρινα), and ελαιον σουσινον, Pap. Berl. II. 249.

tšps as an oil, Br., Wtb., 1602, made from laurus cinnamomum according to Loret, Flore Phar., 2nd ed. p. 51.

bq. v. Loret, Rec. trav., vii. 101.

ⲡⲉⲛⲉⲃⲉ. v. Loret, Rec. trav., xvi. 148 لُبْنَى styrax.

23. wr-mr·t ẖn wʿ ḥn(?) n thne nte-k ʾny wʿ ʿnẖ n . . . . . . ths-f n py nḥe nt ḥry nte-k ʿš

24. ny [sẖ ?]·w ar-f n sp VII mbḥ p rʿ n twe e b-ʾr te-k sz[e wbe] rm nb n p t nte-k šty-f nte-k ths ḥr-k nʾm-f

25. nte-k ẖʿ [p]ʿnẖ ẖn t·t-k nte-k mšʿ a mʿ nb . . . . . ʾwt mšʿ nb ẖr te-f t ẖp n-k

26. ḥs·t ʿo·t ʾwt-w m šs sp-sn py sp n sẖ pa p pr-ʿo [Ntryw (?)]š pe mn p nt (ne-)ʿne-f ar-f

Col. XII.

1. [wʿ ky(?) a t ʾre] s-ḥm·t mr ḥwt hepwbʿlsʿmw sttr(?) I hbʾryr(?) . . . . . sttr(?) I

2. qwšt sttr(?) I . . . . n sty sttr(?) I mrwe sttr(?) I nḥe n mʿ·t lq II e·ʾr-k nt ny [pẖre·tw(?)]

3. e·ʾr-k ty-sw a wʿ [ʿngen(?)] e-f wʿb nte-k t p nḥe n pe-w ḥr·w ẖr t ḥ·t n p wrš wʿ hw a·ʾre p w[rš]

4. ẖp e·ʾr-k ʾny wʿ·t qeš . . . . [k]m(?) e-s ʾr n tbʿ IX ke-z VII n ẖy·t e yr·t-s šel n ʾwn n [p nt(?)]

---

l. 26. The *pa* is for **ⲡⲁ-**. **ⲡⲉⲣⲟ** in O. C. Par. corresponds to *p pr-ʿo* in 21/2. So also we have in B. M. Pap. XLVI, l. 113 *εγω ειμι αγγελος του φαπρω οσορννωφρις*, 'of Pharaoh Osoronnophris,' where *φαπρω* = our *pa p pr-ʿo*. Undoubtedly the initial letter of *pr-ʿo* had already been lost by assimilation to the article. The tautology of *του φα-* is precisely the same as in **Αμενωφις του Παaπιος**, 'Amenophis, son of Hapis,' in Josephus, Contra Ap. i. 26.

. . . . *š*. The only kings whose names end in *š* are Darius, Xerxes, Artaxerxes, and the native Khebbesh. Of these Darius is doubtless the name to be restored here; cf. Diod. Sic. i. 95, and for his reputation as a magician in particular, *μαγικων διδασκαλος*, Porphyry, de Abstin., iv. 16. That kings, as well as aspirants to the throne, used these arts is suggested by the spell 'of Rameses III' being given to the herdsman Penhuyban in order to give him 'valour and respect.' See note to l. 17 above.

Col. XII.

l. 1. Restore [*wʿ ky* (?) *a t ʾre*] *s-ḥm·t* from 25/23, 31.

hepwbʿlsʿmw: cf. *αποβαλσαμινα* (*ξυλα*) Leyden Pap. W. ix. 21 = *οποβαλσαμον*, 'juice of balsam tree'; cf. Sigismund, Aromata, pp. 14, 15.

ⲙⲁⲗⲁⲃⲁⲑⲣⲟⲛ = *μαλαβαθρον*, 'leaf of Laurus Cassia'; Sigismund,

incense together with seeds of (23) 'great-of-love' plant in a metal (?) vase; you bring a wreath of flowers of..... ... and you anoint it with this oil as above, and recite (24) these spells over it seven times before the sun in the morning, before speaking to any man on earth; you extract it, you anoint your face with it, (25) you place the wreath in your hand, and proceed to any place [and be] amongst any people; then it brings you (26) great praise among them exceedingly. This scribe's feat is that of King [Dariu]s (?); there is no better than it.

Col. XII.

(1) [A method for making] a woman love a man. Opobalsamum, one stater(?); malabathrum, one stater(?). (2) *kusht*, one stater(?); scented ...., one stater(?); *merue*, one stater(?); genuine oil, two *lok*; you pound these [medicaments]. (3) You put them into a clean [vessel], you add the oil on the top of them one day before the lunar period (?); when the lunar period (?) (4) comes, you take a black *Kesh* ... -fish measuring nine fingers—another says seven—in length, its eyes being variegated (?) of

---

Aromata, p. 33, and Lemm., Kopt. Apocr. Apostelacten (Mél. Asiat. t. x. p. 351). It occurs in magic prescriptions, Leyden Pap. W. i. 16, ix. 10. The demotic group *hb* .... corresponding to it is strange in form and difficult to read: there seems to be a gap between the *r* and the measure.

Graphically ⊙, ⊙ (fem.) are hieroglyphic equivalents of the demotic for ⲕⲓⲧⲉ, 'didrachma,' but from 24/15, 18 the former should be a small multiple of the latter. *στατηρ* (Copt. ⲥⲁⲧⲉⲉⲣⲉ, fem.) is common as a weight = 'tetradrachma,' in Ptolemaic and Roman papyri.

l. 2. *qwšt*, perhaps *κοστος* (Diosc. i. 15), which follows *μαλαβαθρον* in a prescription, Pap. Bibl. Nat. l. 2680; cf. Leyd. Pap. W. i. 16, ix. 10.

lq. The Hebrew log is ·56 litre, about one pint, and the Coptic ⲗⲟⲕ translates *κοτυλη*, which in all its varieties is no larger than a pint.

ny [*pḫre·tw* (?)]: cf. 29/28, 29.

l. 3. *wᶜ* [*ᶜngen* (*αγγειον* of l. 11) *e*]-*f wᶜb* seems to fill the gap, which is too wide in the Pl. of vol. ii. in this and the following line according to the evidence of the succeeding lines.

4. *qeš* ..., in l. 27 *qš* ..., in both cases broken. In l. 9 it is referred

5. [e·ʾr-k] gm ḫn wʿ mw(?) . , . . . nte-k ty-s a py nḥe nt ḫry n hw II e·ʾr-k ʿš n py ʿš ar-f n twe . . . .

6. e b-ʾr te-k ʾy n p [bl n pe-k(?)] ʿy e b-ʾr te-k sze wbe rm nb n p t a·ʾr p(?) hw II sny [e·ʾr-k]

7. ḫrp a bl n twe e·ʾr[-k še] a wʿ km e·ʾr-k ʾny wʿ šlḥe n elle e b·ʾr te-f wtḥ elle . . . .

8. e·ʾr-k fy·t-f n te-k·t [t·t n] . . . . e·ʾr-k ty-f a te-k·t t·t n wnm e·ʾr-f ʾr n tbʿ VII e·ʾr-k θy·t-f [a pe-k(?)]

9. ʿy nte-k ʾny p [tbt(?)] a ḥry ḫn p nḥe nte-k mr-s (*sic*) a py-s st n tyb n mḥe nte-k ʿyḫ·t-s m-s [zz-f]

10. n p ḫ n elle [nte-k ḫʿ] p nk nt ḫr nḥe ḫrr-s šʿ nte-s zlzl p nt n ḫe·t-s a ḫr[y]

11. e p ʿngen nt ḫr[r-s] ḥr wʿ·t tbe nmy šʿ ke hw III a·ʾre p hw III sny e·ʾr-k [ʾny·t-s]

12. a ḫry e·ʾr-k qs[-s] n ḫl ḥsm ḥbs n š-stn e·ʾr-k ḫʿ-s n wʿ mʿ e-f hep ḫn pe-[k pr]

13. nge e·ʾr-k ʾr ke hw II e·ʾr-k ʿš a p nḥe ʿn a hw VII e·ʾr-k ḥrḥ ar-f e·ʾr[-k wḥ (?)]

14. a t ʾr-f te-f yp·t e[ʾr-k th]s pe-k mt n ḥwt ḥnʿ pe-k ḥr e·ʾr-k str erme t s-ḥm·t nt e·ʾr-k ʾr-f aʾr-s

15. n sḫ nt e·ʾr-k ʿš-w a p nḥe ank šwy(?) glʿbʾn-ʿo ank rʿ ʾnk qm-rʿ ʾnk s rʿ ank

16. syšt s šwy(?) qme(?) n mw n ʾN py srrf nt n ʾBt nte·t tp·t wr·t wr ḥyq

---

to apparently as *p tbt*, 'the fish'; and in l. 31 is written with the fish sign, but with feminine article and termination. It seems characteristically female, the gender of the pronoun changing to fem. ungrammatically immediately after the masculine *tbt*, in l. 9, and no doubt it was sacred to some goddess. The lates niloticus (which according to MM. Lortet and Hugounenq is found of all sizes mummified at Latopolis, and is therefore the Latus, Ann. du Serv. iii. 15) is called in Arabic *qišr*, قشر.

l. 6. *a·ʾr*. The original reads perhaps *a ʾr p*. In either case it is probably a slip for *a ʾre p*.

l. 8. Vice versa of 'Lotus Lion-Ram' is 'Lion-Ram Lotus,' not 'Ram Lion Lotus'; see note to 1/12.

l. 9. *p* [*tbt*]. The remains favour this restoration. The word does

the colour of (?) the . . . (5) [which you (?)] find in a water (?) . . . you put it into this oil above-mentioned for two days; you recite this formula to it (the oil) at dawn . . . (6) before going [out of your] house, and before speaking to any man on earth. When two days have passed [you] (7) rise early in the morning [and go] to a garden; you take a vine-shoot before it has ripened grapes, (8) you take it with your left hand, you put it into your right hand—when it has grown seven digits (in length)—you carry it [into your] (9) house, and you take the [fish] out of the oil, you tie it by its tail with a strip (?) of flax, you hang it up to . . . (10) of (?) the vine-wood. [You place] the thing containing oil under it until it (the fish) pours out by drops that which is in it downwards, (11) the vessel which is under [it] being on a new brick for another three days; when the three days have passed, you [take it] (12) down, you embalm [it] with myrrh, natron, and fine linen; you put it in a hidden place or in [your chamber] (13) You pass two more days; you recite to the oil again for seven days; you keep it; when you [wish] (14) to make it do its work, you anoint your phallus and your face; you lie with the woman for whom you do it. (15) The spells which you recite to the oil, 'I am Shu, Klabano, I am Re, I am Komre, I am son of Re, I am (16) Sisht (?), son of Shu; a reed (?) of the water of On, this gryphon which is in Abydos. Thou (fem.) art Tepe-were (first, great) great of sorcery,

---

not occur elsewhere in the papyrus. For the change of gender in *mr-s* see note to l. 4.

m-s [*zz-f*], see l. 29.

l. 12. *pe*-[*k pr*] restored from the parallel l. 31.

l. 13. *nge* here and in l. 31 seems to be placed after the alternative phrase, as is the case with *r-pw* in older Egyptian.

l. 14. *a'r-s* for *ar-s*, ⲉⲣⲟⲥ, 'to her.'

l. 15. *šwy*. The name of the god Shu (cf. l. 20) is here falsely written like ⲧⲁⲓ.

17. t ʿre·t ʿnḫ·t nte·t [p w]tn p šy n wʿ-pke my n-y ḥs·t mr·t šfe·t ne-ḥr

18. ʿte·t nb s-ḫm·t nb mr·t pe rn n mte ʿš nte-s ʿn ʾnk šwy(?) klʾkyn-ʿo-k ank yʾrn

19. ʾnk gʿmren ʾnk se . . . . . pe pʾeaypʿf ynpen ntynhs gʿm-r-n mw n ʾN ʾnk

20. šwy(?) šʿbw šʿ . . . . . . šʿbʿh-ʿo lʿh-ʾy-lʿhs(?) lʿh-ʿe·t p ntr ʿo nt ḥr pr-ybt·t

21. lʿbrʿthʿʿ a[nk p] srrf nt n ʾBt ky nʾm-y(?) ʿn(?) a t ḥs·t n ḥwt a ḥr s-ḫm·t θs-pḫr a ḥr . . .

22. nte-t t wr·t t wr ḥyq . . . . ʾkš·t s·t n rʿ t nb ʿre·t nte-t Sḫm ʿo·t nb ʾs·t

23. ʾr sḫme sʿbe nb a . . . . . . t n p rʿ n t wz·t a·ms ʿḥ n t XV·t n grḥ nte-t qm . . . .

24. wr nwn nte-t qm . . . . wr·t nt n ḥ·t-bnbn m(?) ʾN nte-t t yʿl n nb [nte-t t]

25. skte·t p wtn n p rʿ . . . . lʿnzʾ p ḫrt p šr n t wʿyʿnʿyne·t t pyt·t n t . . . . .

26. n gwg ny št-t . . . . n by-wekm t ḥs·t t mr·t nta p rʿ pe-t yt ty-s n-t m[y] . . .

27. n-y a ḫry ḫn py nḫe . . . . . ḥr ḥt yr·t nb s-ḫm·t nb nt e-y ʾn·nʿ a ḫn a ḥr-w a wʿ·t qš . . . .

28. n tbʿ IX e-s km nte[-k ty-s a] ḫn wʿ sknn n wrt nte-k ʾr-s n ḥsy ḫn-f nte-k ʾny·t[-s a ḥry]

---

l. 18. *ʿš nte-s ʿn.* The blank before *ʿš* is perhaps for the insertion of a word (*ke* (?)) in red ink; *nte-s* is ⲛⲧⲁⲥ, St., § 299, and the invocation is still to the fish.

l. 20. *lʿh-ʿe·t.* The plural of *ʿe-t*, 'limbs,' is ⲏⲟⲩ in O. C. Par. The singular may have been *ⲏⲉ.

l. 21. *nʾm-y.* Probably an error for *nʾm-f*, but the facsimile would admit of the reading *nʾm-w ʿn.*

l. 22. Thoueris is generally figured as a hippopotamus.

ʾs·t must be the place *ỉs*·t, dem. *ʾs*, mentioned in Brugsch, Dict. Geogr., pp. 70–71, as being under the rule of Sochmet.

l. 23. *wz·t*: sun or moon as eyes of heaven; cf. 8/8, 10/22, 29/23.

l. 24. *Ḥ·t-bnbn* [*m*] *ʾN* is the best restoration. The 'house of the obelisk' was a famous shrine in the temple of Heliopolis.

(17) the living uraeus, thou art the sun-boat, the lake of Ua-peke; grant to me praise, love, and lordship before (18) every womb, every woman. Love (?) is my true name.' [Another (?)] invocation of it again: 'I am Shu, Klakinok, I am Iarn, (19) I am Gamren, I am Se.... Paer(?)ipaf, Iupen, Dynhs, Gamrou, water of On, I am (20) Shu, Shabu, Sha...., Shabaho, Lahy-lahs, Lahei, the great god who is in the East (21) Labrathaa, I am that gryphon which is in Abydos.'

[Another] form of them (?) again (?) to give favour to a man before a woman and vice versa, before.... 'Thou art Thoueris, the great of sorcery, [cat (?)] of Ethiopia, daughter of Re, lady of the uraeus; thou art Sochmet, the great, lady of Ast, (23) who hast seized every impious person.... [eye-ball (?)] of the sun in the *uzat*, born of the moon at the midmonth at night, thou art Kam (?)..... (24) mighty, abyss, thou art Kam (?).... great one (fem.) who art in the House of the obelisk in On; thou art the golden mirror, [thou art ?] (25) the *sektet*-boat, the sun-boat of Re..... Lanza, the youth, the son of the Greek woman, the Amazon (?) in the ... (26) of dûm-palm fruit (?), these .... of Bywekem; the favour and love which the sun, thy father, hath given to thee, send [them] (27) to me down into this oil, before the heart, and eyes of (?) every woman before whom I come in.' [Invocation] to a *Kesh* ...-fish (28) of nine digits and black; [you put it] in an ointment of roses; you drown it therein; you

---

l. 25. *skte·t.* It is interesting to find this clear spelling, not *smkt·t*, which seems to be that of the Pyramid Texts.

w'y'n'yne·t, an extraordinary spelling for **ⲟⲩⲉⲉⲓⲛⲓⲛ**, 'Greek.'

pyt·t. *pdty* in Eg. seems to be a foreign soldier or mercenary. This is evidently a feminine derivative.

l. 26. *gwg* = *kwk* in Kufi, p. xx; probably the dûm-nut, as in Kufi it is evidently the fruit of a tree, so not **ϭⲟⲩϭ : ϫⲟⲩϫ**, carthamus.

l. 28. *sknn n wrt*, μυρον ροδινον of Pap. Bibl. Nat. l. 759. That it was of a consistency to choke a fish is seen by its use as a lamp-oil in 6/9.

29. nte-k ʿyḫ m-s zz[-f] . . . . . e·ʾr-k wḥ e·ʾr-k ty-s a wʿ ḥn(?) n yl e·ʾr-k (*sic*) wʿ ḫm n mw n sʿsmrem

30. erme wʿ ḫm n s-ʾS·t e-f . . . [e-f] nt nte-k ʿš ny ar-f n sp VII n hw VII wbe t pr n p rʿ e·ʾr-k ths ḥr-k nʾm[-f]

31. n p nw nt e·ʾr-k str erme s-ḥm·t [nte-k] qs t . . . ·t n ḫl ḥsm e·ʾr-k tms-s n pe-k pr n wʿ mʿ e-f hep nge

Col. XIII.

1. p ky n prz ḥwt a s-ḥm·t s-ḥm·t a py-s hy

2. wy sp-sn ḫo sp-sn ʾr(?) Gb ḫbr-f n k nq-f . . . . mw·t-f Tfn·t m whm . . .

3. mw wwhe(?) p ʾb n yt-f ḥr-f p ḫyt n p nte by-f m st·t e ḫe-f (*sic*) m ʾn nte-f . . .

4. mḥ p t n st·t nte n tw·w syt n sʿl(?) p ḫyt n ntr nb ntr·t nb ʿnḫ wr lʿlʿt(?)

5. bʿresʿk bel-kš . . . ḥwy mn p šr n t mn . . t mn t šr·t n t mn

6. my t st·t m-s ḥt-f t sḥt·t n pe-f mʿ n str e b(?) . . . . . n st·t n mst . . .

---

l. 29. *t*, or a similar word, has dropped out between *e·ʾr-k* and *wʿ*. Such omissions have often been supplied over the line by the scribe.

sʿsmrem, probably sisymbrium, of which there were two sorts, growing respectively on land and on water, Diosc. ii. 154–5. The former being also known as Αφροδιτης στεφανος, herba venerea (ib.), is very appropriate for this ἀγωγή. It may be mentha sylvestris, and the second species is nasturtium (Sprengel). Unfortunately the determinative is lost of our word, so that we cannot be sure that a plant was intended: cf. V. 13/7.

l. 30. *s-[n?]ʾS·t.* Among the ingredients of a sacred oil, Pap. Boul. I. Pl. 38, col. 1, is a plant called by this name. Here there is no det.

l. 31. *t ḫʾ(?)·t* might mean 'the carcase,' but having no determinative almost certainly represents the *qeš* . . . -fish of ll. 6, 27.

Col. XIII.

l. 1. For the subject, compare Leyd. Pap. Graec. V. col. 11, l. 15 (see Leemans' ed.), headed *wʿ prz*, διακοπος.

l. 2. The first sentence, as far as *p ḫyt*, is in clumsy archaistic language,

take it [out], (29) you hang it up by [its] head [. . . days (?)]: when you have finished you put it on a glass vessel; you [add] a little water of sisymbrium (30) with a little amulet (?)-of-Isis . . . . . and pounded; you recite this to it seven times for seven days opposite the rising of the sun. You anoint your head with [it] (31) in the hour when you lie with [any (?)] woman. [You] embalm the fish with myrrh and natron; you bury it in your chamber or in a hidden place.

Col. XIII.

(1) The mode of separating a man from a woman and a woman from her husband. (2) 'Woe! (*bis*), flame! (*bis*); Geb assumed his form of a bull, coivit [cum filia ?] matris suae Tefnet, again . . . . (3) because (?) the heart of his father cursed (?) his face; the fury of him whose soul is as flame, while his body is as a pillar (?), so that (?) he . . . . (4) fill the earth with flame and the mountains shoot with tongues (?):—the fury of every god and every goddess Ankh-uer, Lalat (?), (5) Bareshak, Belkesh, ... be cast upon (?) N. the son of N. [and (?)] N. the daughter of N., (6) send the fire towards his heart and the flame in his place of

---

employing the obsolete *'b* for heart, *mw* for  or , the suffix with the noun *ḥbr*, the past *stm-f*, &c.

wy sp-sn: cf. Louvre dem. Mag. iii. 16.

Geb is Κρονος, the planet Κρονος being named 'Horus the Bull,' and Nut, daughter of Tefnut, is the heavenly cow in the Destruction des Hommes, &c. The restoration before 'his mother' is, however, very uncertain. Cf. the Greek myth of Κρονος, and Plutarch, de Iside et Or., cap. 12, where 'Ρεα is Nut.

l. 3. *ẖe-f*, 'his body,' must be for *ẖe·t-f*, but this spelling occurs elsewhere in the papyrus. Cf. 21/22.

'n might represent the city of On, but the determinative is apparently a stone.

l. 5. *ḥwy a* (?) *mn*, 'is cast upon (?) N.'

There are traces of writing covering $1\frac{1}{2}$ inches at the end of this line, perhaps erased by the original scribe, and wholly illegible now.

7. a ḫn a ḥt-f n hte·t nb šʿ nte-f ḥwy t(?) mn t šr·t mn (*sic*) a bl ḫn ne-f ʿy·w e·s lk(?)

8. mst n ḥt-f e-s ḫr ḫnt(?) n ḥr-f my n-f p wywy p wʿwʿ p ʾhe(?) p ḫnt ʾwt-w

9. n hte·t nb šʿ nte-w prz a ne-w ʾre·w e bnp-w ḥtp a šwe a nḥe ***ⲕⲙⲉ*** *. . . . **ⲣ***

10. ***ϣⲉⲗ*** nte-k t ʾrp ar-w nte-k ʾr-w n wʿ twt(?) n Gb e wn wʿ ws n t·t-f

11. n p ʿmʿm nt ḫr še-f ar-w e·ʾr-k ʾny wʿ ʿmʿm nte-k ʾr-f n ḥsy ḫn hyn·w ***ⲙⲁⲟⲩ*** nte-k t swr p rm n (*sic*)

12. nʾm-f ḫr ʾr-f ***ϭⲱⲛⲙ*** n p byl II e·ʾr-k nt pe-f ***ⲙⲟⲥⲉ*** ḥr nk nb(?) n wm nte-k t wm-f-s p rm ḫr ʾr-f(?)

13. ***ⲙⲟⲩⲛⲧⲟ*** nte-f ***ϣⲉϥϥⲉ*** nte-f ***ⲙⲟⲩ*** e·ʾr-k ʾr-f a ʾny s-ḥm·t e·ʾr-k ʾny wʿ ʿmʿm e·ʾr-k ḫʿ-f ḥr wʿ·t blz n

14. ḫr nte-k wḥ-f ḥr t θse n wʿ ʿo nte-k t pe-f st ḫn wʿ·t(?) blz n ḫr nge yl ʿn nte-k wrḥ-f e-f ʿnḫ a ḫn

15. n p r n wʿ·t s·t-eyw n t s-ḥm·t nte-k . . . . -f n nb nte-k qs pe-f st nte-k t ḫl e-f nt ar-f nte-k ty-f a ḫn wʿ·t ʾlykt n nb

---

l. 7. At the end read *e-s ḫr* (?).

l. 9. **ⲕⲙⲉ** is probably the true native pronunciation of the word for gum, unaffected by the Greek.

l. 10. *twt* (?). The determinative of a star must mean that the planet form *Ḫr-p-k*, a bull-headed man standing with *was*-sceptre, is intended, Br., Thes., p. 68. With regard to the reading, the sign is the det. of *twt* in Bul. Pap. I. Pl. 37, l. 14, and in l. 15 stands for *twt*. *Twt*, 'figure,' seems to be the reading here, and wherever it occurs with the det. of divinity (15/10, &c.); but without det. (16/22, &c.) it means 'style,' 'method,' and is probably to be read *ky*. Max Müller, however (Rec. trav. ix. 26), shows reason for reading it *qte*, comparing Louvre dem. Mag. v. 1, vi. 19; *qte*, though apparently masc., may be the origin of the fem. **ϭⲟⲧ**.

l. 11. *hyn·w* **ⲙⲁⲟⲩ**, some water: cf. 21/13 *hyn·w ʾrt·t*.

l. 12. The word in cipher reads **ⲙⲟⲥⲉ́**, a word unknown in Egyptian. Probably it is a mis-writing for **ⲥⲱⲙⲉ** (l. 17)=*swmʿ* (*σωμα*) of V. 32/5.

sleeping, the . . . of fire of hatred never [ceasing to enter] (7) into his heart at any time, until he cast N. daughter of N. out of his abode, she having (?) (8) hatred to his heart, she having quarrel to his face; grant for him the nagging (?) and squabbling (?), the fighting and quarrelling between them (9) at all times, until they are separated from each other, without agreeing again for ever.' Gum, . . . , (10) myrrh; you add wine to them; you make them into a figure of Geb, there being a *was*-sceptre in his hand.

(11) [The uses (?)] of the shrew-mouse (?) to which it is put (goes). You take a shrew-mouse (?), you drown it in some water; you make the man drink (12) of it; then he is blinded in his two eyes. Grind its body (?) with any piece of food, you make the man eat it, then he makes a (13) . . . and he swells up and he dies. If you do it to bring a woman, you take a shrew-mouse (?), you place it on a Syrian (14) pot, you put it on the back-bone (?) of a donkey, you put its tail in a Syrian pot or in a glass again; you let it loose (?) alive within (15) the door of a bath of the woman, you gild (?) it (*sic*) and embalm its tail, you add pounded myrrh to it, you

---

wm-f-s p rm: note the superfluous *f*.

l. 13. **ⲙⲟⲩⲛⲧⲟ**, probably a compound word, **ⲙⲟⲩ-ⲛ-ⲧⲟ**. It might mean 'water of spot (**ⲧⲟⲉ**)' or 'death of spot,' referring to a disease with spots or blisters.

blz n ḫr. Wine was imported from Syria in amphorae, but probably some special ware was denoted by this name.

l. 15. The word for bath is determined with the sign of fire: its name in Coptic is **ⲥⲓⲟⲟⲩⲛⲉ : ⲥⲉⲓⲱⲟⲩⲛⲓ** with variations; in the demotic there is no trace of the **ⲛ**, and it evidently means 'place o fwashings,' ***ⲥⲉ-ⲉⲓⲟⲟⲩⲉ**.

'You gild and embalm its tail' is perhaps the meaning.

l. 15. *'lykt* (fem.), an unknown word, apparently the *gswr*, 'ring,' of l. 27. It is perhaps to be connected with ἕλιξ or ἑλικτός. **ϩⲁⲗⲁⲕ**, 'ring,' and **ⲁⲗⲕⲟⲩ**, 'vase,' have been suggested, but these are both masculine, and ignore the *t*, which seems to be firm. The determinative appears to be that of silver, also found in *znf*, &c.

16. nte-k ty-s a pe-k tbʿ bn-s ʿš ny sḫ·w ar-f nte-k mšʿ a mʿ [nb ?] erme-f a(?) s-ḥm·t nb nt e·ʾr-k a mḥt nʾm-s ḫr [wḫ ?]-s m-s-k

17. ḫr ʾr-k-f e ʿḥ mḥ e·ʾr-k ʾr-f a t ʾre s-ḥm·t lyb m-s ḥwt e·ʾr-k fy pe-f ***ⲥⲟⲙⲁ*** e-f šwy e·ʾr-k nt[-f e·ʾr-k] fy

18. wʿ ḫm nʾm-f erme wʿ ḫm n snf n pe-k tbʿ n mḥ II n p sʿlʿpy[n] n tek·t t·t n . . . . e·ʾr-k tḫ-f erme-f e·ʾr-k ty-f

19. a wʿ z n ʾrp e·ʾr-k ty-f n t s-ḥm·t nte-s swr-f ḫr ʾr-s lyb [m-]s-k e·ʾr-k t pe-f ***ⲥⲁϣⲉ*** a wʿ ʾrp

20. nte p rm swr-f ḫr ***ⲙⲧⲉϥ*** ty hte·t nge ty-f a nk nb [n wm] e·ʾr-k t pe-f ***ϩⲉⲧ*** a wʿ ḫtm(?)

21. n nb nte-k ty-f a t·t-k nte-k mšʿ a mʿ nb ḫr te-f t ḫp n-k [ḥs·t mr·t šfe·]t e·ʾr-k ʾr wʿ ***ⲃⲉϭ*** n ḥsy ḫn

22. wʿ ʾrp nte-k t swr-s p rm ḫr ***ⲙⲧⲉϥ*** e·ʾr-k t p ***ⲥⲁϣⲉ*** n [wʿ gʿl]e n rʿqt a nk nb n wm

23. ḫr ***ⲙⲧⲉϥ*** e·ʾr-k t wʿ·t ***ϩⲁϥⲗⲉⲗⲁ*** n st II a p nḫe [nte-k psy·]t-s nte-k ths p rm nʾm-f ḫr . . . .

24. e·ʾr-k wḫ a t ḫp ***ⲡⲁⲉⲓϣⲉ*** ḥr rm nte-s tm lʿk-s wʿ·t *[**ϩ**]**ⲁⲛⲧⲟⲩⲥ*** [erme ?] ***ϩⲁϥⲗⲉ**[**ⲗⲁ**]* nte-k psy·t-w ḥr . . . .

25. nte-k zqm p rm nʾm-w e·ʾr-k wḫ a t ʾr-f ***ⲧⲟⲩⲣ***(?) e·ʾr-k t . . . . ḫr ʾr-f ***ⲧⲟⲩⲣ***(?) e·ʾr-k ty ḥnk(?) . . .

26. a yr·t-f n rm ḫr ʾr-f ***ϭⲱⲛⲙ***

---

l. 16. 'The charms' are those at the foot of the column, l. 27 et seqq. There seems scarcely space for the *a* before *s-ḥm·t*, and it should no doubt be omitted.

l. 17. There is a variant version in V. col. 32 of the prescriptions in ll. 17–20.

l. 18. *sʿlʿpyn*. The finger is always thus elaborately described in the pap., the blood being used in erotica as here 15/4, 22, V. 32/7. It is evidently the Boh. **ⲥⲉⲗⲟⲩⲡⲓⲛ.** الخنصر 'middle finger' in Kircher. But Sah. **ⲥⲉⲗⲉⲡⲓⲛ** is 'heart,' also *ὑποχόνδρια* (cf. 21/25, 33); and that a nerve connected the third (ring-) finger of the left hand with the heart is said

put it in a gold ring (?), (16) you put it on your finger after reciting these charms to it, and walk with it to any place, and any woman whom you shall take hold of, she [giveth herself (?)] unto you. (17) You do it when the moon is full. If you do it to make a woman mad after a man, you take its body, dried, you pound [it, you] take (18) a little of it with a little blood of your second finger, (that) of the heart (?), of your left hand; you mix it with it, you put it (19) in a cup of wine; you give it to the woman and she drinks it; then she has a passion for you. You put its gall into a (measure of) wine (20) and the man drinks it; then he dies at once; or (you) put it into any piece [of food]. You put its heart (?) into a seal-ring (?) (21) of gold; you put it on your hand, and go anywhere; then it brings you [favour, love, and] reverence. You drown a hawk in (22) a (measure of) wine; you make the man drink it, then he dies. You put the gall of an Alexandrian [weasel] into any food, (23) then he dies. You put a two-tailed lizard into the oil and [cook] it, and anoint the man with it; then [he dies (?)]. (24) You wish to produce a skin-disease on a man and that it shall not be healed, a *hantous*-lizard [and (?)] a *hafleele*-lizard, you cook them with [oil (?)], (25) you wash the man with them. If you wish to make it troublesome (?), you put . . . . . , then it is troublesome (?). You put beer (?) . . . . . (26) to the eye of a man, then he is blinded.

(Apion, frag. 7, Macrob. Saturn. vii. 13) to be a discovery of Egyptian anatomy. For fingers of the right hand see 16/29, 29/5.

l. 20. *ḫr* ⲙⲧⲉϥ. It is very interesting to obtain the *stm-f* form following *ḫr*; but whether it would be *ⲙⲧⲟϥ or *ⲙⲧⲁϥ in Sah. may be a little doubtful. The vowel seems however to represent ⲉ, not ⲁ, and should therefore correspond to ⲁ, not ⲟ, in Sah.; but a Sah. form *ⲙⲧⲉϥ, or even *ⲙⲧⲏϥ, would be conceivable.

l. 21. *t* over the line seems to be a correction of *ḫp*.

27. n sh̬·w nt h̬r ʾr-k ʿš-w a p gswr n p nw nt e·ʾr-k mḥt n(?) t s-ḥm·t nʾm[-f . . . .] yʿh-ʿo ʾbrʿsʿks

28. my ʾre mn a·ms mn mryt my ʾr-s mḥ m-s-y a p myt nte-k zrp(?) . . . . h̬r ʾr-s wḥ-s m-s-k h̬r sh̬-k[-s ?] . . .

29. ʿn a t tys nt h̬r ʾr-k qs p [ʿmʿm(?)] nʾm-f

Col. XIV.

1. p-e·ze ke rm n-y z a·wn n yr·t sp-sn šʿ sp IV(?)

2. . . . . . . a·wn n yr·t-yt a·wn n yr·t-k θs-ph̬r šʿ . . . sp III a·wn tt a·wn nʿp III sp

3. a·wn . . . . III(?) z ʾnk ʾrtʿm-ʿo a·ms ḥme-ʿo p syt ʿo n pr-ybt [nt] h̬ʿ erme pe-k yt

4. n twe hy sp-sn ḥḥ(?) a·wn n-y hʿh h̬r z-k-f e·ʾr-k sq n h̬rw-k ʾrtʿm-ʿo a·wn n-y hʿh e·ʾr-k

5. tm a wn n-y hʿh e-y a t ʾr-k wn n-y hʿh hb sp-sn nwzh̬ nte nw [a] p ntr ʿo ʾNp p nʿš

6. nt n-ne-zz-y p nʿšt ʿo n wz·t p nʿš ʾNp p mr ʾḥ nfr a·wn nb e·ʾr-y

7. wnḥ-k a·ʾr-y z ʾnk nesthom neszot neshotb b-ʿo-rylʿmmʿy sp-sn

---

l. 27. See l. 16 above for the employment of this spell.

l. 29. *qs*: the only embalming is of the tail of the shrew-mouse in l. 15.

Col. XIV.

l. 1. This line is merely a gloss on l. 2.

l. 2. The mark over *sp* occurs also in 29/22 and V. 9/8. In 29/22 it is placed over *sp* without any number following, in the other instance over a blank space where a numeral would be expected. Here a number has been written under *sp*, but below the line, as if inserted later, and the inference may be drawn that the sign in question indicates that a number is wanting.

l. 3. *Ham-o* might mean 'great carpenter,' but many Egyptian words in these magic names are no doubt almost meaningless, and it is difficult in translating to decide whether to give English equivalents or to transcribe them phonetically.

l. 5. *tm a wn.* The *a* is a mistake, or at least superfluous.

(27) The charms which you recite to the ring at the time of taking hold of the woman . . . . . 'Yaho, Abrasax, (28) may N. daughter of N. love me, may she burn for me by the way (?).' You . . . . . Then she conveys herself (?) after you; you write it (29) again on the strip with which you wrap up the [shrew-mouse (?)].

Col. XIV.

(1) That which another man said to me: 'Open my eyes,' unto four times. (2) [A vessel-divination:] 'Open my eyes; open thy eyes,' (and) vice versa, unto three times. 'Open, Tat; Open, Nap,' three times; (3) 'open [unto me?]' three [times?], 'for I am Artamo, born of Hame-o (?), the great basilisk of the East, rising in glory together with thy father (4) at dawn; hail (*bis*), Heh, open to me Hah,' you say it with a drawling(?) voice 'Artamo, open to me Hah; if thou dost (5) not open to me Hah, I will make thee open to me Hah. O Ibis (*bis*), sprinkle (?), that I may (?) see the great god Anubis, the power, (6) that is about (?) my head, the great protector (?) of the Uzat, the power, Anubis, the good ox-herd, at every opening (?) (of the eye?) which I have (?) made, (7) reveal thyself to me; for I am Nasthom,

---

nwzḥ is used of sprinkling a floor with water for the reception of visitors.

ⲛⲧⲁ would mean 'that I may,' the demotic equivalent of which is usually written *nte-y*, though the *y* was not pronounced. Here we have *nte* alone written, unless the group be read *nte-w* 3rd pl., which would give the meaning 'that the god may be seen.'

l. 6. *n-ne-zz-y*: the *n* is a doubling of the initial.

'That I may see the god every time I open my eyes (?).' *e·'r-y* is only past relative in ordinary demotic, but in early demotic is often future. Possibly it retains this meaning here, but if so it is a very exceptional usage.

Arian is repeated three times, each time with a different epithet, but the reading of the second is uncertain: it might mean 'this bringer of prosperity.'

8. mʿstsynks ʾNp mekyste ʾryʿn p nt ʿy ʿryʿn py n(?)-wzy ʾryʾn

9. p nt n bl hy phryks yks ʿnʿksybr-ʿo-ks ʿmbr-ʿo-ks eb-ʿo-rks ks-ʿo-n

10. nbr-ʿo-khrʿ . . p ḫrt wr ʾNp z ʾnk py mty ne-ʾtef ne-pephnwn mʿsph-ʿo-nege

11. hy my ḫp n-e·z-y nb ty n p-hw ze hy nte-k thʿm thʿmth-ʿo-m thʿmʿth-ʿo-m

12. thʿmʿthwmthʿm thʿmʿthwtsy ʾMn sp-sn pe-k rn n mte nt e-w(?) z rn-f z th-ʿo-m

13. ʾnkth-ʿo-m nte-k yt·th thwtsy rn-yk sythom ʿnythom ʾp-sʾ . . . šʿtn-sr

14. km a·wn n-y n n r·w n pe hne ty n p-hw ʾm n-y a n r·w n pe hne pe swt my ʾre

15. pe ʾpt ʾr p(?) w[be ?] n t p·t my ʾre n wḥr·w n p hwlot t n-y p nt n mʿ·t n p nwn my z-w n-y

16. p nt e-y šn ḫrr-f ty n p-hw n mʿ·t sp-sn e mn mt·t n ʿze nʾm-w ⲁ·ⲉ·ⲏ·ⲓ·ⲟ·ⲩ·ⲱ· mʿkh-ʿo-pnewmʿ

17. z-mt·t ḫr ʾny-k wʿ z n ḥmt nte-k ptḥ wʿ twt n ʾNp ḫn-f nte-k mḥ-f n mw n str n

18. mnt(?) b-ʾr p rʿ gm·t-f nte-k zq ḥr-f n nḥe n mʿ·t nte-k wḥ-f ḥr tb·t nmy ė ḫrr-w prḫ

19. n šʿ nte-k t ke tb·t IV·t ḫr p ḫm-ḫl nte-k t ʾre p ḫm-ḫl str a ḥr ḫe·t-f

20. nte-k t ʾr-f(?) wḥ te-f mrt a t tb·t n p hne nte-k t ʾr-f kšp a ḫn p nḥe e wn wʿ ḥbs prḫ a zz-f

---

l. 13. *šʿtn-sr-km* looks like 'sacrifice of black ram.'

l. 15. *wbe* (?). The facsimile gives *e* as the last letter of the word, and so excludes *wyn*. The previous group, apparently written *ʾre*, we have taken as *ʾr p*.

p hwlot has the determinative of locality.

l. 18. *mnt* (?), perhaps 'custodian,' as in I Kham. iv. 7. It might represent the name of the god Mônth.

b-ʾr with final sense? Cf. I Kham. iv. 12, note, and below 22/3. The facsimile would perhaps admit of a reading *e b ʾr*.

Naszot, Nashoteb, Borilammai (*bis*), (8) Mastinx, Anubis, Megiste, Arian, thou who art great, Arian, Pi-anuzy (?), Arian, (9) he who is without. Hail, Phrix, Ix, Anaxibrox, Ambrox, Eborx, Xon, (10) Nbrokhria, the great child, Anubis; for I am that soldier. O ye of the Atef-crown, ye of Pephnun, Masphoneke; (11) hail! let all that I have said come to pass here to-day; say, hail! thou art Tham, Thamthom, Thamathom, (12) Thamathom-tham, Thamathouthi, Amon (*bis*), thy correct name, whom they call Thom, (13) Anakthom; thou art Itth; Thouthi is thy name, Sithom, Anithom Op-sao (?), Shatensro (14) black; open to me the mouths of my vessel here to-day; come to me to the mouths of my vessel, my bandage (?), let (15) my cup make the reflection (?) of heaven; may the hounds of the *hulot* give me that which is just in the abyss; may they tell me (16) that about which I inquire here to-day truly (*bis*), there being no falsehood in them ⲁⲉⲏⲓⲟⲩⲱ, Makhopneuma.' (17) Formula: you take a bowl of bronze, you engrave a figure of Anubis in it; you fill it with water left to settle (?) and (18) guarded (?) lest (?) the sun should reach it; you finish its (sur-)face (of the water) with fine oil, you place it on [three ?] new bricks, their lower sides being sprinkled (19) with sand; you put four other bricks under the child; you make the child lie down upon (?) his stomach; (20) you cause him (?) to place his chin on the brick of the vessel; you make him look into

---

zq: reading not quite certain, but probably *zq ḥr-f* means ϫⲱⲕ, 'complete its (sur-)face,' i. e. fill up the vessel with a thin layer of oil on the top of the water.

tb·t: the facsimile shows a numeral III (?) following, and 'a brick' is always *wꜥ·t tbe·t*. The plural *ḫr-w* also follows; yet in l. 20 'the brick of the vessel' is spoken of in the singular.

l. 19. *a ḥr ḫe·t-f*, a curious expression, possibly meaning 'on his face-and-stomach.'

21. e wn wʿ ḫbs e-f θ-r·t ḥr pe-f wnm wʿ ʿb ḫr st·t ḥr pe-f . . . . nte-k t wʿ ḫlp n sym n

22. ʼNp ḥr p ḫbs nte-k t py sty a ḥry nte-k ʿš ny sḫ·w nt ḥry a p hne n sp VII p sty nt e·ʼr-k t·t-f

23. a ḥry ʼlbwnt mrḥe(?) ʼmwnyʿk trymyʿmʿ-t-s bne nt-w ḥr ʼrp nte-k ʼr-w n

24. bnn nte-k t a ḥry nʼm-w e·ʼr-k wḥ e·ʼr-k t ʼre p ḫm-ḫl wn yr·t-f e·ʼr-k šn·t-f ze ne(?) p ntr ʼy a ḫn e-f

25. z ḥr p ntr ʼy [a ḫn] e·ʼr-k ʿš ḥ·t-f z-mt·t pe-k qʼ mʿo ʼy ʼNp py . . . oy py gʿm

26. py km pe(?) . . . . py srytsy sp-sn srytsy sp-sn ʼbrytsy rn-yk n pe-k rn n mte

27. nte-k šn·t-f a p nt e·ʼr-k [wḫ-f] e·ʼr-k wḥ n pe-k šn nt e·ʼr-k šn ḫrr-f e·ʼr-k ʿš ar-f n sp VII e·ʼr-k wt [p ntr] a pe-f ʿy pe-f wt z-mt·t

28. wt nfr sp-sn ʼNp p mr ʼḥ nfr ʼNp sp-sn p šr n nw wnš wḥr p(?)[-e·ze ?] ke-zm(?) z p šr n ne te(?)

29. ʼS·t wḥr nʼbryš-ʿo-tht(?) p gerwb n ʼmnt pr-ʿo n te . . . . z sp VII e·ʼr-k fy

30. p ḫbs a p ʿlw e·ʼr-k fy p hne nt ḫr mw e·ʼr-k fy t šnto·t [ḥr] ʼ·t-f ḫr ʼr-k-f ʿn

31. n šn-hne [wʿe]t-k nfr sp-sn ʼp e-f znt n sp IX p sym n ʼNp ḫr rt-f n hhe n mʿ

32. te-f gbe·t m q[ty t] gbe·t [n sym ?] n ḫr e-f θy wbḫ te-f ḥrre m q·t[y t ḥ]rre n ʼnq

---

l. 21. *sym n ʼNp*, the ανουβιαδα την του σταχυν of Pap. Bibl. Nat. l. 901. Cf. below, l. 31.

l. 22. *t a ḥry* is the regular expression for putting incense on the censer or brazier.

l. 23. *ʼmwnyʿk trymyʿmʿ-t-s* ʼΑμμωνιακὸν πόα ἐστὶν ὅθεν τὸ ἀμμωνιακὸν θυμίαμα, Diosc. iii. 98. The very slight alteration of *r* to *h* in the demotic would produce θυμιάματος.

l. 28. *p šr n nw wnš wḥr . . . . . p šr n ne te* (?) *ʼS·t wḥr*. For *te* = ⲧⲁ- cf. 8/13, 'the son of those of (?) a (?) jackal and (?) hound . . ., the son of those of Ta-Ese and (?) hound'; possibly a form of pedigree in breeding animals.

the oil, he having a cloth spread over his head, (21) there being a lighted lamp on his right, and a censer with fire on his left; you put a leaf of (22) Anubis-plant on the lamp, you put this incense on (the fire); you recite these spells, which are above, to the vessel seven times. The incense which you put (23) on (the fire): frankincense (?), wax (?), styrax, turpentine (?), date-stone (?); grind them with wine; you make them into a (24) ball and put them on (the fire). When you have finished, you make the child open his eyes, you ask him, saying, 'Is the god coming in?' If he says (25) 'The god has come in,' you recite before him: formula: 'Thy bull (?) Mao, ho! Anubis, this soldier (?), this Kam, (26) this Kem . . . Pisreithi (*bis*), Sreithi (*bis*), Abrithi is thy name, by thy correct name.' (27) You ask him concerning that which you [desire]; when you have finished your inquiry which you are asking about, you call to him seven times; you dismiss the god to his home. His dismissal: formula: (28) 'Farewell (*bis*) Anubis, the good ox-herd, Anubis (*bis*), the son of a (?) jackal (and ?) a dog . . . another volume saith: the child of . . . (29) Isis (?) (and ?) a dog, Nabrishoth, the Cherub (?) of Amenti, king of those of . . . . .' Say seven times. You take (30) the lamp from (?) the child, you take the vessel containing water, you take the cloth off him. You do it also (31) by vessel-inquiry alone, excellent (*bis*), tried (?), tested nine times.

The Anubis-plant. It grows in very numerous places;

---

l. 29. *gerwb* probably = כְּרוּב. Cf. Pap. Bibl. Nat. l. 3061; Leyd. Pap. Gr. V, col. 9, l. 16.

l. 30. *fy* must refer to the removal of the apparatus.

l. 32. [*sym*] *n ḫr*. There seems hardly room for more than the sign *sym*, and some slight remains agree with it.

The leaves of stachys are λευκά (Diosc. iii. 110), coloris in luteum inclinati (Pliny, N. H., xxiv. 86). The former compares it with the

33\. . . . . e·ʾr-k . . . . yr·t . . . . e b-ʾr te-k . . . . . . p hne

Col. XV.

1\. wʿ t swr e·ʾr-k ʾny wʿ ḫm n ḫḫ n ʿpe·t n wʿ rm e-f mw·t n ḫtb·t

2\. erme VII n blbyle·t n yt(?) n tms ḫn wʿ·t be·t n rm e-f mw·t nte-k nt-w erme ʾp·t X·t

3\. ke-z IX·t pr·w n zpḫ nte-k t snf n wʿ·t hʿlʿmʿtʿ n wʿ ʾʾe(?) km a ḫ·t-w erme wʿ ḫm n

4\. snf n pe-k tbʿ n mḥ II n p sʿlʾpyn n te-k·t t·t n gbyr erme te-k·t mt·t nte-k

5\. hm-w n wʿ sp nte-k ty-sw a wʿ z n ʾrp nte-k t·t wtḥ III ar-f n t

6\. ḥʿyt·t n p ʾrp e b-ʾr te-k tp-f e b-ʾr te-w wtne ḫn-f nte-k ʿš py ʿš ar-f n sp VII

7\. nte-k t swr-s t s-ḥm·t nʾm-f nte-k mr p ḫʿr n p syb nt ḥry n wʿ·t tys n š-stn

8\. nte-k mr-s a pe-k znḥ n gbyr pe-f ʿš z-mt·t ʾnk pa(?) ʾBt n mʿ·t n

9\. mnqe n ms n rn-s n ʾS·t t sbb hh ta t s·t-sbḥ n p šʿy

10\. ʾnk py twt n p rʿ s-tʿme-sr rn-yt ʾnk py twt n mr mšʿ a-pḥt py

---

marrubium, the latter (through misunderstanding of *πράσιον*) with the leek. Here we have it compared to the *ʾnqe* ⲉⲛⲩ : (ⲉⲛⲟⲩⲕ ?) *κόνυζα*, Bsciai, Rec. trav., vii. 25; Loret, Flore Phar., 2nd ed., p. 68. Curiously enough, amongst the synonyms of *κονυζα* in Diosc. iii. 126 *ἀνουβιας* occurs. Evidently there is some confusion here with stachys.

θy wbḫ probably 'tends to whiteness.'

Col. XV.

l. 1. *ḫtb·t*: this might represent an Achmimic infinitive ending in ⲉ, but in the Hist. Rom. no. 245 there is a fem. subst. *ḫtby*.

l. 2. *rm e-f mw·t*, no doubt again a man slain or murdered. Parts of the body of those who had suffered a violent death were considered peculiarly efficacious for magical purposes. Cf. P. S. B. A. xiii. 169–70.

l. 3. *pr·w*, a genitive *n* has probably been omitted by mistake.

(32) its leaf is like the leaf of Syrian [plant (?)]; it turns (?) white; its flower is like the flower of conyza.

(33) . . . you . . . eye . . . before you . . . the vessel.

Col. XV.

(1) A potion. You take a little shaving of the head of a man who has died a violent death, (2) together with seven grains of barley that has been buried in a grave of a dead (?) man; you pound them with ten *oipe*, (3) otherwise nine, (of) apple-seeds (?); you add blood of a worm (?) of a black dog to them, with a little (4) blood of your second finger, (that) of the heart (?), of your left hand, and with your semen (?), and you (5) pound them together and put them into a cup of wine and add three *uteh* to it of (6) the first-fruits of the vintage, before you have tasted it and before they have poured out from it; and you pronounce this invocation to it seven times (7) and you make the woman drink it; and you tie the skin of the parasite aforesaid with a band of byssus (8) and tie it to your left arm. Its invocation, formula: 'I am he of Abydos in truth, (9) by formation (?) (and ?) birth in her (?) name of Isis the bringer (?) of fire, she of the mercy-seat of the Agathodaemon. (10) I am this figure of the sun, *Sitamesro* is my name. I am this

---

hʿlʿmʿtʿ, referred to in l. 7 as *syb*. *Syb*, cf. 25/25, 28, = **cıϐ : cıπ** (Eg. *sp*), the meaning of which seems vague—parasitic worms and insects and even sores. Possibly our word may be connected with ἑλμινς.

a ḫ·t-w: see chapter on Grammar.

l. 7. *swr-s*: *s* is duplicated either as the object by *n'm-f* or as the subject by *t s-ḥm·t*.

l. 9. *n mnqe n ms* is difficult.

n rn-s: it seems as if Abydos were here personified as Isis, cf. l. 13, or else we may translate 'by the name of Isis'; see 19/16.

ταπ : τα- represents Eg. *tnt*, to which *τα*- corresponds in Ptolemaic transcriptions of proper names. But possibly the *n* was retained in O. C. in looser combinations.

11. štʿ py sḫr-ʿo·t t ḫo ʿo·t rn-yt ʾnk py twt n Ḥr py štʿm py štʿ py

12. sḫr-ʿo·t rn-t ʾnk py twt n ḥsy-ntr(?) nt mtr n sḫ nt ḥtp a mr ty ḫr

13. t ḥtp·t ʿo·t n ʾBt nta mtr p snf n Wsr a rn-s n ʾS·t e-w ty-f a ḫry ḫn

14. py z py ʾrp my nʾm-f snf n Wsr te-f n ʾS·t a t ʾr-s wʿ mr n ḥt-s ar-f

15. n grḥ mre·t n nw nb e mn nw šr my nʾm-f p snf n mn a·ms mn a ty-f

16. n mn a·ms mn ḫn py z py ʾpt n ʾrp n p-hw a t ʾr-s wʿ mr n ḥt-s ar-f

17. p mr nta ʾr-s ʾS·t a Wsr e-s qte m-s-f a mʿ nb my ʾr-s mn t šr n mn

18. e-s qte m-s mn p šr n mn a mʿ nb p pz nta ʾr-s ʾS·t a Ḥr Bḥtt my

19. ʾr-s t mn s(?) mn e-s mr nʾm-f e-s lby m-s-f e-s rqh n t·t-f e-s qte m-s-f

20. a mʿ nb e wn wʿ·t ḫo n st·t ḫn ḥt-s n ty-s wne·t n tm nw ar-f

21. ke ky nʾm-f ʿn p znf n p ḫbys n te-k·t ʿne·t n pr·w zpḫ ḥnʿ snf

22. n pe-k tbʿ nt sḫ a ḥry ʿn nte-k nt p zpḫ nte-k t snf ar-f nte-k ty-f a p z n ʾrp

23. nte-k ʿš ar-f n sp VII nte-k t swr-s t s-ḥm·t n p nw n rn-f

---

l. 12. *ḥsy*:  inserted after the *ḥ* seems to be a kind of determinative, also in 19/24. The reference here is, of course, to Osiris.

a mr: the geographical significance of this is difficult to grasp, but cf. 9/23.

l. 13. *t a ḫry ḫn*, 'pour into,' of liquids: cf. 19/29.

nt a seems to be the form for the relative before *stm-f* in this papyrus when used instead of the old relative form *a·stm-f*. Cf. l. 17, &c.

l. 14. *my nʾm-f*: above this is a letter resembling ⲁ erased by two lines; the following words are very difficult to understand. *Te-f* may be intended for the past relative *a·te-f*, 'which he gave.'

figure of a Captain of the host, very valiant, this (11) Sword (?), this Overthrower (?), the Great Flame is my name. I am this figure of Horus, this Fortress (?), this Sword (?), this (12) Overthrower (?) is my name. I am this figure of One Drowned, that testifieth by writing, that resteth on the other side (?) here under (13) the great offering-table (?) of Abydos; as to which the blood of Osiris bore witness to her (?) name of Isis when it (the blood) was poured into (14) this cup, this wine. Give it, blood of Osiris (that?) he (?) gave to Isis to make her feel love in her heart for him (15) night and day at any time, there not being time of deficiency. Give it, the blood of N. born of N. to give it (16) to N. born of N. in this cup, this bowl of wine to-day, to cause her to feel a love for him in her heart, (17) the love that Isis felt for Osiris, when she was seeking after him everywhere, let N. the daughter of N. feel it, (18) she seeking after N. the son of N. everywhere; the longing that Isis felt for Horus of Edfu, (19) let N. born of N. feel it, she loving him, mad after him, inflamed by him, seeking him (20) everywhere, there being a flame of fire in her heart in her moment of not seeing him.'

(21) Another method of doing it again. The paring (?) of your nail's point (?) from an apple-fruit (?), and blood (22) of your finger aforesaid again; you pound the apple and put blood on it, and put it in the cup of wine (23) and invoke it seven times, and make the woman drink it at the moment named.

---

l. 21. *znf*: an obscure word; cf. 25/32, V. 7/1. It occurs also in a Philae inscription (Br., Thes., 1017), perhaps with the meaning of a 'small portion.'

pr·w: cf. perhaps Sah. ⲉϭⲣⲁ, pl. ⲉϭⲣⲏⲩⲉ. It is not clear whether the fruit or the pips are intended.

l. 22. *a ḥry*. The MS. appears to have the *a*, but it must be a mistake of the scribe.

24. n še ne-ḥr ḥry e-f ⟨sre-w(?)⟩ myẖ erme-k nte-f tm sze ar-k

25. *μη με διωκε οδε· ανοχ παπιπετου μετουβανες· βασταζω*

26. *την ταφην του οσιρεως και υπαγω καταστησαι αυτην εις αβιδος*

27. *καταστησαι εις ταστας και καταθεσθαι εις [α]λχας εαν μοι ο ⳁ κοπους*

28. *παρασχη προσρεψω αυτην αυτω* pe-f ʿš n mt·t rm n kmy ʿn pe py nt [ẖr]y

29. mpr ptt m-s-y t mn ank pʿpypetw metwbʿnes e-y fy ẖr t qs·t n Wsr

30. e-y ʾnnʿ a θy·t-s a ʾBt a ty ḥtp-s n ʿLghʿh e-f ẖp nte t mn myẖ erme-y n p-hw

31. e-y a hwy·t-s abl z sp VII

Col. XVI.

1. ke-zʿm thew ye ʿo-e ʿo-n yʿ wʿ ke-zʿm elon nfr sp-sn

2. n mt·wt n p ẖbs b-ʿo-th thew ye we ʿo-ʿo-e yʿ wʿ pthʿkh el-ʿo-e

3. yʿth e-ʿo-n peryphʿe yew yʿ y-ʿo yʿ ywe ʾm a ẖry

4. a p wyn n py ẖbs nte-k wnḥ a py ʿlw nte-k šn n-y ẖr p nt e-y šn ẖrr-f

---

l. 24. *ḥry* probably means 'Sovereign,' 'king,' but may perhaps only mean a 'superior officer.' *sre-w* would seem to mean 'range soldiers,' 'array battle.'

l. 25. The Greek formula, ll. 25–28, is translated into demotic in ll. 29–31.

ανοχ, &c. This passage invites interpretation as Old Coptic, but if it really meant anything it must be corrupt, and the demotic version in l. 29 renders it phonetically as if it consisted of magic names. One may perhaps suggest *ʾnk pe pa p nt ʿo my t wʿb n-s*, 'I am the servant of him that is great; give discharge (ⲙⲁⲧⲟⲩⲃⲟ) (of the fault or the liability) to her' (*sic* for 'to me'?).

l. 26. *ταφην*. At this time *ταφή* in Egypt = 'mummy,' as is seen by the mummy tickets (Pap. Rainer Mitth. V. 14).

(24) [A spell] of going to meet a sovereign (?) when he fights with you and will not parley(?) with you. (25) 'Do not pursue me, thou! I am Papipetou Metoubanes. I am carrying (26) the mummy of Osiris and I am proceeding to take it to Abydos, (27) to take [it] to Tastai (?) and to deposit it in Alkhai; if N. deal blows at me, (28) I will cast it at him.' Its invocation in Egyptian also is this as below: (29) 'Do not pursue me, N., I am Papipetu Metubanes. I am carrying the mummy of Osiris, (30) I am proceeding to take it to Abydos, to cause it to rest in Alkhah. If N. fight with me to-day, (31) I will cast it away.' Say seven times.

Col. XVI.

(1, 2) The words of the lamp: 'Both, Theou, Ie, Oue, O-oe, Ia, Oua—otherwise, Theou, Ie, Oe, Oon, Ia, Oua —Phthakh, Eloe—otherwise, Elon, excellent (*bis*)— (3) Iath, Eon, Puriphae, Ieou, Ia, Io, Ia, Ioue, come down (4) to the light of this lamp and appear to this boy

---

l. 27. *ταστας*: an unknown name. This phrase is not translated in the demotic.

[*α*]*λχας*: the *λ* is sufficiently recognizable in the facs.; see the note on 1/16. The *ς* of *κοπους* is likewise seen in the facs.

εαν μοι, &c. Wünsch, in the Supplement on magic tablets to the Corp. inscript. Attic., quotes in his preface an inscription from the Collections du mus. Alaoui I. p. 57 (publ. also Maspero, Et. myth. arch. ii. 297), a Latin eroticon of the 2nd cent. A.D. from Hadrumetum written in Greek characters: 'Si minus descendo in adytus Osyris et dissolvam *τὴν ταφήν* et mittam ut a flumine feratur. Ego enim sum magnus decanus magni dei Achrammachalala,' i.e. as Wünsch says, a sepulcro Osiridis arcam illius eripiet et in Nilum coniiciet, idem quod olim Typho fecerat.

Col. XVI.

l. 1. This is only a gloss on the second line.

l. 2. The apparent *n* at the beginning before *n mt·wt* is probably false.

l. 4. *šn*. In this papyrus this word is often used in such a way as to suggest the meaning 'answer' rather than 'inquire.' Perhaps it may mean both 'to inquire' and 'to be inquired of.'

5. ty n p-hw yʿ-ʿo yʿ-ʿo-mr therenth-ʿo psykšymeʿkhe-mr blʿ

6. khʿnsplʿ yʿe we-by bʿrbʿrethw yew ʿrp-ʿo-n·ghnwph

7. bryntʿten-ʿo-phry heʿ gʾrhre bʿlmenthre menebʿry-ʿkhegh yʿ

8. khekh bryn·sk(?) ʾlmʿ ʿrwnsʿrbʿ meseghryph nyptw-mykh

9. mʿ-ʿo-rkhʿrʿm ʾy lʿʿnkhekh ʿo-mph brymbʾynwy-ʿo

10. th sengenbʿy gh-ʿo-wghe lʿykhʿm ʾrmy-ʿo-wth nte-k zt-f

11. e-f wʿb n py smte p ntr nt ʿnḫ p ḫbs nt θ-r·yt tʾgrtʾt pa zt wy

12. b-ʿo-el a ḫn šʿ sp III ʾrbeth bʾy wtsy-ʿo p ntr ʿo ʿo a·(?)wy b-ʿo-el

13. a ḫn tʾt sp-sn a·wy b-ʿo-el a ḫn šʿ sp III tʾgrtʾt pa zt [a·]wy

14. b-ʿo-el a ḫn šʿ sp III bewtsy p ntr ʿo a·wy b-ʿo-el a ḫn sʿ sp III

15. p ʿš nt e·ʾr-k ʿš-f a ḥr p rʿ n ḫrp e b-ʾr te-k ʿš a p ʿlw z a·ʾr p nt e·ʾr-k ʾr-f a ḫp

16. p ntr ʿo tʾbʾ-ʿo bʾswkhʿm ʿm-ʿo ʿkhʿ·ghʿr·khʿn·-grʿbwnsʿ

17. nwny·etsyqme-t gʿthwbʿsʿthwry·thmylʿʿl-ʿo sp VII

18. ke gy nʾm-f ʿn e·ʾr-k twn-k n twe ḥr pe-k klk n ḫrp n p hw nt e·ʾr-k a ʾr-f nʾm-f nge hw nb

19. z a·ʾr p nt e·ʾr-k a ʾr-f nb a mte n t·t-k e·ʾr-k wʿb a bte nb e·ʾr-k ʿš py ʿš a ḥr p rʿ n sp III nge sp VII

20. y-ʿo·tʾ·bʾ-ʿo s·ʿo-khʿm·mwʾ ʿo-kh·ʿo-kh·khʿn·bwnsʿ-nw ʿn

21. yesy eg-ʿo-m-p-t geth-ʿo sethwry thmylʿ ʾlwʾp-ʿo-khry my ʾre hb nb

---

l. 5. The demotic sign corresponding to the glosses λο, λω is identical with that for *r* in *R-qty* = **Ρακοτε**, and with that for *mr-* = **λε-**, 'superintendent'; λο, λω is evidently the absolute form of the construct **λε-**.

and inquire for me about that which I ask (5) here to-day, Iao, Iaolo, Therentho, Psikhimeakelo, (6) Blakhanspla, Iae, Ouebai, Barbaraithou, Ieou, Arponknouph, (7) Brintatenophri, Hea, Karrhe, Balmenthre, Menebareiakhukh, Ia, (8) Khukh, Brinskulma, Arouzarba, Mesekhriph, Niptoumikh, (9) Maorkharam. Ho! Laankhukh, Omph, Brimbainouioth, (10) Segenbai, Khooukhe, Laikham, Armioouth.' You say it, (11) it (*sic*) being pure, in this manner: 'O god that liveth, O lamp that is lighted, Takrtat, he of eternity, bring in (12) Boel!'—three times—'Arbeth-abi, Outhio, O great great god, bring Boel (13) in, Tat (*bis*), bring Boel in!' Three times. 'Takrtat, he of Eternity, bring (14) Boel in!' Three times. 'Barouthi, O great god, bring Boel in!' Three times.

(15) The invocation which you pronounce before Phre in the morning before reciting to the boy, in order that that which thou doest may succeed: (16) 'O great god, Tabao, Basoukham, Amo, Akhakharkhan-kraboun-zanouni-(17)edikomto, Kethou-basa-thouri-thmila-alo.' Seven times.

(18) Another method of it again. You rise in the morning from your bed early in the day on which you will do it, or any day, (19) in order that everything which you will do shall prosper in your hand, you being pure from every abomination. You pronounce this invocation before Phre three times or seven times. (20) 'Io, Tabao, Sokhom-moa, Okh-okh-khan-bouzanau, An-(21) iesi, Ekomphtho, Ketho, Sethouri, Thmila, Alouapokhri,

---

l. 7. καρρε: the aspiration of the second ρ is interesting. Cf. note to 1/20.

l. 11. *e-f wʿb*: the lamp must be pure as described in ll. 22 et seqq.

a·wy, sometimes perhaps written *wy*, is ⲁⲩ-, ⲁⲩⲉⲓ⸗, St., § 384, and is synonymous with *a·ʾny*: cf. 17/10, &c.

l. 15. *z a·ʾr* = ϫⲉⲣⲉ, 'final.'

22. nt e-y a θy t·t ar-f ty n p-hw my ʾr-f ẖp pe-f ky ẖr ʾny-k wʿ ẖbs nmy e bnp-w t prš ar-f nte-k (*sic*)

23. wʿ sʿl e-f wʿb ar-f nte-k mḥ-f n nḥe n mʿ·t e-f wʿb nte-k wḥ-f n wʿ mʿ e-f wʿb n mw n ḥsm e-f hep

24. nte-k wḥ-f ḥr wʿ·t tbe·t nmy nte-k ʾny wʿ ʿlw nte-k t ḥms-f ḥr k·t tbe·t nmy e ḥr-f

25. st a p ẖbs nte-k ẖtm n yr·t-f nte-k ʿš ny nt ḥry a ẖry ẖn zz-f n p ʿlw n sp VII e·ʾr-k t ʾr-f wn

26. yr·t-f e·ʾr-k z n-f ʿn e·ʾr-k nw a p wyn e-f z n-k te-y nw a p wyn ẖn t st·t n p ẖbs e·ʾr-k ʿš ty hte z

27. hewe **ϫοϫε** n sp IX e·ʾr-k šn·t-f a p nt e·ʾr-k wḫ-f nb bn-s ʿš p ʿš a·ʾr-k t ḥ·t mbḥ p rʿ n ẖrp

28. ẖr ʾr-k-f n wʿ mʿ e r wn a pr(?)-ybt nte-k ẖʿ ḥr-f n p ẖbs e-f st nte-k ẖʿ ḥr-f n p ʿlw

29. e-f·st a ḥr p ẖbs e·ʾr-k ḥr . . . . nʾm-f e·ʾr-k ʿš a ẖry ẖn zz-f e·ʾr-k qlh a zz-f n pe-k tbʿ n mḥ II n p (?) ẖyne (?) n te-k·t t·t

30. n wnm

Col. XVII.

1. ke ky nʾm-f ʿn nfr sp-sn a p ẖbs e·ʾr-k (z ?) b-ʿo-el sp III y·y·y· ʿ·ʿ·ʿ· tʾt tʾt tʾt p šmsy ḥyt n p ntr ʿo p nt t wyn m šs sp-sn

2. p ẖbr n t st·t nte t st·t n r-f pa t st·t nte my-s htm p ntr nt ʿnḫ nte b-ʾr-f mw p ntr ʿo ⟨p⟩ nt ḥms ẖn t st·t nt n t mt·t n t st·t nt

---

l. 22. *θy t·t a*, 'undertake,' 'apply hand to': cf. 17/26 *θ wʿb a.*
pe-f ky: this seems to correspond to *py smt* in l. 11.
t has been omitted by the scribe at the end of the line.

l. 28. *f* is omitted after *r* and *pr* is incomplete before *ybt*. The scribe has moreover been confused in describing the positions of the lamp and the boy.

l. 29. Thus the middle finger of the right hand must have had a different name from that of the left, see 13/18 and cf. 29/5 with this passage. *ẖyne* (?) has the det. of flesh and should be some part of the body.

let everything (22) that I shall apply (?) my hand to here to-day, let it happen.' Its method. You take a new lamp in which no minium has been put and you (put) (23) a clean wick in it, and you fill it with pure genuine oil and lay it in a place cleansed with natron water and concealed, (24) and you lay it on a new brick, and you take a boy and seat him upon another new brick, his face being (25) turned to the lamp, and you close his eyes and recite these things that are (written) above down into the boy's head seven times. You make him (26) open his eyes. You say to him, 'Do you see the light?' When he says to you 'I see the light in the flame of the lamp,' you cry at that moment saying (27) 'Heoue' nine times. You ask him concerning everything that you wish after reciting the invocation that you made previously before Phre in the morning. (28) You do it in a place with (its) entrance open to the East, and put the face of the lamp turned (*blank*). You put the face of the boy (29) turned (*blank*) facing the lamp, you being on his left hand. You cry down into his head, you strike his head with your second finger, (that) of the . . . . , of your (30) right hand.

COL. XVII.

(1) Another method of it again, very good, for the lamp. You (say ?): 'Boel,' (*thrice*), 'I, I, I, A, A, A, Tat, Tat, Tat, the first attendant of the great god, he who gives light exceedingly, (2) the companion of the flame, in whose mouth is the flame which is not quenched,

---

COL. XVII.

l. 1. *e·ʾr-k*. 'Thou art Boel' would need *nte-k*: probably *e·ʾr-k z* was intended.

l. 2. *pa t st·t*: the stroke over the *t* is merely a line separating off the interlineation.

nte my-s = ετε ⲙⲉⲥ-, elsewhere (l. 27, &c.) written etymologically *nte b ʾr-s*. Cf. ο ασβεστος λυχνος Pap. Bibl. Nat. l. 1218.

3. n p šy n t p·t nte p ʿw erme p nʿš n p ntr n t·t-f ʾm a ḫn n t mt n ty st·t nte-k wnḥ-k ⟨wnḥ-k⟩ a py ʿlw ty n p-hw nte-k t ʾr-f šn n-y ḫr mt·t nb nt e-y

4. a šn·t-f [a]r-w ty n p-hw z e-y a šʿš-k n t p·t ne-ḥr p rʿ e-y a šʿšʿ-k ne-ḥr ʿḥ e-y a šʿš-k n p t

5. e-y a šʿš-k ne-ḥr p nt ḥr p bḥt nte b-ʾr-f htm pa p šʿš ʿo nte p ʿw erme p nʿš n p ntr n t·t-f pa p

6. šʿš ʿo petery sp-sn pʿter emphe sp-sn p ntr ʿo ʿo nt n t rʿ ḥry·t n t p·t nte p šbt nt ne-(ne-)ʿne-f n t·t-f p-e·ʾr t ḫp ntr e bp ntr

7. t ḫp-f ʾm n-y a ḫn erme b-ʿo-el ʾnyel nte-k t p zr n n byl·w n py ʿlw nt ḫr pe hne

8. n p-hw a t nw-f ar-k a t stm msz-f ar-k e·ʾr-k sze nte-k šn n-f ḫr hb nb mt·t nb nt e-y a šn·t-f ar-w ty n p-hw

9. p ntr ʿo sy·sʾ-ʿo-th ʾkhrem-p-t ʾm a ḫn n t mt·t n ty st·t p nt ḥms ḥr p tw

10. n gʾbʾ-ʿo-n tʾgrtʾt pa zt p nte b-ʾr-f mw nt ʿnḫ šʿ nḥḥ ⟨a·wy⟩ a·ʾny b-ʿo-el a ḫn b-ʿo-el sp-sn

11. ʾrbethbʾy·nwtsy ʿo p ntr ʿo sp-sn ⟨a·(?)wy⟩ a·ʾny b-ʿo-el a ḫn tʾt sp-sn ⟨a·wy⟩ a·ʾny b-ʿo-el a ḫn e·ʾr-k

12. z ny sp VII a ḫry ḫn zz-f n p ʿlw e·ʾr-k t ʾr-f wn yr·t-f e·ʾr-k šn·t-f z ʿn ḥr p wyn ḫp

13. e-f ḫp e bnp p wyn pyr e·ʾr-k t ʾre p ʿlw ḥ-f sze n r-f a p ḥbs z-mt·t ʿw p wyn pr

14. p wyn θs p wyn ḫy p wyn pr p wyn n p ntr wnḥ-k a·ʾr-y p šmsy n p ntr nte p wḥ-sḥne n p-hw [n t·]t-f

15. nt ne šn n-y ḫr ʾr-f wnḥ-f a p ʿlw n p nw n rn-f ḫr ʿš-k ny a ḫry ḫn zz-f n p ʿlw e-f nw

---

l. 12. *ʿn ḥr* = Boh. ⲁⲛ ⲁ- cf. 2/24.

the great god that dieth not, the great god he that sitteth in the flame, who is in the midst of the flame, (3) who is in the lake of heaven, in whose hand is the greatness and might of the god, come within in the midst of this flame and reveal thyself to this boy here to-day; cause him to inquire for me concerning everything about which I shall (4) ask him here to-day; for I will glorify thee in heaven before Phre, I will glorify thee before the Moon, I will glorify thee on Earth, (5) I will glorify thee before him who is on the throne, who perisheth not, he of the great glory, in whose hand is the greatness and might of the god, he of the great glory, (6) Petery (*bis*), Pater, Emphe (*bis*), O great great god, who is above heaven, in whose hand is the beautiful staff, who created deity, deity not having (7) created him, come in to me with Boel, Aniel; do thou give strength to the eyes of this boy who has my vessel (8) to-day, to (?) cause him to see thee, cause his ears to hear thee when thou speakest; and do thou inquire for him concerning everything and every word as to which I shall ask him here to-day, (9) O great god, Sisaouth, Akhrempto, come into the midst of this flame, he who sitteth on the mountain (10) of Gabaon, Takrtat, he of eternity, he who dieth not, who liveth for ever, bring Boel in, Boel (*bis*), (11) Arbethbainouthi, great one, O great god (*bis*) ⟨bring⟩ fetch Boel in, Tat (*bis*) ⟨bring⟩ fetch Boel in.' You (12) say these things seven times down into the head of the boy, you make him open his eyes, you ask him saying, 'Has the light appeared?' (13) If it be that the light has not come forth, you make the boy himself speak with his mouth to the lamp. Formula: 'Grow, O light, come forth (14) O light, rise O light, lift thyself up O light, come forth O light of the god, reveal thyself to me, O servant of the god, in whose hand is the command of to-day, (15) who will ask for me.' Then he reveals himself to the boy in the moment named.

16. m-s p ḫbs mpr t ʾr-f nw m-s ge mʿ m-s p ḫbs wʿe·t-f e-f tm nw m-s-f ḫr ʾr-f htye·t

17. e·ʾr-k ʾr ny tre-w e·ʾr-k wḥ n pe-k šn e·ʾr-k st-k e·ʾr-k t ʾr-f ḫtm yr·t-f e·ʾr-k sze a ḫry ḫn zz-f n py ke

18. ʿš nt ḫry ze a·ʾre n ntr·w še n-w nte p ʿlw lk-f e-f nw ar-w ʾ·rkhe·khem·phe nsew

19. hele sʿtrʿpermt ḥrḥ a py ʿlw nte-k tm t ʾr-f htye·t ḥnwḥe škll·t nte-k t

20. st-f a pe-f myt n ḫrp a·wn ty·t a·wn ty te-y z nʾm-s z ne-(ne-)ʿne py šn-hne n p ḫbs (?)

21. a p ḫrp py smt ʿn pe pe-f ky ḫr ʾny-k wʿ ḫbs nmy e·bp-w t prš ar-f nte-k t wʿ sʿl n

22. ḥbs e·f wʿb ar-f nte-k mḥ-f n nḥe n mʿ·t e-f wʿb nte-k wḥ-f ḥr wʿ·t tbe·t nmy nte-k t ḥms p ʿlw ḥr k·t tbe·t

23. wbe p ḫbs nte-k t ʾr-f ḫtm yr·t-f nte-k ʿš a ḫry ḫn zz-f a ḫ p ke ky ʿn ke ʿš e·ḫr

24. ʾr-k ʿš-f wbe p rʿ n twe n sp III nge sp VII z-mt·t y-ʿo·tʾbe-ʿo s-ʿo-kh-ʿo-mmwʾ ʿo-kh

25. ʿo·kh·khʿn bwnsʿ-nw ʿn yesy eg-ʿo-mth-ʿo geth-ʿo seth-ʿo-ry thmy

26. lʿ·ʾlwʾp-ʿo·khry my ḫp mt·t nb nt e-y a ʾr-w n p-hw nte-w ḫp e-f ḫp nte-k tṃ θ wʿb ar-f b-ʾr-f ḫp te-f mt·t ʿo·t wʿb ke

27. ʿš a ḫ p nt ḥry ʿn z-mt·t b-ʿo-el sp III ⲓ·ⲓ·ⲓ·ⲁ·ⲓ· ⲓ·ⲓ·ⲁ· tʾt sp III p nt t wyn m šs sp-sn p ḫbr n t st·t pa t st·t nte b-ʾr-s

28. htm p ntr nt ʿnḫ nte b-ʾr-f mw p nt ḥms ḫn t st·t nt n t mt·t n t st·t nt n p šy n t p·t nte p ʿw erme p nʿš

29. n p ntr n t·t-f wnḥ-k a py ʿlw hew ϭⲟϭ sp-sn he-ʿo

---

l. 19. *hele* has the Greek symbol of the sun (ἥλιε) above it.

l. 20. The demotic sign for  at the end apparently stands for *ḫbs*, 'lamp.'

l. 26. *θ wʿb a*: cf. 14/32.

te-f mt·t ʿo·t: cf. εστιν δε το αγαθον ζωδιον B. M. Pap. XLVI. 171.

You recite these things down into the head of the boy, he looking (16) towards the lamp. Do not let him look towards another place except the lamp only; if he does not look towards it, then he is afraid. (17) You do all these things, you cease from your inquiry, you return, you make him close his eyes, you speak down into his head this other (18) invocation which is below, that is, if the gods go away and the boy ceases to see them: 'Arkhe-khem-phai, Zeou, (19) Hele, Satrapermet, watch this boy, do not let him be frightened, terrified, or scared, and make (20) him return to his original path. Open Teï (the Underworld), open Taï (Here).' I say it that this vessel-inquiry of the lamp is better (21) than the beginning. This is the method again; its form: you take a new lamp in which no minium has been put and you put a wick of (22) clean linen in it; you fill it with genuine clean oil; you place it on a new brick, you make the boy sit on another brick (23) opposite the lamp; you make him shut his eyes, you recite down into his head according to the other method also.

Another invocation which (24) you recite towards Phre in the morning three times or seven times. Formula: 'Iotabao, Sokh-ommoa, Okh-(25)-okh-Khan, Bouzanau, Aniesi, Ekomphtho, Ketho, Sethori, (26) Thmilaalouapokhri may everything succeed that I shall do to-day,' and they will (?) succeed. If it be that you do not apply (?) purity to it, it does not succeed; its chief matter is purity.

Another (27) invocation like the one above again. Formula: 'Boel,' (*thrice*), 'I, I, I, A, I, I, I, A, Tat (*thrice*), he who giveth the light exceedingly, the companion of the flame, he of the flame which does not (28) perish, the god who liveth, who dieth not, he who sitteth in the flame, who is in the midst of the flame who is in the lake of heaven, in whose hand is the greatness and might (29) of the god, reveal thyself to

nte-f šn n-y nte-k ty ʾr-f nw nte-f kšp nte-f stm a mt·t nb nt e-y

30. šn·t-f ar·w z e-y a šʿš-k n t p·t e-y a šʿš-k n p t e-y a šʿš-k ne-ḥr p nt ḥr p bḥt nte b-ʾr-f htm

31. py ʿw petery sp-sn emphe sp-sn p ntr ʿo nt n ḥry (?) n t p·t nte p šbt nt ne-(ne-)ʿne-f n t·t-f ʾr t ḫp ntr

32. e bnp ntr t ḫp-f ʾm a ḫn n t mt·t n ty st·t erme b-ʿo-el ʾnyel nte-k t p zr n n byl·w n hew sp-sn

Col. XVIII.

1. n hew sp-sn p šr n hew sp-sn z e·f a nw ar-k n yr·t-f nṭe-k t stm msz-f

2. nte-k sze wbe-f n hb nb e-f a šn·t-k ar-f nte-k z n-y wḥ n mt·t mʿ·t nte-k p ntr ʿo sʿ

3. bʿ-ʿo-th ʾm a ḫry erme b-ʿo-el tʾt sp-sn a·wy b-ʿo-el a ḫn ʾm a ḫn n t mt·t n ty st·t

4. nte-k šn n-y ḫr p nt ne-(ne-)ʿne-f tʾgrtʾt py zt a·wy b-ʿo-el a ḫn šʿ sp III ʾrbth

5. bʿynwtsy-ʿo p ntr ʿo a·wy b-ʿo-el a ḫn sp III e-ʾr-k z ny a ḫry ḫn zz-f n p ʿlw

6. e-ʾr k t ʾr-f wn yr·t-f e-ʾr-k šn·t-f a mt·t nb a ḫ p ky nt n bl ʿn

7. šn-hne e te-s n-y wʿ syn ḫn p ṭše n pr-mz ḫr ʾr-k-f ʿn n šn-hne wʿ·t-k

8. sʾbʾ nm nn (?) byrybʾt hy sp-sn p ntr sysyʾh-ʿo nt ḥr p tw n qʾbʾh-ʿo

9. nte t wt·t n p šʿy n t·t-f šm a py ḫm-ḫl my pḫr-f p wyn z ʾnk

---

l. 32. Gloss ϩⲟⲩ ϩⲟⲩ: the word is spelt in the demotic like ϩⲏⲟⲩ, 'money,' with the det. of silver.

Col. XVIII.

l. 6. *n bl*: ἔξω in the Revenue Pap., Wilck., Ostr., i. 19 n., 'on the verso,' 'on the other side.' Cf. V. 15/7. The verso columns I and II are on the back of this Col. XVIII, but they do not contain the passage here indicated.

this boy, Heou (*bis*), Heo, that he may inquire for me, and do thou make him see and let him look and let him listen to everything which I (30) ask him, for I will glorify thee in heaven, I will glorify thee on earth, I will glorify thee before him who is on the throne, who does not perish, (31) he of greatness, Peteri (*bis*), Emphe (*bis*), O great god who is above heaven, in whose hand is the beautiful staff, who created deity, (32) deity not having created him, come into the midst of this flame with Boel, Aniel, and give strength to the eyes of Heu (*bis*).

Col. XVIII.

'(1) Of Heu (*bis*), the son of Heu (*bis*), for he shall see thee with his eyes, and thou shalt make his ears to hear, (2) and shalt speak with him of everything; he shall ask thee about it, and thou shalt tell me answer truly; for thou art the great god (3) Sabaoth; come down with Boel, Tat (*bis*); bring Boel in, come into the midst of this flame (4) and inquire for me concerning that which is good; Takrtat, he of eternity, bring Boel in,' three times, 'Arbeth, (5) Bainouthio, O great god, bring Boel in,' three times. You say these things down into the head of the boy, (6) you make him open his eyes, you ask him as to everything according to the method which is outside, again.

(7) [Another ?] vessel-inquiry which a physician in the Oxyrhynchus nome gave me; you (can) also make it with a vessel-inquiry alone by yourself: (8) 'Sabanem, Nn, Biribat, Ho! (*bis*) O god Sisiaho who (art) on the mountain of Kabaho, (9) in whose hand is the creation of the Shoy, favour (?) this boy, may he enchant the

l. 9. *t wt·t n p šʿy*: 'the generation of the Agathodaemon' probably signifies 'the fortune produced by the god of Fate.'

10. ḥr ʿnw pe p ze k-zʿm z ʾnk ḥr nwn n twe hʾlʾ-ḥr n mre·t ʾnk

11. ʾh n ḥr rhwe ʾnk p rʿ p ẖrt šps nt e-w z n-f gʾrtʾ n rn ank p-e·ʾr pyr a bl

12. ẖr p znḥ n t rpy·t n pr-ybt ʾnk ʿo sp-sn rn-yt ʿo pe pe rn n mte ʾnk . . . .

13. rn-yt ʾw pe pe rn n mte ank l-ʿo-t mw l-ʿo-t pe p ʾr-y gʿm sp-sn p nte te-f

14. gʿm·t ẖn t st·t pa py qlm n nb nt n zz-f th-ʾy-yt sp-sn t sp-sn

15. hʿtrʿ sp-sn p ḥr n ʾʾe sp-sn hy ʾNp p pr-ʿo n t ty·t my še n-f p kke

16. a·ʾny p wyn n-y a ẖn a pe šn-hne z ʾnk Ḥr s Wsr a·ms ʾS·t

17. p ẖrt šps nte mr-s ʾS·t nt šn m-s pe-f yt Wsr wn-nfr hy ʾNp

18. p pr-ʿo n t ty·t my še n-f p kke a·ʾny p wyn n-y a ẖn a pe šn-hne

19. pe swt ty n p-hw my wz-y my wz p nte ḥr-f pẖt a py hne ty n p-hw

20. šʿ nte n ntr·w ʾy a ẖn nte-w z n-y wḥ n mt·t mʿ·t ẖr pe šn nt e-y šn

21. e-tbe·t-f ty n p-hw n mt·t mʿ·t n wš n mt·t n ʿze twn hy ʾNp

22. p snt nẖne mšʿ a bl ty wne·t a·ʾny n-y n ntr·w n ty bk·t erme

23. p ntr nt θ wḥ n p-hw nte-f z n-y pe šn nt e-y šn ẖrr-f n p-hw n sp IX

24. e·ʾr-k wn yr·t-k nge p ẖm-ẖl nte-k nw a p wyn e·ʾr-k ʿš a p wyn z ʾwe·t-f

---

l. 10. *ḥr ʿnw* possibly means 'ape-headed'; the word *šm* (l. 9) occurs with the name of the ape also in 11/2. The copula usually follows *ʾnk* and *nte-k* immediately in this papyrus, but is separated here as in l. 13 *ʾnk l-ʿo-t mw l-ʿo-t pe*.

l. 12. *t rpy·t*: either the goddess Triphis or possibly the constellation Virgo.

light, for I am (10) Fair-face'—another roll says, 'I am the face of Nun—in the morning, Halaho at midday, I am (11) Glad-of-face in the evening, I am Phre, the glorious boy whom they call Garta by name; I am he that came forth (12) on the arm of Triphis in the East; I am great, Great is my name, Great is my real name, I am Ou, Ou (13) is my name, Aou is my real name; I am Lot Mulot, I have prevailed (?) (*bis*), he whose (14) strength is in the flame, he of that golden wreath which is on his head, They-yt (*bis*), To (*bis*), (15) Hatra (*bis*), the Dog-face (*bis*). Hail! Anubis, Pharaoh of the underworld, let the darkness depart, (16) bring the light in unto me to my vessel-inquiry, for I am Horus, son of Osiris, born of Isis, (17) the noble boy whom Isis loves, who inquires for his father Osiris Onnophris. Hail! Anubis, (18) Pharaoh of the underworld, let the darkness depart, bring the light in unto me to my vessel-inquiry, (19) my knot (?) here to-day; may I flourish, may he flourish whose face is bent down to this vessel here to-day (20) until the gods come in, and may they tell me answer truly to my question about which I am inquiring (21) here to-day, truly without falsehood forthwith (?). Hail! Anubis, (22) O creature (?), Child, go forth at once, bring to me the gods of this city and (23) the god who gives answer (?) to-day, and let him tell me my question about which I am asking to-day.' Nine times.

(24) You open your eyes or (those of) the boy and you see the light. You invoke the light, saying, 'Hail,

---

ⲟⲩ ⲟⲩ: the hieratic (?) symbols below are of uncertain meaning.

l. 13. *p 'r-y*. It is difficult to make sense of this as it stands. Possibly the *p* may be a copyist's error for *e*, in which case the meaning could be that given above.

g'm sp-sn read *g'mg'm* = **ϫⲉⲙϫⲟⲙ**, cf. 3/10.

l. 17. *nte mr-s*: perhaps present relative, see chapter on Grammar.

l. 23. *nt θ wḥ n p-hw* seems to correspond to *nte p wḥ sḥne n t·t-f n p-hw* 6/17, &c., and so may mean 'who governs to-day': see 21/2.

25. p wyn pr sp-sn p wyn θs sp-sn p wyn ʿw sp-sn p wyn p nt n bl ʾm a ḫn e·ʾr-k z·t-f n sp IX

26. šʿ nte p wyn ʿw nte ʾNp ʾy a ḫn a·ʾre ʾNp ʾy a ḫn nte-f smne nʾm-f

27. e·ʾr-k z n ʾNp z twn mšʿ a bl a·ʾny n-y n ntr·w n ty bk·t tym

28. a ḫn ḫr še-f a bl n t hte·t n rn-s nte-f ʾny n ntr·w a ḫn e·ʾr-k rḫ-s

29. z a n ntr·w ʾy a ḫn e·ʾr-k z n ʾNp z a·ʾny wʿ tks a ḫn ḫr n ntr·w

30. nte-w ḥms e-w ḥms e·ʾr-k z n ʾNp a·ʾny wʿ ʾrp (?) a ḫn erme hyn·w t·w my wm-w my swr-w

31. e-f t wm-w nte-f t swr-w e·ʾr-k z n ʾNp z n se ne šn n-y n p-hw e-f z se ʿn e·ʾr-k z n-f z

32. p ntr nt ne šn n-y my ʾr-f t ʿḥʿ t·t-f n-y nte-f z n-y rn-f e-f z rn-f n-k e·ʾr-k

33. šn·t-f a p nt e·ʾr-k wḫ-f e·ʾr-k wḥ e·ʾr-k šn ḫr p nt e·ʾr-k wḫ-f e·ʾr-k wt-w

Col. XIX.

1. [r (?)] n mt·t a p phs n p wḥr

2. a·ʾr-y ʾy a bl n ʾrq-ḥḥ e r-y mḥ n snf n ʾʾe(?) km

3. e-y syt nʾm-f p (?) tšer (?) n whr py whr nt ḫn p X n whr

4. nte wn-te ʾNp s-f n ḫet-f šte n te-k·t mt·t ʿl n pe-k zʾk nʾm-y (?) ʿn

5. e·ʾr-k tm šte n te-k·t mt·t nte-k ʿl n pe-k zʾk e-y a θy·t-k

6. a ḥry a p ḫft-ḥ n Wsr pe nw e-y a ʾr n-k n p-e·ʾr-e-p-e ge·t (?) ʾpt·w (?)

---

l. 27. *bk·t tym*: cf. Matt. ix. 35, x. 11, 14.

l. 31. *se*, lit. 'they' (are so), = ϲⲉ, 'yes.'

Col. XIX.

l. 1. Supply *r*, 'spell,' before *n mt·t*: cf. l. 32.

(25) O light, come forth (*bis*) O light, rise (*bis*) O light, increase (*bis*) O light, O that which is without, come in.' You say it nine times, (26) until the light increases and Anubis comes in. When Anubis comes in and takes his stand, (27) then you say to Anubis, 'Arise, go forth, bring in to me the gods of this city (or ?) village,' (28) then he goes out at the moment named and brings the gods in. When you know (29) that the gods have come in, you say to Anubis, 'Bring in a table for the gods (30) and let them sit down.' When they are seated, you say to Anubis, 'Bring a wine-jar in and some cakes ; let them eat, let them drink.' (31) While he is making them eat and making them drink, you say to Anubis, 'Will they inquire for me to-day ?' If he says 'Yes' again, you say to him, (32) 'The god who will ask for me, let him put forth his hand to me and let him tell me his name.' When he tells you his name, you ask him as to that which you desire. When you have ceased asking him as to that which you desire, you send them away.

COL. XIX.

(1) [Spell] spoken to the bite of the dog. (2) 'I have come forth from Arkhah, my mouth being full of blood of a black dog. (3) I spit it out, the . . . of a dog. O this dog, who is among the ten dogs (4) which belong to Anubis, the son of his body, extract thy venom, remove thy saliva (?) from me (?) again. (5) If thou dost not extract thy venom and remove thy saliva (?), I will take thee (6) up to the court of the temple of Osiris, my watch-tower (?). I will do for thee the *parapage* (?) of

---

l. 4. *šte* seems to mean 'extract' rather than 'enchant.'

l. 6. *p-e-ʾr-e-p-e ge·t* might mean 'that which he of *ge·t* did.'
ge·t, perhaps 'sort,' II Kham. vii. 7.
ʾpt·w. REUVENS has clearly *ʾptḥ·w*, the *ḥ* being apparently inserted by error between *t* and the determination of birds.

7. a ḫ p ḫrw n ʾS·t t šte·t t nb šte nt šte n nt nb nte b-ʾr-w šte

8. n-s n rn-s n ʾS·t t šte·t   nte-k nt *ϩϫⲁⲛ* ḥr *ϭⲙⲟⲩ*

9. nte-k ty-f a t tm·t n p phs n p whr nte-k mt·t ar-f n mne šʿ nte-f (ne-)nfr

10. [r (?)] n mt·t a šte n t mt·t ḥr ḥt-f n rm e·ḥr-w t swr-f pḫre·t nge (?)

11. zw·t   ʾwe·t-f sp-sn yʾblw p z n nb n Wsr

12. e swr ʾS·t Wsr p šʿy ʿo n ḫe·t-k e swr-w p III ntr·w e swr-y

13. m-s-w ḥ·t ze n-k t ʾr-y tḫ n-k t ʾr-y byk n-k t ʾr-y hy

14. a bl n-k t ʾr-y hbrbr n-k t ʾr-y the n ḥt n-k t ʾre r-y

15. z wʿ my wz-y a krʿo (?) mw-bn mtw·t nb a·e-w ḫt (?)-w a ḥt-y

16. e-y swr-k my te-y hwy·t-w a ḥry n rn-s n sʿrbythʿ t šr·t

17. n p šʿy z ʾnk sʾbrʿ bryʾthʿ brysʿrʾ her

18. rn-yt ank Ḥr šʿ-r-n (?) e-f n·ʾw n p θ ʾwe·t-f yʿh-ʿo

19. p ḫrt rn-yt n pe rn n mte   a wʿ z n ʾrp

20. nte-k t *ⲃⲉϣⲟⲩϣ* e-f knn nte-k ty-f ar-f nte-k mt·t ar-f n sp VII nte-k t swr-f

21. p rm n twe e b-ʾr te-f wm [r (?)]n mt·t a p rm e wn qs zthe

22. ḥr te-f šnbe·t   nte-k pe šlʾte lʿte bʿlʿte

---

l. 7. *ʾS·t tʾ šd·t* is figured on a stela of Horus and the crocodiles in the British Museum, Budge, Mummy, p. 359; Wilkinson, Anc. Eg., 3rd ed., vol. iii. Pl. 33. For *šte* see note to l. 4.

l. 8. *πρασον* is prescribed for *θηριοδηκτοις*, Diosc., ii. 178.

ϭⲙⲟⲩ (ϭⲙⲟϩ?): cf. *kmw*, Br., Wtb. Suppl., 1245; or *qmḥ*, *kmḥ*, ib., Suppl., 1249; Wtb., 1455, 1495 = קֶמַח, 'fine meal.'

l. 9. *tm·t*, 'wound'; the word is best known in the Eg. *ḫr dm·t* = person stung, bitten, or wounded, written out in the Metternich stela, l. 32.

birds (?) (7) like the voice of Isis, the sorceress (?), the mistress of sorcery (?), who bewitches (?) everything and is not bewitched (?) (8) in her name of Isis the sorceress (?).' And you pound garlic with *kmou* (?) (9) and you put it on the wound of the bite of the dog; and you address it daily until it is well.

(10) [Spell] spoken for extracting the venom from the heart of a man who has been made to drink a potion or (?) (11) . . . 'Hail to him! (*bis*) Yablou, the golden cup of Osiris. (12) Isis (and) Osiris (and) the great Agathodaemon have drunk from thee; the three gods have drunk, I have drunk (13) after them myself; for, dost thou make me drunk? dost thou make me suffer shipwreck? dost thou make me perish? (14) dost thou cause me confusion? dost thou cause me to be vexed of heart? dost thou cause my mouth (15) to speak blasphemy? May I be healed of all poison, pus (and) venom which have been . . . . ed to my heart; (16) when I drink thee, may I cause them to be cast up in the name of Sarbitha, the daughter (17) of the Agathodaemon; for I am Sabra, Briatha, Brisara, Her (18) is my name. I am Horus Sharon (?) when he comes from receiving acclamation (?), Yaho, (19) the child is my name as my real name.' (Pronounced) to a cup of wine (20) and you put (*sic*) fresh rue and put it to it; and you make invocation to it seven times, and make (21) the man drink it in the morning before he has eaten.

[Spell] spoken to the man, when a bone has stuck (22)

---

l. 15. *kr'o* (?): the reading is very uncertain, and the remains will admit of reading *gl'o*, i. e. **κλo**.

a·e-w, perhaps for **ϵⲁⲩ**, or simply **ϵⲩ**.

l. 16. *n rn-s*: there is no fem. word preceding to which this can be attached. Apparently the pronoun is explained by the subsequent *S'rbytha*, and the passage may be translated 'by the name of Sarbitha.'

l. 20. Seeds or leaves of rue as an antidote to poison, &c., Diosc., 3/45. *knn* is a word applied to leaves and flowers in this papyrus.

23. p msḥ wbḫ nt ḫr t stp-p·t(?) n p yʿm n h-ʿo-h nte ḫe·t-f

24. mḥ n qs n ḥsy nb hʿy e·ʾr-k a syt n py qs n-y a ḥry n p-hw e-f ʾr

25. qs e-f ʾr wšym (?) e-f ʾr l . . . s n tys·t e-f ʾr nge nb e mn n

26. ge šre z ʾnk wʿ ḥʿ·t n my ank wʿ tp n sr ank wʿ šʿl

27. n ʾbyw srrf pe pe rn n mte z Wsr p nt m t·t p rm n rn-f

28. p nt . . . . . sp VII nte-k mt·t a wʿ ḫm n *ⲛⲉϩ* nte-k

29. t ḥr-f n p rm a ḥry nte-k ty-f a ḫry ḫn r-f nte-k ḥn pe-k tbʿ erme

30. te-k·t ʿne mwt II n te-f šnbe·t nte-k t ʾr-f ʿm p nḥe nte-k t

31. twn-f-s n ḫtp nte-k t p nḥe nt ḫn te-f šnbe·t a bl ty hte·t

32. ḫr ʾw p qs a ḥry erme p *ⲛⲉϩ* r n mt·t a p phs n p whr

33. p ḫyt(?) n ʾMn t rp·t z ʾnk py hkr nḫt šlʿmʿlʿ mʿlet št (?)

34. a-pḥt št-ʿe·t grš-ʿe·t grš-ʿe nb rnt tʿhne (?) bʿhne (?) py ʾʾe (?)

35. py km p ʾʾe (?) ʾr (?) št (?) py ʾʾe (?) pa ty IV·t ʿlw·t p wnš n šr wpy

36. p šr n ʾNp glz n pe-k šʿl ḫʿ n pe-k ryt a ḫry e·ʾr-k n ḥr

37. n St a Wsr e·ʾr-k n ḥr n ʿpp a p rʿ Ḥr s Wsr a·ms ʾS·t nta e·ʾr-k mḥ r-k ar-f

---

l. 25. Copies and the original seem to admit the reading *wšym*, which may be connected with Eg. *wšm*, meaning perhaps a fine point; and *qs* in Egyptian is a harpoon-head.

l. 26. *ʾnk*, perhaps possessive 'mine is'; *tp*, parallel to *šʿl*, may here be 'horn': see 3/22.

in his throat. 'Thou art Shlate, Late, Balate, (23) the white crocodile, which is under (?) the . . . of the sea of fire, whose belly (24) is full of bones of every drowned man. Ho! thou wilt spit forth this bone for me to-day, which acts (?) [as] (25) a bone, which . . . . ., which . . . . . as (?) a bandage, which does everything without (26) a thing deficient; for I am (?) a lion's fore-part, I am a ram's head (?), I am a leopard's tooth; (27) Gryphon is my real name, for Osiris is he who is in my hand, the man named (28) is he who gives (?) my . . . . .' Seven times. You make invocation to a little oil. You (29) put the face of the man upwards and put it (the oil) down into his mouth; and place your finger and (30) your nail [to the ?] two muscles (?) of his throat; you make him swallow the oil and make him (31) start up suddenly, and you eject the oil which is in his throat immediately; (32) then the bone comes up with the oil.

Spell spoken to the bite of the dog. (33) The exorcism (?) of Amen (and ?) Thriphis; say: 'I am this Hakoris (?) strong, Shlamala, Malet, secret (?) (34) mighty Shetei, Greshei, Greshei, neb Rent Tahne Bahne (?) this [dog ?] (35) this black [one], the dog which hath bewitched (?), this dog, he of these four bitch-pups (?), the jackal (?) being (?) a son of Ophois. (36) O son of Anubis, hold on (?) by thy tooth, let fall thy humours (?); thou art as the face (37) of Set against Osiris, thou art as the face of Apop against the Sun; Horus the son of Osiris, born of Isis (is he ?) at whom thou didst fill thy

---

l. 27. *m t·t*, or 'beside me,' ⲚⲦⲞⲞⲦ.

l. 31. *n ẖtp*: in older demotic *n ẖp*, II Kham. 3/18; possibly the *t* may be an error.

l. 33. *ẖyt* (?): cf. 21/30.

hkr is determined with the signs of a foreigner and a man. It is perhaps the same word that constituted the name of king Akoris (*Hgr*) of the twenty-ninth dynasty.

l. 37. Apop, the dragon-enemy of the sun.

38. mn a·ms m[n nta (?)] e·ʾr-k mḥ r-k ar-f stm n py sze Ḥr ʾr t ʿlk ḫmm ʾr še a p nwn

39. ʾr snt p t stm p yʿh-ʿo sʿbʿh-ʿo ʾbyʾh-ʿo n rn e·ʾr-k lšlš (?) t tm·t e·ʾr-k nt

40. ḥm ʾh tt t ar-f ke e·ʾr-k nt bšwš ḥr ʾby t ar·f nte-k z·t-f ʿn a wʿ z n mw nte-k t swr-f-s

Col. XX.

1. n mt·t a t plege

2. ʾnk pe s stn wr tp ʾNp te mw Sḫm·t ʾS·t (?) ʾre-s (?) ʾy m-s-y

3. a bl a p t n ḫr a p sbt n p t n ḥḥ a p tš n ny wm-rm z

4. ys sp-sn tkr sp-sn pe šr s stn wr tp ʾNp z twn·t-k nte-k ʾy

5. a Kmy z pe-k yt Wsr e-f n pr-ʿo ⟨a⟩ n Kmy e-f n wr a (*sic*) p

6. t tre-f n ntr·w tre·w n Kmy swh a θ t grep·t n t·t-f

7. t wne·t n z ny a·ʾre-s fy n-y n wʿ·t fks·t hy te nmte·t a·ʾr-y

---

l. 38. This seems to imply an original chaos of burning.

l. 39. *p* seems distinct, *stm* is extremely doubtful.

lšlš (?): the reading is from Reuvens' copy. ⲧⲟⲩⲃⲟ, 'purify,' is determined by  in 5/3, and 'cleanse' fits the sense here.

Col. XX.

l. 1. *plege* = πληγή, as Max Müller, Rec. tr., viii. 174. πληγη is used especially of the sting of a scorpion, B. M. Gr. Pap. CXXI, l. 193, &c., but also of bites and stings of venomous animals in general, Diosc., Περι Ιοβολ. 19, and of wounds in general. Except that it bleeds (l. 14) there is little here to show what is meant by *plege* so long as ll. 7–8 remain unintelligible.

l. 2. According to this Anubis was the eldest son of Osiris (l. 5), and his mother was Sekhemt-Isis, called in l. 9 Isis. The liaison of Osiris with Nephthys (cf. Plutarch) is referred to in the O. C. of Pap. Bibl. Nat.

nte-s(?)*ʾy* is a possible reading, *a·ʾr-s* is not possible.

l. 3. *wm-rm*: there were Anthropophagi and Cynamolgi caninis capitibus (cf. 21/7) associated in Africa, apparently on the Upper Nile, Plin.,

mouth (i.e. bite), (38) N. son of N. (is he) (?) at whom thou hast filled thy mouth; hearken to this speech. Horus who didst heal burning pain (?), who didst go to the abyss, (39) who didst found the Earth, listen, O Yaho, Sabaho, Ȧbiaho by name.' You cleanse (?) the wound, you pound (40) salt with . . . ; apply it to him. Another: you pound rue with honey, apply it; you say it also to a cup of water and make him drink it (?).

Col. XX.

(1) [Spell] spoken to the sting: (2) 'I am the King's son, eldest and first, Anubis. My mother Sekhmet-Isis (?), she came (?) after me (3) forth to the land of Syria, to the hill of the land of Heh, to the nome of those cannibals, saying, (4) "Haste (*bis*), quick (*bis*) my child, King's son, eldest and first, Anubis," saying, "Arise and come (5) to Egypt, for thy father Osiris is King of Egypt, he is ruler over (6) the whole land; all the gods of Egypt are assembled to receive the crown from his hand." (7) The moment of saying those things she brought me a blow (?),

---

H. N., 6. 35 ad fin. Northward, Anthropophagi were placed in Syria, ib. 7. 2, or in Parthia (Robinson, Apocr. Gosp., p. 23, and Preface): cf. Rec. tr., xxv. 41. The land of Hah (Millions) is not known.

l. 5. *a n Kmy . . . a p t* must be for *n Kmy . . . n p t*. Possibly the Faiyumic pronunciation ⲉ for ⲛ̄ has produced this exceptional writing.

l. 7. The following may be suggested as an alternative translation for this difficult passage: 'At the moment when she said this, a wasp (?) flew to me, my spittle (?) fell down upon me (from fright); it (the wasp) drew near (or gathered itself together) to me, coming unto me with a sting.' Here *a·ʾre-s* is taken as a relative attached to *z* as regularly in other demotic texts (I Kham. v. 1, &c.); the *n* before *fks·t* is omitted. *fy* is taken in the sense of 'fly' (see Griff., H. Priests, p. 178, note to l. 19), and *fks·t* as possibly an Egyptian rendering of σφήξ. The Coptic ϥⲟⲩⲕⲁⲥⲓ, meaning an aquatic (?) animal of some kind, can hardly be the same word for phonetic reasons; for the form of the *f* see l. 21. The word recurs in 21/7.

nmte·t as 'power' = ⲛⲟⲙϯ: this makes no sense. Cf. Kufi, xii. 30, 'he swallowed his *nmty·t*' (of the monkey when terrified).

8. a·ʾr-s swḥ a·e-s ʾy n-y n nw plege a·e-y ḥms a ẖry a·e-y

9. rym ḥms ʾS·t te mw·t n pe mte a bl e-s z n-y mpr

10. rym sp-sn pe šr s stn wr tp ʾNp lkh n ls·t-k a ḥt-k θs-pẖr

11. šʿ n r·w n t ẖt-s (?) lkh n n r·w n t ẖt-s (?) šʿ n r·w n te-k·t

12. nmte·t p nt e·ʾr-k a lkh-f e·ʾr-k ʿm-f bn pʿy nʾm-f a p t z pe-k

13. ls p ls n p šʿy pe-k sʿl pa ʾTm

14. nte-k lkh-f n pe-k ls e-f ẖr snf ty hte·t m-s-s e·ʾr-k mt·t a wʿ ẖm

15. n nḥe nte-k mt·t ar-f n sp VII e·ʾr-k t nʾm-f a t plege m-mne e·ʾr-k

16. sp wʿ·t tys n ʿyw e·ʾr-k ty-s ar-f

17. nt e·ʾr-k zt-f a p nḥe a ty-f a t plʾge m-mne

18. ḥms ʾS·t e-s mt·t a p nḥe ʿbʿrtʿt e-s tyt a p nḥe

19. n mʿ·t z e·ʿr-k ḥsy te-y ne ḥys·t-k p nḥe te-y ne ḥys

20. nʾm-k e·ʾr-k ḥse n t p šʿy e·ʾr-k mẖy n t·t ḥ·t te-y ne ḥys-k

21. šʿ zt p nḥe sp-sn n sym ke-z mʿ·t p fty n p šʿy p s n Gb ʾS·t t nt

22. mt·t a p nḥe p nḥe n mʿ·t t tltyle·t n hwm-p·t p zlẖ n Ḥr-št

---

l. 10. *ls·t-k.* This form seems due to a confusion in endeavouring to write in archaic style. The *t* is quite unwarranted by Egyptian. We may compare the *t* added before the object pronouns following *stm-f*: cf. also note to l. 20. We have here a passage in which very modern forms ⲙⲡⲁⲙⲧⲟ ⲉⲃⲟⲗ are mixed with older forms *ḥms ʾS·t* (past *stm-f*) and this *ls·t-k.*

l. 12. *nmte·t*: if this means 'tail' we may compare Pist. Sophia, p. 323 ⲧⲧⲁⲡⲣⲟ ⲙⲡⲥⲁⲧ, 'the point of the tail of the dragon.'

bn pʿy: the Achmimic vetitive ⲙⲡ=ⲙⲡⲣ, cf. 21/23, probably derived from the old vetitive *m*. It occurs in Eg. as *bn*, Pap. Mag. Harris 8/7.

fell my tail (?) upon me. (8) It (?) gathered together (?), it (?) coming to me with a sting (?): I sat down and (9) wept. Isis, my mother, sat before me, saying to me, " Do not (10) weep (*bis*), my child, King's son, eldest and first, Anubis; lick with thy tongue on thy heart, repeatedly (?) (11) as far as the edges of the wound (?); lick the edges of the wound (?) as far as the edges of thy (12) tail (?). What thou wilt lick up, thou swallowest it; do not spit it out on the ground; for thy (13) tongue is the tongue of the Agathodaemon, thy tongue (?) is that of Atum."'

(14) And you lick it with your tongue, while it is bleeding, immediately; thereafter, you recite to a little (15) oil and you recite to it seven times, you put it on the sting daily; you (16) soak a strip of linen, you put it on it.

(17) [The spell] which you say to the oil to put it on the sting daily: (18) ' Isis sat reciting to the oil Abartat and lamenting (?) to the true oil, (19) saying, " Thou being praised, I will praise thee, O oil, I will praise (20) thee, thou being praised by the Agathodaemon; thou being applauded (?) by me myself, I will praise thee (21) for ever, O herb-oil—otherwise true oil—O sweat of the Agathodaemon, amulet (?) of Geb. It is Isis who (22) makes invocation to the oil. O true oil, O drop of

---

l. 17. *pꜣge*: the word has been extensively corrected; *p*, originally ꜣ, and *g* and *e* being written above the line—see the facsimile.

l. 18. *ṭyṭ* = ⲧⲟⲉⲓⲧ, plangere. The songs at funerals both in ancient and modern Egypt are in praise of the deceased, so the word may really mean, or at least imply, 'pronounce eulogy.'

l. 19. *ḥys·ṭ-k*, and in l. 20 *ḥys-k*. It seems as if in one case the *ṭ* was preserved and in the other lost. Compare the fact that this ⲧ of verbs iiiae inf., is often preserved in Sah. when lost in Boh.

l. 21. *nḥe n sym* = ⲛⲉϩ ⲛⲥⲓⲙ, i. e. ῥαφάνινον, Diosc. i. 45 and Peyr. Lex.

fty, cf. 21/16, is the reading = ϥⲱⲧⲉ, not *šty*, ϣⲓϯ. For the form of *š* in this papyrus see *šty* in 19/7, 8; *f* over another sign has the tail very short.

l. 22. *zlḫ* means to pump, draw water.

23. nt ʾn·ʿw a ẖry n p wtn n twe e·ʾr-k a ʾr p nfr n t yt·t n twe a hwy

24. t p·t a p ʾytn a ḥr šn nb e·ʾr-k a t nfr t ʿe·t ʾr wḥ (?) e·ʾr-k a ʾr pẖret

25. a p nt ʿnẖ z e-y a bk-k a t plege n s stn wr tp ʾNp pe šr

26. z e·ʾr-k a mḥ-s n e·ʾr-k t nfr-s z e-y a bk-k a plege n mn a·ms mn

27. z e·ʾr-k a mḥ-s n e·ʾr-k t nfr-s sp VII r n mt·t a ʾny qs a bl ẖn šnbe·t

28. ʾnk p nte zz-f θy n t p·t e rt·t-f θy a p nwn ʾr nhe n py msḥ mrh (?) ẖn pr-zm (?)

29. n N z ʾnk sʾ syme tʾmʿh-ʿo pe pe rn n mte ʿnwg sp-sn z swḥ·t n bk

30. p nt n r-y swḥ·t n hb p nt n ẖe·t z qs n ntr qs n rm qs n hʿlet qs n rym

31. qs n ʾw qs n nk nb e mn nk ge z p nt n ẖe·t-k my ʾw-f a ḥt-k p nt n ḥt-k

32. my ʾw-f a r-k p nt n r-k my ʾw-f a t·t ty n p-hw z ʾnk p nt ẖn t VII n p·t nt smne·t

33. ẖn t VII n qnḥ·t z ʾnk p šr n p ntr nt ʿnẖ a wʿ z n mw n sp VII nṭe-k t swr-s t s-ḥm·t

---

l. 24. *ʾr wḥ,* past part. perhaps of ⲟⲩⲱ, cessare, or of ⲟⲩⲱϩ, permanere.

l. 25. *bk* would seem here to mean 'employ,' 'apply.'

l. 27. *a bl*: or *a ḥry* would be a possible reading.

l. 28. *θy n . . θy a*: cf. note to l. 5.

ʾr nhe n py msḥ meaning very uncertain; perhaps 'who has risen, ⲛⲁϩⲥⲉ, as this crocodile,' or, if *nhe* = ⲛⲟⲩϩⲉ, 'who has expelled this crocodile.' Cf. note to 2/25.

pr-zm. This, though usually written without the *pr,* must be the ϫⲏⲙⲉ, situated on the west bank of the Nile at Thebes, and well known in Coptic literature. The name *zm* may be written with the figure of a crocodile.

rain, O water-drawing of the planet Jupiter (23) which cometh down from the sun-boat at dawn, thou wilt make the healing effect (?) of the dew of dawn which heaven hath cast (24) on to the earth upon every tree, thou wilt heal the limb which is paralysed (?), thou wilt make a remedy (25) for him that liveth; for I will employ thee for the sting of the King's son, eldest and first, Anubis, my child, (26) that thou mayest fill it; wilt thou not make it well? For I will employ thee for (the ?) sting of N. the son of N., (27) that thou mayest fill it; wilt thou not make it well?"' Seven times.

Spell spoken to fetch a bone out of a throat.

(28) 'I am he whose head reaches the sky and his feet reach the abyss, who hath raised up (?) this crocodile . . . in Pizeme (?) (29) of Thebes; for I am Sa, Sime, Tamaho, is my correct name, Anouk (*bis*), saying, hawk's-egg (30) is that which is in my mouth, ibis-egg is that which is in my belly; saying, bone of god, bone of man, bone of bird, bone of fish, (31) bone of animal, bone of everything, there being nothing besides; saying, that which is in thy belly let it come to thy heart; that which is in thy heart, (32) let it come to thy mouth; that which is in thy mouth, let it come to my hand here to-day; for I am he who is in the seven heavens, who standeth (33) in the seven sanctuaries; for I am the son of the god who liveth.' (Say it) to a cup of water seven times: thou causest the woman (*sic*) to drink it.

---

l. 29. Egg of ibis and hawk, the same collocation in B. M. Pap. XLVI. 241.

l. 31. *e mn nk ge*, 'there being nothing else,' i. e. nothing not included in my words—a curious expression: cf. *emn nge šre*, 19/26.

Col. XXI.

1. p šn-hne n Wsr

2. ʾwe·t-f Wsr p pr-ʿo n t ty·t p nb n t qs·t p nte zz-f n Tny e rt·t-f n N p nt θ wḥ n ʾBt

3. e te-f ʾwhe·t pr-šylem p nt ḥr p nbs n mrwe p nt ḥr p tw n p-ʿo-rʿnws p nt ḥr pe pr šʿ nḥe

4. p pr n Ne-tbew šʿ z·t p nte ḥr-f m sn n ḥr n bk n š-stn a-pḥte·t nte pe-f st n st n ḥf(?)

5. e te-f ʾ·t n ʾ·t n mnt(?) e te-f gyz n rm nt elθ(?) n py mzḥ n ryt nte py bʿ n wḥ-sḥne n te-f gyz

6. ·ʾwe·t-f yʿhw sʿbʿh-ʿo ʾt-t-ne mystemw yʿwyw ʾwe·t-f mykhʿel sʿbʾel

7. ʾwe·t-f ʾNp n p tše n n ḥr-n-ʾʾe(?)·w p nte pe-f pe py qh p nt fy fks ḥr t rt·t wʿt·t

8. hp p kke n t mt·t a·ʾny p wyn n-y a ḫn ʾm n-y a ḫn a·z·y n-y p wḥ n p nt e-y šn ḫrr-f ty n p-hw n sp IX

9. šʿ nte p ntr ʾy nte p wyn ḫp ḫr ʾr-k-f a ḫ p ky n p sp nt ⟨bl⟩ ḥry ʿn e ḥr-f n p ʿlw a pr-ybt e ḥr-k ḥ-k a pr-ʾmnt e·ʾr-k ʿš a ḫry ḫn zz-f

---

Col. XXI.

l. 1. The first lines of this column have been made the subject of special study in connexion with the Old Coptic texts of Paris (written on the first pages of the Pap. Bibl. Nat., edited by Wessely), which contain a variant version of them: Erman, A. Z., 1883, 89; Griffith, A. Z., 1900, 85; 1901, 86.

l. 2. Parallel to this line the O. C. (A. Z., 1883, Pl. 3) gives ⲉⲟⲩⲱⲧϥ ⲟⲩⲥⲓⲣⲉ. ⲡⲉⲣⲟⲛ̄ⲧⲏ ⲡⲛⲏⲃ ⲛ̄ⲧⲕⲁⲏⲥⲉ ⲡⲉⲧⲛ̄ⲛⲣⲏⲥⲛ̄ⲧⲓⲛ ⲉⲧϯⲓⲟⲩⲱ ⲛ̄ⲡⲉⲃⲱⲧ ⲡⲉⲧⲍⲁ ⲍⲫ̄ⲁ ⲛⲛⲟⲩⲃⲥ. ⲛ̄ⲡⲉⲣⲟϯⲉ. ⲉⲧⲉ ⲡⲉϥ. ⲉ̀ⲟⲟⲩ ⲛ̄ ⲡⲁ ϭⲁⲗⲱⲙ. The notes to the foregoing in A. Z., 1900, 86 seq., may be consulted by those who wish to study its connexion with the demotic text.

Tny. The Edfu geographical list (Br., Dict. Geogr., 1359) states that the head of Osiris was preserved at Abydos (in the nome of This) and a *sbq*, 'foot (?),' at Thebes.

θ wḥ, O. C. ϫⲓⲟⲩⲱ: cf. 18/23.

l. 3. *ʾwhe·t* has the determinative of wood: cf. *ʾwhy*, Kufi, xi. 21.

pr-šylem, ⲡⲁϭⲁⲗⲱⲙ, perhaps Jerusalem, or Siloam. Probably *n pr-šylem* is to be read.

Col. XXI.

(1) The vessel-inquiry of Osiris. (2) 'Hail to him! Osiris, King of the Underworld, lord of burial, whose head is in This, and his feet in Thebes, he who giveth answer (?) in Abydos, (3) whose .... is (in ?) Pashalom, he who is under the *nubs* tree in Meroë, who is on the mountain of Poranos, who is on my house to eternity, (4) the house of Netbeou for ever, he whose countenance is as the resemblance (?) of the face of a hawk of linen, mighty one whose tail is the tail of a serpent, (5) whose back is the back of a crocodile (?), whose hand is a man's, who is girded (?) with this girdle of bandage, in whose hand is this wand of command, (6) hail to him Iaho, Sabaho, Atonai, Mistemu, Iauiu; hail to him, Michael, Sabael, (7) hail to him, Anubis in the nome of the dog-faces, he to whom this earth belongs, who carries a wound (?) on one foot, (8) hide the darkness in the midst, bring in the light for me, come in to me, tell me the answer to that about which I am inquiring here to-day.'— Nine times, (9) until the god come and the light appear. You must do it in the manner of the remainder as above again; the boy's face being to the East and your own face to the West; you call down into his head.

---

p nbs n mrwe: cf. Maspero in P. S. B. A., xiii. 496. Cf. *n pr-wt* in l. 36.

p-ʿo-rʿnws, perhaps *οὐρανός*, in the sense of Olympus.

l. 4. *Ne-tbew*: see note on 2/9.

ḥf: a 'snake's' head or tail is regularly described as *n ḥf* in Eg.: cf. Leyd. I. 384, V. II*. 12.

l. 5. *mnt*: some monster or reptile with spiny back, perhaps a crocodile, to judge by the determinative, for which cf. 3/23. It may mean a guardian (**ⲙⲛⲟⲩⲧ**) dragon, as in I Kham. iv. 7.

nt elθ (?): very obscure, though the writing is clear.

l. 7. *ḥr-n-ʾʾe·w*: cf. **ϩⲟⲛⲟⲩϩⲱⲣ**, Z., 235, and see the note to 20/3 and A. Z., 1900, 88 (Hdt. iv. 191).

t rt·t wʿt·t, **ⲟⲩⲉ-ⲣⲏⲧⲉ** is thus perhaps one foot as opposed to dual **ⲣⲁⲧ-**.

l. 9. *nt n bl* and *nt ḥry* have both been written.

10. n p mḫrr n p z n ʾrp a t (*sic*) s-ḥm·t mr ḥwt e·ʾr-k ʾny wʿ mḫrr n ḥr (?)  ★ nte py mḫrr ḫm pe nte mn-te-f tp e-f θ n III n ʾkym

11. ḥr t ḥ·t n zz-f ḫr gm-k pe-f ḥr e-f šm a bl nge p nt θ tp II ʿn e·ʾr-k ʾny·t-f n t pr n p rʿ e·ʾr-k mr-k n wʿ ḥbs(?) n p ḥrw n ʾ·t-k

12. nte-k mr-k a pe-k ḥr n wʿ·t pke·t n šr-bne·t e p mḫrr ḥr t ḫ·t n t·t-k nte-k mt·t ar-f a ḥr p rʿ e-f a pr n sp VII e·ʾr-k wḥ e·ʾr-k θ-f n ḥsy

13. ḫn hyn·w ʾrt n ʾḥ·t kme·t e·ʾr-k ḥn a zz-f n wʿ . . . n ḫ n zyt e·ʾr-k ḫʿ-f šʿ rhwe ḫn p ʾrte a·ʾre rhwe ḫp e·ʾr-k

14. ʾn·t-f a ḥry e·ʾr-k prḫ ḫrr-f n šʿ nte-k t wʿ·t mnfre(?) n ḥbs (?) ḫrr-f ḥr p šʿ šʿ hw IV e·ʾr-k ʾr ʿnte ʾh st·t mbḥ-f a·ʾre p hrw IV sny nte-f šwy

15. e·ʾr-k ʾn·t-f ne (?)-rt·t-k e wn wʿ ḥbs (?) prḫ ḫrr-f e·ʾr-k prz-f n te-f mt·t n wʿ tk n ḥmt e·ʾr-k fy te-f pše·t n wnm erme ne-k yb·w n t·t-k rt·t-k n wnm

16. e·ʾr-k zfzf-w ḥr wʿ·t blz n ššw nmy n ḫ n elle e·ʾr-k nt-w ḥr IX·t n blbyle·t n zpḫ erme te-k·t mt·t nge te-k·t fty n wš n nḥe

17. n t s·t-eyw·t nte-k ʾr-f n wʿ·t bnn·t nte-k ty-f a p ʾrp nte-k mt·t ar-f n sp VII nte-k t swr-s t s-ḥm·t nte-k fy te-f ke pše·t n . . . . ḥnʿ ne-k yb·w n t·t-k

18. rt·t-k n . . . ʿn nte-k mr-w n wʿ·t tys n š-stn ḥr

---

l. 10. *a t s-ḥm·t mr*: supply *ʾre* after *t*; cf. 25/31, V. 3/14, 13/10.

'Fish-faced (?)': possibly the weevil as having the oxyrhynchus' snout. In Horap. the weevil (?) is *μονόκερως καὶ ἰδιό-* (*ἰβιό-* ?)*μορφος*.

tp: cf. 3/22; *ʾkym* probably = Eg. *ỉkm*, 'shield.'

l. 11. *p nt θ tp II* = 'stag-beetle (?).' Cf. Pap. Bibl. Nat. l. 65 *κανθαρον τον ταυρομορφον*, and see Horap. I. 10 for Scarabaeidae, Lucanidae (*δίκερως καὶ ταυροειδής*) and Rhynchophora.

l. 12. *mr* sometimes means 'wrap,' but see 11/33.

ḫ·t must be a mistake for *ḥ·t*, probably through confusion of the sounds *ḫ* and *ḥ*.

θ-f, not from ϫⲓ : ϭⲓ, which would give *θy·t-f*, but a false writing for *t še-f* above 3/31 = *ϫⲟϥ from ϫⲟ : ϭⲟ.

(10) [The method] of the scarab of the cup of wine, to make a woman love a man. You take a fish-faced (?) scarab, this scarab being small and having no horn, it wearing three plates (11) on the front of its head; you find its face thin (?) outwards—or again that which bears two horns—. You take it at the rising of the sun; you bind (?) yourself with a cloth on the upper part of your back, (12) and bind (?) yourself on (?) your face with a strip of palm-fibre, the scarab being on the front (?) of your hand: and you address it before the sun when it is about to rise, seven times. When you have finished, you drown it (13) in some milk of a black cow; you approach (?) its head with a hoop (?) of olive wood; you leave it till evening in the milk. When evening comes, you (14) take it out, you spread its under part with sand, and put a circular strip of cloth under it upon the sand, unto four days; you do frankincense-burning before it. When the four days have passed, and it is dry, (15) you take it before you (lit. your feet), there being a cloth spread under it. You divide it down its middle with a bronze knife; you take (?) its right half, and your nails of your right hand and foot; (16) you cook them on a new potsherd with vine wood, you pound them with nine apple-pips together with your urine or your sweat free from oil (17) of the bath; you make it into a ball and put it in the wine, and speak over it seven times, and you make the woman drink it; and you take its other half, the left one, together with your nails of your left hand (18) and foot also, and bind them in a strip of fine linen, with myrrh and saffron, and bind them to your

---

l. 15. *ne-rt·t-k*: a strange spelling.

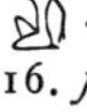 *fy*: so also in l. 17.

l. 16. *fly*, &c. ῥύπος βαλανείων was actually prescribed as a drug, Diosc., i. 34.

ḫl grwgws nte-k mr-w a pe-k znḥ n gbyr nte-k str erme t s-ḥm·t e-w mr ar-k

19. e-f ḫp e·ᵓr-k wḫ a ʾr-f ʿn n wš n še-f n ḥsy ḫr ʾr-k-f ʿn n p mḥ III n p wrš e·ᵓr-k ʾr n py smte nt ḥry n-f ʿn e·ᵓr-k ʿš pe-f ʿš ar-f a ḥr p rʿ n twe e·ᵓr-k zfzf

20. e·ᵓr-k prz-f e·ᵓr-k ʾr-f a ḫ p nt ḥry ʿn n mt·t nb nt e·ᵓr-k ʿš-f ar-f mbḥ p rʿ n twe nte-k pe p mḫrr n ḫstb n m·ʿt a·ᵓn-y·t-k a bl n p r n pe ʾrpe e·ᵓr-k

21. θy(?) zmyz ḥmt a šy·t-k nta rḫ wm p sym e-f hm p sʾḫʿt e-f gmʿ a n sšt(?)·w ʿy·w n na Kmy e-y hb nʾm-k a mn a·ms mn

22. a myḫ·t-s n ḥt-s a ḫe-s sp-sn a ty-s mḫt sp-sn a ty-s ʿte·t z nte-s p-e·ᵓr ʾr ty-s mʾ·t a ḥr p rʿ n twe e-s z n p rʿ

23. z bn pr n p ʿḥ z bn wbn n p mw z bn ʾy n na Kmy n t sḫ·t z bn wlʿlʿ n šn·w ʿy·w n na Kmy z bn wtwt

24. e-y hb nʾm-k a mn a·ms mn a šʿkʿ-s n ḥt-s a ḫe-s sp-sn a ty-s mpt (*sic*) sp-sn a ty-s ʿte·t nte-s wḥ-s a p myt m-s mn a·ms mn n nw nb(?)

25. nt e·ᵓr-k ʿš-f ar-f e-f ḫn p ʾrte a·wy ʿo sp-sn a·wy pe ʿo sp-sn a·wy nwn-f(?) a·wy mr-f p mḫrr sp-sn nte-k t yr·t n p rʿ p sʾlʿpyn

26. n Wsr t sḥn-t·t(?) n šwy e·ᵓr-k nʿy n py ky nta Wsr pe-k yt še nʾm-f e-tbe mn a·ms mn šʿ nte-w t t st·t m-s ḥt-s t ḫo·t

27. m-s ny-s ef-w šʿ nte·s ⟨ne⟩ še mn a·ms mn a mʿ

---

l. 23. Read (*n*) *n šn·w*.

l. 24. *mpt* (*sic*) for *mḫt*.

The last group is  *n nw nb*: cf. l. 43; but in 27/10 we have *stm* written similarly.

l. 25. *sʾlʿpyn*, see note to 13/18.

l. 26. *sḥn-t·t* looks like a compound with *sḥ*, 'the toes' collectively, or 'a toe.' *sḥ-n-t·t* may therefore mean the toes, or the fingers (collectively) of Shu, referring perhaps to his hands which support the sky. The eyes of Ra and Atum were the most important instruments of their rule.

py ky, i. e. the condition of one drowned, Εσιης, cf. 6/12.

left arm, and lie with the woman with them bound upon you. (19) If you wish to do it again without its being drowned, then you do it again on the third of the lunar month. You do it in this manner that is above for it again. You pronounce its invocation to it before the Sun in the morning, you cook (it), (20) you divide it, you do it according to that which is above again in everything. [The invocation] which you pronounce to it before the Sun in the morning: 'Thou art this scarab of real lapis-lazuli; I have taken thee out of the door of my temple; thou carriest (?) (21) . . . . . of bronze to thy nose (?), that can eat (?) the herbage that is trampled (?), the field-plants (?) that are injured for the great images of the men of Egypt. I dispatch thee to N. born of N. (22) to strike her from her heart to her belly (*bis*), to her entrails (*bis*), to her womb; for she it is who hath wept (?) before the Sun in the morning, she saying to the Sun, "Come not forth," to the Moon, "Rise not," to the water, "Come not to the men of Egypt," to the fields, "Grow not green," and to the great trees of the men of Egypt, "Flourish not." (24) I dispatch thee to N. born of N. to injure her from her heart unto her belly (*bis*), unto her entrails (*bis*), unto her womb, and she shall put herself on the road (?) after N. born of N. at every time (?).'

(25) [The spell] that you pronounce to it, while it is in the milk. 'Woe (?), great (*bis*), woe (?), my (?) great, woe (?) his (?) Nun, woe (?) his (?) love. O scarab (*bis*), thou art the eye of Phre, the heart (?) (26) of Osiris, the open-hand (?) of Shu, thou approachest in this condition in which Osiris thy father went, on account of N. born of N. until fire is put to her heart and the flame (27) to

---

l. 27. *ne*. This group occurs in a similar phrase in l. 41 and in l. 32, if the reading in the latter instance be correct. If it stands, then *ne* is difficult to explain; it looks like a preposition 'to,' but if l. 32

nb nt e-f nʾm-w   nt e·ʾr-k ʿš-f ar-f e·ʾr-k kk nʾm-f hy pe ḫrt nfr p syf n wm·w(?) nḥe(?)

28. p-e·ʾr syt nt syt ʾwt n ntr·w tre-w py nta p nt n ḫm erme p nt ʿy gm·t-f ʿwt t pʾt(?) ʿo·t II·t ḥr pr-ybt n Kmy

29. e-f pr n nw mḫrr km ḥr wʿ·t bw n qme zwf te-y ʾr-rḫ n pe-k rn te-y ʾr-rḫ n te-k·t ḥm·t(?) t yp·t n syw II (?) rn-k

30. te-y ḥwy ḫyt(?) ar-k n p-hw nphʿlʿm bʿllʿ bʿlkhʿ y-ʿo-phphe z zf nb ḫmm nb sḥt nb nt e·ʾr-k nʾm-w

31. n p-hw e·ʾr-k-sw ḫn p ḥt p wef p mws p nyš t ʿte·t p mḫt ʿo p mḫt ḫm n spyr·w n ef·w n qs·w n ʿe nb

32. n p ḫʿr n mn a·ms mn šʿ nte-s še(?) ne(?) mn a·ms mn a mʿ nb nt e-f nʾm-w   nt e·ʾr-k ʿš- ar-f ḫn p ʾrp   p mḫrr sp-sn nte-k pe p mḫrr

33. n ḫstb n mʿ·t nte-k t yr·t n p rʿ nte-k p byl n ʾTm t sḥn-t·t(?) n šwy p sʾlʿpyn n Wsr nte-k py k km ḥyt ʾr pyr n p nwn

34. e p nfr n ʾS·t erme-k nte-k rʿks rʿpʿrʿks p snf n py ʾʾš ḥwt a·ʾn-w-f n p t n ḫr a Kmy ḥr p bl(?) a p ʾrp(?)

---

be left out of the question, the fact that both in **21/27** and **21/41** *š̌* is written over *ne*, as if by an afterthought, suggests that *ne*, which is identical in spelling with **ⲛⲁ** the auxiliary of the future, must be the verb **ⲛⲁ**, 'go' (attaching itself to **ⲛⲟⲩ : ⲛⲟⲩⲓ**, 'futurus esse'), as opposed to **ⲛⲏⲟⲩ**, 'come' (which is qualitative of **ⲉⲓ**; see KABIS, A. Z., 75. 107). **ⲛⲁ** is practically the qualitative of **ϣⲉ** (STERN, § 348). The correction of *ne* to *š̌* in both passages would therefore be particularly remarkable. Although, according to STEINDORFF, § 251, the qualitative is admissible in the conjunctive it seems difficult after **ϣⲁⲛⲧⲉ-**: hence no doubt the correction; but if it be possible, the meaning would be 'until she be going,' while *š̌* expresses 'until she go.' It would seem that the scribe was puzzled by the *ne*, hence the mistakes and corrections. The following table of forms of the verbs 'come' and 'go' may be useful:—

		Inf.	Inf.		Qual.	Stm-f.
'go'	Copt.	ϣⲉ : ϣⲉⲓ	ⲛⲟⲩ : ⲛⲟⲩⲓ,	ⲛⲁ-	ⲛⲁ	(ⲧ)ⲉⲛⲛⲟ(ⲟⲩ)?
	Dem.	*š̌*	*nʿ*	*ne-*	*ne* (?)	*nʿ-f*
'come'	Copt.	ⲉⲓ : ⲓ	—		ⲛ-ⲛⲏⲟⲩ	(ⲧ)ⲁⲩⲟ
	Dem.	*ʾy*	—		*ʾn-ʾw*	*ʾw-f*

her flesh, until she shall follow (?) N. born of N., unto every place in which he is.' [The spell] which you utter to it when you cook it: 'O my beautiful child, the youth of oil-eating (?), (28) thou who didst cast semen and who dost cast semen among all the gods, whom he that is little (and ?) he that is great found among the two great enneads in the East of Egypt, (29) who cometh forth as a black scarab on a stem of papyrus-reed; I know thy name, I know thy . . . . "the work of two stars" is thy name, (30) I cast forth fury upon thee to-day: Nephalam, Balla, Balkha (?), Iophphe; for every burning, every heat, every fire that thou makest (31) to-day, thou shalt make them in the heart, the lungs, the liver (?), the spleen, the womb, the great viscera, the little viscera, the ribs, the flesh, the bones, in every limb, (32) in the skin of N. born of N. until she follow (?) N. born of N. to every place in which he is.'

[The spell] that you pronounce to it in the wine: 'O scarab (*bis*), thou art the scarab (33) of real lapis-lazuli, thou art the eye of Phre, thou art the eye of Atum, the open-hand (?) of Shu, the heart (?) of Osiris, thou art that black bull, the first, that came forth from Nun, (34) the beauty of Isis being with thee; thou art Raks, Raparaks, the blood of this wild boar (?) which they brought from the land of Syria unto Egypt . . . .

---

l. 28. *p'ṯ ʿo·t.* It is very rarely that the Ennead is written without the addition of the word 'gods.' The double Ennead of eighteen gods is frequently mentioned from the earliest times onwards.

l. 29. **πο**. Can this gloss represent a qualitative of **πιρε** as **ο** of **ειρε**? The usual qual. is **πορε**.

n nw mẖrr for *n wʿ mẖrr*: cf. 14/28, 20/8.

ḥm·t (?), 'trade,' 'art' (?).

l. 30. *ẖyt.* In spite of its peculiar form this word can scarcely be other than *ẖyt*, both on account of its meaning and of its association with *ḥwy.* We may translate 'fury of Phalam,' &c.

l. 31. *mws*, O. C. **ⲙⲁⲟⲩⲥ**, probably from Eg. fem. *mỉs·t*, 'liver' or 'kidneys.' *p mẖt ẖm* named *p ky mẖt* in Pap. Rhind. iv. 6.

35. e-y hb-k n e·ʾr-k nʿ n pe hb n e·ʾr-k a ʾy-f ḫr-k hb·t a p ʾb nte-w tḫm-f a t ḥny·t nte-w t šwy-s a p šʿ n p snyt nte-w ḫḫ-f n wš

36. n tw p zwf n(?) pr-wt nte-w t p ḥmt m-s-f e Ḥr wz n ʾS·t n ḫyrḫr·w ʿy·w n na Kmy nte-w tm ḫʿ ḥwt s-ḥm·t n te-w mt·t e-y hb

37. n·ʾm-k yn a ny e-y hb nʾm-k a ḫry a p ḥt n mn a·ms mn nte-k ʾr st·t n ḫe-s sḥt ḫn ny-s mḫt my p lyb m-s ḥt-s

38. p trwš m-s ny-s ef·w my ʾr-s m qte n p ḫpš m-s t ryr·t my ʾr-s

39. n [p?] mšʿ n p ḫy m-s t̄ḫyb·t e-s qte m-s mn a·ms mn a mʿ nb nt e-f nʾm-w e-s mr nʾm-f e-s lby m-s-f e b-ʾr-rḫ-s mʿ n p t

40. e-s nʾm-f θy ty-s qt n grḥ my n-s p ʾhm p rwš n mre·t mpr t wm-s mpr t swr-s mpr t str-s mpr t ḥms-s ḫr

41. t ḫyb·t n ny-s ʾy·w šʿ nte-s ⟨ne⟩ še n-f a mʿ nb nt e·f nʾm-w e ḥt-s ʾbḫ e yr·t-s ḥl e ny-s nw pnʿ e·b-ʾr-rḫ-s mʿ

42. n p t e-s nʾm-f šʿ nte-s nw ar-f e yr·t-s m-s yr·t-f ʾb-s m-s ʾb-f t·t-s m-s t·t-f e-s t n-f ty . . . nb my ḥr t ḥ·t n rt·t-s

43. m-s ne-f tbs·w n p [ḫ]yr n nw nb e mn nw šr ys sp-sn tkr sp-sn

Col. XXII.

1. tey-s n(?) p rn n wr-ty nt e-w ʿš-w a ʾyḫ nb e mn p nte

---

l. 35. *ʾy-f* here and in V. 12/5–8 must represent the infinitive form of *ʾr*, 'do,' with suffix ⲁⲁϥ : ⲁⲓϥ.

ḫr-k: cf. V. 33/3.

tḫm seems to be the actual reading in the original, but if so it must be an error for *ʿḫm*.

ḥny·t: cf. ⲗⲉ-ϩⲱⲛⲉ, Crum, Pap. Fay. No. 34.

l. 37. ⲉⲓⲛⲉ : ⲓⲛⲓ, 'be like,' takes ⲛ in Coptic, but here is used with *a*.

l. 38. The reading is uncertain: perhaps *my ʾr-s p qte*, or more likely the plural *n qte*. The Shoulder and Hippopotamus are the two well-known constellations: cf. Brugsch, Thes., i. 126–7; Maspero, Les Origines, p. 94.

l. 39. The first words may be *n n mšʿ*, hardly *n p mšʿ*.

to the wine, (35) I send thee; wilt thou go on my errand? Wilt thou do it? Thou sayest, "Send me to the thirsty, that his thirst may be quenched, and to the canal that it may be dried up, and to the sand of the *snyt* that it may be scattered without (36) wind, and to the papyrus of Buto that the blade may be applied to it, while Horus is saved for (?) Isis, catastrophes grow great for the Egyptians, so that not a man or woman is left in their midst." I (37) send thee; do like unto these; I send thee down to the heart of N. born of N. and do thou make fire in her body, flame in her entrails, put the madness to her heart, (38) the fever (?) to her flesh; let her make the pursuit of the "Shoulder"-constellation after the "Hippopotamus"-constellation; let her make (39) the movements of the sunshine after the shadow, she following after N. born of N. to every place in which he is, she loving him, she being mad for him, she not knowing the place of the earth in which (40) she is. Take away her sleep by night; give her lamentation and anxiety by day; let her not eat, let her not drink, let her not sleep, let her not sit under (41) the shade of her house until she follow (?) him to every place in which he is, her heart forgetting, her eye flying, her glance turned (?), she not knowing the place (42) of the earth in which she is, until she see him, her eye after his eye, her heart after his heart, her hand after his hand, she giving to him every ..... Let fly (?) the tip of her feet (43) after his heels in the street at all times without fail at any time. Quick (*bis*), hasten (*bis*).'

COL. XXII.

(1) Behold! (spell?) of the name of the Great-of-Five which they pronounce to every spirit. There is none

---

COL. XXII.

l. 1. No more than the heading has been written. It can hardly refer to the spell in 2/25.

2. n-nḫt-f ar-w(?) ḫr n zʿm·w e·ʾr k ʿš ny sḫ·w a hne nb

3. b-ʾre n ntr·w še n-w e bnp-k šn·t-w a mt·t nb nte-w z n-k

4. p wḥ ḫr t p·t p t t ty·t šn e-f wwy p mw

5. t sḫ·t sḫ e-f n t·t-f n rm a ʿš-f

Col. XXIII.

1. wʿ r a t hy . . . . z-mt·t

2. ḫr ʾny-k wʿ tp n ʿo nte-k smn·t-f ʾwt rt-k wbe p rʿ n twe e-f a pr

3. wbe-f ʿn n rhwe e-f ʾn·nʿ a p ḥtp nte-k ths te-k·t rt·t n wnm n st

4. n ḫr te-k·t rt·t n . . . . n sʿn n ʿršyn(?)·w n te-k pt ʿn nte-k smn te-k·t wnm

5. ḥr t ḥ·t te-k·t . . . . ḥr pḥ e p tp n te-w mte·t nte-k ths t·t-k n te-k·t t·t II·t n snf n

6. ʿo ḥnʿ t fnz II·t n r-k nte-k ʿš ny sḫ·w a ḥr p rʿ n twe rhwe n hw IV ḫr

7. str-f e·ʾr-k wḫ a t ʾr-f *ⲙⲟⲩ* e·ʾr-k ʾr-f n hw VII e·ʾr-k ʾr pe-f θ-ʾwe·t e·ʾr-k mr wʿ·t ʿy n šr-

8. bne·t a t·t-k wʿ·t pk n šr-bne ḥwt a ḥn·t-k ḥnʿ zz-k nfr nfr pw py(?) (p ?) ʿš nt e·ʾr-k ʿš-f a ḥr p rʿ

9. *επικαλουμαι σε τον εν τω κενεω πνευματι δεινον αορατον*

10. *παντοκρατορα θεον θεων φθοροποιον και ερημοποιον ο μισων*

---

l. 2. Reading *n-nḫt-f e·ʾr-w* (?).

l. 3. Or final 'that the gods depart not.'

l. 5. Probably this spell was never copied out, the remainder of the page having been left blank.

Col. XXIII.

l. 1. . . . . (?). The signs are , suggesting catalepsy or an evil dream, but the reading is quite uncertain. The result is sleep (l. 7), and, if further prolonged, death.

l. 5. *ḥr bl* or *ḥr pḥ* (?).

t·t-k n te-k·t t·t II·t: probably meaning 'your two hands.' Cf. V. 10/4, 5, of the feet.

that is (2) stronger than it in the books. If you pronounce these charms to any vessel, (3) then the gods depart not before you have questioned them concerning every word and they have told you (4) the answer about heaven, earth, and the underworld, a distant inquiry (?), water, (5) (and) the fields. A charm which is in the power(?) of a man to pronounce.

Col. XXIII.

(1) A spell to inflict (?) catalepsy (? Formula. (2) You take an ass's head, and you place it between your feet opposite the sun in the morning when it is about to rise, (3) opposite it again in the evening when it goes to the setting, and you anoint your right foot with *set*-stone (4) of Syria, and your left foot with clay, the soles (?) of your foot also: and place your right hand (5) in front and your left hand behind, the head being between them. You anoint your hand, of your two hands, with ass's blood, (6) and the two *fnz* of your mouth, and utter these charms towards the sun in the morning and evening of four days, then (7) he sleeps. If you wish to make him die, you do it for seven days, you do its magic, you bind a thread of palm-fibre (8) to your hand, a mat (?) of wild palm-fibre to your phallus and your head; very excellent. This is the invocation which you utter before the sun: (9) 'I invoke thee who art in the void air, terrible, invisible, (10) almighty, god of gods, dealing destruction and making desolate, O thou

---

l. 6. *fnz*: possibly the corners of the mouth.

l. 7. *θ-'we·t* seems to mean literally 'taking pledge,' ϫⲓ-ⲉⲟⲩⲱ : ϭⲓ-ⲁⲟⲩⲱ, so as to get power over a man or god; hence 'magic.' See I Kham. iv. 32.

l. 9. See a very similar invocation in διακοπαί, Leyd. Gr. Pap. V. 11/17, 15/21.

11. *οικιαν ευσταθουσαν ως εξεβρασθης εκ της Αιγυπτου και εξω*

12. *χωρας επενομασθης ο παντα ρησσων και μη νικωμενος*

13. *επικαλουμαι σε τυφων σηθ τας σας μαντειας επιτελω*

14. *οτι επικαλουμαι σε το σον αυθεντικον σου ονομα εν οις ου δυνη*

15. *παρακουσαι ιω ερβηθ ιωπακερβηθ ιωβολχωσηθ ιωπαταθναξ*

16. *ιωσωρω ιωνεβουτοσουαληθ ακτιωφι ερεσχιγαλ νεβοποσοαληθ*

17. *αβεραμενθωου λερθεξαναξ εθρελυωθ νεμαρεβα αεμινα*

18. *ολον ηκε μοι και βαδισον και καταβαλε τον* ⇧ *η την* ⇧ *ριγει και πυ*

19. *ρετω αυτος ηδικησεν με και το αιμα τουφυωνος εξεχυσεν παρ εαυ*

20. *τω η αυτη δια τουτο ταυτα ποιω κοινα*

21. a šn wbe ʿḥ e·ʾr-k ʾr-f n šn hn wʿe·t nge ḫm-ḫl e-f ḫp e nte-k nt ne šn e·ʾr-k mḥ yr·t-k

22. n wyt mstme e·ʾr-k ʿḥ ḥr zz wʿ mʿ e-f θse ḥr zz pe-k pr e·ʾr-k sze wbe ʿḥ e-f mḥ

23. wz·t n . . . . . e·ʾr-k wʿb n hw III e·ʾr-k ʿš py ʿš wbe ʿḥ n sp VII nge sp IX šʿ nte-f wnḥ ar-k

24. nte-f sze wbe-k h'y s-ʿks ʾMn s(t)-ʿks ʿbrʿ-s(t)-ʿks ze nte-k ʿḥ

25. p wr n n syw·w p-e·ʾr ms·t-w stm m-s n-e·z-y mšʿ m-s na r-y wnḥ-k a·ʾr-y tʾhʾnw

26. tʾheʾnwnʿ tʾhnwʿthʿ pfe pe rn n mtr IX n z·t-s šʿ nte-s wnḥ-s ar-k

---

l. 13. *σηθ*: the name of the brother of Osiris is usually written in the Greek papyri with the line over it. Cf. B. M. Pap. CXXI. 965, &c.

l. 15. Cf. Brit. Mus. Gr. Pap. CXXI. l. 893 *ονομασιν σου α ου δυνασαι παρακουσαι*.

l. 18. Frost and fire—probably ague and fever, as REVILLOUT suggests. Cf. *ῥιγοπύρετος* GALEN; *ριγοπυρετιον* Brit. Mus. Gr. Pap. CXXI. l. 218.

l. 19. Read *τυφωνος* (?).

l. 20. *κοινα*: cf. WESSELY, N. gr. Zauberpap., numerous references in index.

l. 22. *sze wbe* is not *ἀποκρίνεσθαι* here.

that hatest (11) a household well established. When thou wast cast out of Egypt and out of (12) the country thou wast entitled, " He that destroyeth all and is unconquered." (13) I invoke thee, Typhon Set, I perform thy ceremonies of divination, (14) for I invoke thee by thy powerful name in (words?) which thou canst not (15) refuse to hear: Io erbeth, Iopakerbeth, Iobolkhoseth, Iopatathnax, (16) Iosoro, Ioneboutosoualeth, Aktiophi, Ereskhigal, Neboposoaleth, (17) Aberamenthoou, Lerthexanax, Ethreluoth, Nemareba, Aemina, (18) entirely(?) come to me and approach and strike down Him or Her with frost and (19) fire; he has wronged me, and has poured out the blood of Typhon (?) beside (?) him (20) or her: therefore I do these things.' Common form.

(21) To divine, opposite the moon. You do it by vessel-inquiry alone or (with) a child. If it is you who will inquire, you fill your eye (22) with green eye-paint (and) stibium, you stand on a high place, on the top of your house, you address the moon when it fills (23) the *uzat* on the 15th day, you being pure for three days; you pronounce this invocation to the moon seven or nine times until he appear to you (24) and speak to you: 'Ho! Sax, Amun, Sax, Abrasax; for thou art the moon, (25) the chief of the stars, he that did form them, listen to the things that I have(?) said, follow the (words) of my mouth, reveal thyself to me, Than, (26) Thana, Thanatha, otherwise Thei, this is my correct name.' Nine (times) of saying it until she (*sic*) reveal herself to thee.

l. 24. The acrophonic use of the group  *st* in ⲁϩ is remarkable.

l. 26. 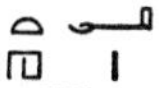 is read first ⲑⲁ and then ⲑⲏⲓ.

After IX probably *sp* should be supplied.

nte-s wnḥ-s: it seems as if the feminine referred to the Greek moon σελήνη, the Egyptian being masculine.

27. ke ky nʾm-f ʿn a ʿš-f wbe ʿḥ e·ʾr-k smt yr·t-k n py smt e·ʾr-k a ḥry a ḥr ʿḥ e-f mḥ wz·t ḫr nw-k a p sšt n p ntr ḫn t wz·t

28. e-f sze wbe-k ʾnk hʿh qʿ ʿm(?)-r mʿ-ʿmt mtė pe pe rn z ʾnk . . . by s-ʿo ʿgʾnʿgwp

29. mlḫ ʾḫ(?) ʾḫ(?) hy mlḫ rn-yt n mʿ·t sp-sn . . . z·t ank ḫl(?)-by stt ḫn(?) m nfr rn-yt sr ʿo šnbt pe rn n mte

30. z m sp IX e·ʾr-k ʿḥ wbe ʿḥ e yr·t-k mḥ n py kys wy(t) mstme nt ḥr ʾby n ḫr nte-k t wʿ sḫy n wʿ ppy

31. ʿo ar-f nte-k ty-f a wʿ nk n yl nte-k ḫʿ-f n-k n wʿ mʿ e-f hep šʿ p nw nt e·ʾr-k a ʿḥ n-f ḫr ʾr-k-f ʿn a ḫ p nt ḥry

Col. XXIV.

1 *a*. a . . . . k·t

2 *a*. nyt n bne ḥwt

3 *a*. e-f šʾkh n ʾrte

4 *a*. *ⲉ(?)ⲕⲓⲗ*

5 *a*. nte-k ʾr-w n wʿ m bnn t a p ʾrp(?)

1. pḫre·t e·ʾr-k wḫ a . . . . . *ⲣⲱⲙⲉ* e-f znt

2. *ⲥⲕⲁⲙⲟⲩⲛⲁ ⲣⲓⲛ* (δραχμή) I

3. *ⲟⲡⲓⲟⲩ* (δραχμή) I nt ḥr ʾrte

4. nte-k ʾr-f n bnn nte-k ty-f a wʿ *ⲕⲛⲟⲩⲙ*

5. e-f zf(?) nte-f *ⲟⲩⲁⲙϥ* ḫr ʾr-f *ⲙⲕⲁϩ*

6. k·t e·ʾr-k wḫ a t str rm n hw II

7. *ⲙⲁⲛⲇⲣⲁⲕⲟⲣⲟⲩ ⲣⲓⲍⲁ* (οὐγκία) I

8. *ⲙⲉⲗⲁⲕⲣⲉⲧⲓⲕⲟⲩ* (οὐγκία) I

---

l. 29. The group before *z·t* is difficult to read.

l. 31. *ʿḥ n-f*, 'wait for, be ready for, it.'

Col. XXIV.

l. 1 *a*. The five short lines at the top corner have been taken first and numbered 1 *a*, &c.

l. 1. *e-f znt* seems to belong to ⲣⲱⲙⲉ, but may perhaps be loosely attached, like *nfr* in l. 17 to *pḫre·t*, without reference to its gender.

l. 2. Convolvulus scammonia, Diosc. iv. 168, found chiefly in Syria

(27) Another form of it again, to be pronounced to the moon. You paint your eye with this paint, you (going ?) up before the moon when it fills the *uzat*, then you see the figure of the god in the *uzat* (28) speaking unto you. 'I am Hah, Qo, Amro, Ma-amt, Mete is my name; for I am . . . bai, So, Akanakoup, (29) Melkh, Akh, Akh, Hy, Melkh is my true (*bis*) . . . . eternity, I am Khelbai, Setet, Khen (?)-em-nefer is my name, Sro, Oshenbet, is my correct name.' (30) Say it nine times. You stand opposite the moon, your eye being filled with this ointment :—green eye-paint (and) stibium, grind with Syrian honey and put the gall of a chick (31) full grown to it, and put it on a thing of glass, and lay it (by) for yourself in a hidden place till the time when you are ready for it; then you do it again as above.

Col. XXIV.

(1 *a*) For catalepsy (?)—another: (2 *a*) flour of wild dates (3 *a*) which has been beaten up (?) with milk, (4 *a*) . . . . (5 *a*) you make them up together into a ball, (and) put in the wine.

(1) A medicament, when you wish to drug (?) a man—tested :—(2) scammony root, 1 drachm, (3) opium, 1 drachm; pound with milk, (4) you make it into a ball and put it into some food (?), (5) which is cooked (?), and let him eat it; then he is upset.

(6) Another, when you wish to make a man sleep for two days :—(7) mandragora root, 1 ounce, (8) liquorice (?),

---

and Asia Minor; a strong cathartic, very griping. The root is used, and from it is obtained a gum resin (Brit. Pharmacop.). **ριι** is probably a mistake for **ριϩ** *ῥίζα*, *σκαμβωνίας ῥίζα* occurring amongst the synonyms in Diosc., l. c.

l. 7. Mandragora, Diosc. iv. 76.

l. 8. **ⲙⲉⲗⲁⲕⲣⲉⲧⲓⲕⲟⲩ** might be *μῆλα κρητικά* (?) (*κυδώνια*), meaning quinces.

9. *ⲩⲟⲥⲕⲩⲁⲙⲟⲩ* (*οὐγκία*) I

10. *ⲕⲓⲥⲥⲟⲩ* (*οὐγκία*) I

11. e·ʾr-k nt-w a ḫ wᶜ lq n ʾrp e·ʾr-k wḫ ʾr.f n mt·t rm-rḫ

12. e·ʾr-k t ḫt(?) IV·t a p wᶜ sp-sn nʾm-w erme(?) wᶜ wth n ʾrp nte-k

13. ⟨nte-k⟩ tḫb-w n *θ* n twe šᶜ rhwe nte-k stf-w

14. nte-k t swr-w-s nfr sp-sn k·t III·t *ⲕⲉⲩⲟⲣ*

15. *ϫⲡⲟϩ* sttr·t (?) I qt I t nᶜ ḥr *ϣⲱⲧⲓ*

16. nte-k ʾr-f n *ϭⲁϭⲓ* nte-k t wm-s p rm nt e·ʾr-k wḫ-f

17. pḫr·t a t ʾre rm ʾn-q⟨te⟩tk nfr sp-sn

18. pr·w *ϫⲡⲱϩ* sttr·t(?) I $\frac{1}{2}$qt·t I nn·t n mᶜntrᶜgwrw IV·t $\frac{1}{2}$qt·t

19. gyss-ᶜo-s IV·t $\frac{1}{2}$qt·t nt n wᶜ sp nte-k t

20. wth n ʾrp XV ar-f nte-k ty-f a wᶜ·t glyt·t n yl

21. nte-k ḥrḥ ar-f e.ʾr-k wḫ a ty-f e·ʾr-k t wᶜ ḫm a wᶜ z n ʾrp

22. e·ʾr-k ty-f n p rm p gyss-ᶜo-s ḫr rt-f ḫn n km·w

23. te-f gbe·t m qty gbe·t n škʾm e-s prz n III ḫlp

24. m qty gbe·t n elle ḫr ʾr-s šp I n ḫy te-f ḥrre

25. m qty ḥt ke-z nb k·t sḫy n *ϭⲁⲗⲉ* n Rᶜqt

26. nte-k (?)t a nk nb n wm k·t wᶜ·t *ϩⲁϥⲗⲉⲗⲉ ⲛⲥⲉⲧ* II

27. pḫre a . . . . . sḫy n fy pr·w zpḫ n pr-ʾmnt sym(?) n *ⲕⲗⲟ*

28. nt-w n wᶜ sp ʾr m bnn t a p wm(?)

But more probably it is the μελίκρητον, 'honey and water,' of Hipp., Aph. v. 41 &c.; cf. also γλυκὺ κρητικόν, Galen, de Antid. i. 12, &c., 'liquorice.'

l. 9. Hyoscyamus, henbane, Diosc. iii. 69, used as hypnotic, &c., Brit. Pharm.

l. 10. κισσος, Diosc. ii. 210.

l. 11. *a ḫ*: a curious usage.

mt·t rm-rḫ: cf. I Kham. iv. 37.

l. 12. The meaning may be that you take each of the four ingredients separately and soak it in wine. Perhaps the four *uteh* of wine make the *lok*.

1 ounce, (9) hyoscyamus, 1 ounce, (10) ivy, 1 ounce; (11) you pound them like (*sic*) a *lok*-measure of wine. If you wish to do it cleverly (?) (12) you take four portions to each one of them with an *uteh* of wine, (13) you moisten them from morning to evening; you clarify them, (14) you make them drink it; very good.

Another, the fourth (?):—pips (?) [of ?] (15) apple, 1 stater (?), 1 *kite*, pound with flour. (16) You make it into a cake (?); you make the man eat it, whom you wish.

(17) A medicament for making a man sleep; very good:—(18) pips (?) of apple, 1 stater (?), 1 drachma, mandragora root, 4 drachmas, (19) ivy, 4 drachmas; pound together; you put fifteen (20) *uteh* of wine to it; you put it into a glass *glyt*; (21) you keep it. If you wish to give it, you put a little into a cup of wine, (22) you give it to the man.

Ivy: it grows in gardens; (23) its leaf is like the leaf of *shekam*, being divided into three lobes (24) like a vine-leaf; it (the leaf) is one palm in measurement; its blossom (25) is like silver—another says gold.

Another: gall of an Alexandrian weasel, (26) you add it to any food.

Another: a two-tailed lizard.

(27) A medicament for catalepsy (?): gall of cerastes, pips (?) of western apples, herb of *klo*, (28) pound them together; make into a pill, put (it) into the food (?).

---

wᶜ sp-sn = ⲟⲩⲁ ⲟⲩⲁ.

l. 14. *t swr-w-s*, 'let them absorb it,' or 'let the patient (?) drink it.'

l. 18. ½*qt·t*. This group of the *kite*, written with the sign for ½ either over it, as twice in this line, or preceding it, as in l. 19 and V. 7/5, 9/3, doubtless represents the Coptic ϭⲓⲥⲕⲓⲧⲉ : ϫⲉϩⲕⲓϯ, which is also a fem. word, meaning half a didrachma, or drachma.

l. 26. *nte-k* seems superfluous, see note on plate.

ll. 27–28. A parallel passage, V. 3/1–3.

l. 27. *ⲕⲗⲟ*: Lemm., Kl. Kopt. Stud. x. (Bull. St. Pet. xiii. 12) has shown that ⲕⲗⲟ was the name of a vegetable arrow poison.

29. k·t e·ʾr-k t snf n *ϭⲉⲙⲟⲩⲓ(?)ⲗ* ḥr snf n rm e-f mw·t

30. a p ʾrp nte·k t swr-f p rm ẖr *ⲙⲧⲉϥ*

31. k·t e·ʾr-k t snf n ʾmwlz a *ⲓⲉⲧϥ* ẖr ʾr-f *ϭⲱⲛⲙ*

32. k·t e·ʾr-k t snf n *ϭⲉⲛϭⲗⲱ* py smt ʿn pe

33. k·t e·ʾr-k ʾr wʿ *ⲃⲉϭ* n ḥsy ẖn wʿ ʾrp nte-k t swr-f p rm

34. ẖr ʾr-f te-f yp·t wʿ *ⲉⲙⲓⲙ* n py smt ʿn ẖr ʾr-f

35. te-f yp·t ʿn pe-f *ⲥⲉϩⲉ* ʿn e·ʾr-k ty-s a p ʾrp

36. ẖr ʾr-f te-f yp·t m šs e·ʾr-k t *ⲥⲉϩⲓ* n

37. gʿle·t n Rʿqt a nk nb n wm ẖr ʾr-f te-f yp·t e·ʾr-k t wʿ·t

38. *ϩⲁϥⲗⲉⲗⲉ* n st II a p nḥe nte-k st(?)·t-s erme-f nte-k ths

39. p rm nʾm-f ẖr ʾr-f te-f yp·t

Col. XXV.

1. n mt·tw n p ẖbs a šn n p ʿlw

2. z-mt·t te·te yg tʿtʿk thethe

3. sʿty sʿn·tʿskl kr-ʿo-mʿkʿt

4. pʿtʿksurʿy kʿlew·pʿnkt ʿ·ʿ·tsyewy

5. mʿkt·sytʿkʿt ḥt-y ḥt r y-ʿo-y

6. ḥʿ·w (?) y my z-w n-y wḥ ⟨a⟩ n mt·t nb nt e-y šn ẖrr-w ty n p-hw

7. z ʾnk Ḥr p ẖrt ḥr ʾb tt z ank ʾS·t t rẖ·t

8. n n z n r-y ẖp z sp VII ḥr ʾny-k wʿ·t mšprt·t (?) nmy

9. nte-k t wʿ sʿl n ḥbs (?) e-f wʿb ar-s n ʾny a bl ẖn ḥ·t-ntr nte-k

10. smn·t-s ḥr wʿ·t tbe·t nmy n ʾny n p myẖl e-s wʿb e bnp

---

l. 30. *t swr-f* (*sic*) *p rm*: so also l. 33.

l. 35. *ty-s* for *ty-f*.

l. 38. *st-s*: can *ps·t-s* be intended? Cf. 27/14.

(29) Another: you put camel's blood with the blood of a dead man (30) into the wine; you make the man drink it; then he dies.

(31) Another: you put a night-jar's blood into his eye; then he is blinded.

(32) Another: you put a bat's blood; this is the manner of it again.

(33) Another: you drown a hawk in a jar of wine; you make the man drink it; (34) then it does its work. A shrew-mouse (?) in the same way; it does (35) its work also. Its gall also, you add it to the wine, (36) then it does its work very much. You put the gall (37) of an Alexandrian weasel into any food; then it does its work. You put a (38) two-tailed lizard into the oil and you cook it with it; you anoint (39) the man with it; then it does its work.

Col. XXV.

(1) The words of the lamp for inquiry of the boy. (2) Formula: 'Te, Te, Ik, Tatak, Thethe, (3) Sati, Santaskl, Kromakat, (4) Pataxurai, Kaleu-pankat, A-a-tieui, (5) Makat-sitakat, Hati, Hat-ro, E-o-e, (6) Hau (?), E; may they say to me an answer to everything concerning which I ask here to-day, (7) for I am Harpocrates in Mendes, for I am Isis the Wise; (8) the speech of my mouth comes to pass.' Say seven times. You take a new lamp (?), (9) you put a clean linen wick into it brought from a temple, (10) and you set it on a new brick, brought from the mould (?) and clean, on which

---

Col. XXV.

l. 6. ⲧⲁⲧ: the demotic group is probably a ligature for some divine name.

l. 8. *n n z*, probably for ⲉⲛϫⲱ, pronounced ⲛ̄ⲛ̄ϫⲱ.

mšprt-t: here and in l. 11 the first sign might be *ḫ* as in the facs.

l. 10. *myḫl*, possibly ⲙⲁϭⲟⲧⲗ, المنقر, in any case probably means the brick-maker's mould; *my* may well represent ⲙⲁ, as in imperative ⲙⲁ-.

11. rm ʿly ar-s nte-k t ʿḥ-s a rt-s nte-k smn t mšprt·t

12. ḥr ʾt-s nte-k t nḥe n mʿ·t ar-s nge nḥe n whe

13. nte-k smn tbe·t II·t nmy ḫrr-k nte-k ḫʿ p ʿlw ʾwt

14. rt-k nte-k ʿš n sḫ·w nt ḥry a ḥry ḫn zz-f n p ʿlw

15. e t·t-k ḥr r yr·t-f nte-k t ḫl a ḥry ḥr gbe·t n twre·t

16. ne-ḥr p ḫbs ḫr ʾr-k-f n wʿ mʿ e·f n kke e-f (*sic*) pe-f r

17. wn a pr-ybt nge p rs e mn ʿy n p ʾytn ḫrr-f

18. nte-k tm ḫʿ wyn a ʾy a ḫn a p mʿ n rn-f nte-k s·wʿb p mʿ n rn-f a t ḥ·t

19. nte-k ḥwy ʾ·t-f n p ʿlw a p r n t ry·t e·ʾr-k wḥ e·ʾr-k ʿš sḫ

20. e·ʾr-k fy t·t-k ḥr r yr·t-f wʿ ʿlw e b-ʾr te-f še erme s-ḥm·t

21. [p] nt e·ʾr-k t še-f ne-t·t-f nte-k šn·t-f z ʾḫ p nt e·ʾr-k nw ar-f

22. ḫr mt·t-f erme-k n mt·t nb nt e·ʾr-k šn·t-f a·ʾr-w

23. wʿ ky a t ḥt s-ḥm·t m-s ḥwt ʾr n wʿ·t wne·t nte-f ḫp ty hte·t ḫr ʾny-k

24. wʿ·t *ⲃⲉϣ(?)ⲉ* ⟨e-s ʿnḫ⟩ erme *ⲕⲟⲩⲕⲟⲩⲡ(?)ⲁⲧ* e-w ʿnḫ kys n ʾr n-w

25. snfe n ʿo ḥwt snf n syb n ʾḥ·t km nte-k ths ne-w

26. ʿpe·t·w n skn sšn nte-k ʿš wʿ skp a ḥr p rʿ n te-f wne·t n ḫʿ

27. e·ʾr-k ḫt(?) zz-w n t II·t e·ʾr-k ʾny pe-w ḥt a bl n ne-w spyr n wnm

28. n t II·t nte-k ths-f n p snf n ʿo ḥnʿ p snfe (?) n syb n ʾh·t km·t

29. nt ḥry e·ʾr-kt y-sw a ḫn wʿ ḫʿr n ʿo e·ʾr-k ḫʿ-w n p rʿ šʿ nte-w

---

l. 11. *ʿly* would seem to represent ⲁⲗⲉ : ⲁⲗⲏⲓ ; the gloss ⲁⲗⲟ is strange.

a rt-s presumably means 'set it up on end.'

l. 17. *ʿy n p ʾytn*, probably to be taken together, meaning 'cellar.'

(11) no man has mounted (?); you set it upright, you place the lamp (?) (12) on it; you put genuine oil in it, or Oasis oil, (13) and you set two new bricks under you; you place the boy between (14) your feet; you recite the charms aforesaid down into the head of the boy, (15) your hand being over his eyes; you offer myrrh upon a willow leaf (16) before the lamp. You do it in a dark place, the door of it (17) opening to the East or the South, and no cellar being underneath it. (18) You do not allow the light to come into the place aforesaid; you purify the said place beforehand. (19) You push the boy's back to the opening of the niche. When you have finished, you recite a charm, (20) bringing your hand over his eyes. A boy who has not yet gone with a woman, (21) is he] whom you make come before you (?); you question him, saying, 'What do you see?' (22) then he tells you about everything that you ask him.

(23) A method to put the heart of a woman after a man; done in one moment (?), and it comes to pass instantly. You take (24) a swallow (?) alive, together with a hoopoe, (both) alive. Ointment made for them: (25) blood of a male ass, blood of the tick (?) of a black cow; you anoint (26) their heads with lotus ointment; you utter a cry before the sun in his moment of rising; (27) you cut off the heads of the two; you take the heart out of the right ribs (28) of both of them; you anoint it with the ass's blood and the blood of the tick (?) of a black cow, (29)

---

l. 21. Read [*p*] *nt e·ʾr-k*, which is required by the space and the meaning.

ne-t·t-f: either *-f* must refer to the lamp, or to the action in general, or else it is a slip for *-k*.

l. 23. *wᶜ·t wne·t*: the preparation of the materials would take several days, but they could be kept ready for immediate use.

l. 24. **Ⲃⲏⲛⲉ** seems a likely word, but there is no authority for reading the third sign in the cipher word as **ⲛ**.

e-w ᶜnḫ does not mean that several hoopoes were required. There were only two birds: see l. 27.

30. šewy n hw IV a·ʾre (?) p hw IV sny e·ʾr-k nt-w e·ʾr-k ty-sw a wʿ

31. ʾrkyʿ e·ʾr-k ḫʿ-f n pe-k ʾy e·ʾr-k wḫ a t ʾre s-ḥm·t mr ḥwt e·ʾr-k θy

32. p znf n wʿ ḫ n hr e·ʾr-k ʿš ny rn·w n mte a ḥr-w

33. e·ʾr-k ty-f a wʿ z n ʾrp nge ḥnke e·ʾr-k ty-f n t s-ḥm·t nte-s swr-f

34. ank byrʿ·ʿqhl lʾ·ʾqh sʾsmryʾ-mr

35. pls·plwn ank ʿo-ʿn-ne sʾbʾʾthl sʾswpw

36. nythy my ḥt mn a·ms mn m-s mn a·ms mn ḫn

37. ny wne·t·w n p-hw sp VII ḫr ʾr-k-f n p mḥ XIV n p wrše nfr sp-sn

Col. XXVI

1. ke ʿš ʿn n py z n ʾrp
2. byrʿgetht
3. sʿmʿrʿ
4. pylpywn
5. yʿhwt
6. sʿbʿwth
7, 8. sʿypwnythʿs
9. ke ʿš nte-f ʿn ḫr ke-zm
10. ank byrʿgʿtht
11. lʿtht
12. sʿsmyrʿ
13. plyprn
14. ʿo-hw
15. sʿbʿqht
16. sʿswpwnythʿ
17. my ḥt mn m-s

Col. XXVII.

1. ke šn-hne wʿe·t a nw a p wtn n p rʿ p ʿš nt e·ʾr-k ʿš-f a·wn n-y t p·t t mw·t n n ntr·w

2. my nw-y a p wtn n p rʿ e-f ḫt-ḫnt ḫn-s z ʾnk Gb ʾrpe ntr·w šll p nt e-y ʾr nʾm-f mbḥ p rʿ pe yt

as aforesaid; you put them into an ass's skin; you lay them in the sun until they (30) are dry for four days; when the four days have passed, you pound them, you put them into a (31) box; you lay it in your house.

When you wish to make a woman love a man, you take (32) the shaving (?) of a pleasure-wood (?); you recite these correct names before them; (33) you put it into a cup of wine or beer; you give it to the woman and she drinks it. (34) 'I am Bira, Akhel, La-akh, Sasmrialo(?), (35) Ples-plun, Ioane, Sabaathal, Sasupu, (36) Nithi, put the heart of N. born of N. after N. born of N. in (37) these hours to-day.' Seven times. You do it on the fourteenth of the lunar month. Very excellent.

Col. XXVI.

(1) Another invocation again of this cup of wine: (2) 'Birakethat, (3) Samara, (4) Pilpioun, (5) Iahout, (6) Sabaouth, (7, 8) Saipounithas.'

(9) Another invocation belonging to it again, in another book: (10) 'I am Biraka-that, (11) Lathat, (12) Sasmira, (13) Plipron, (14) Takou, (15) Sabakhot, (16) Sasoupounitha, (17) send the heart of N. after (18) Sasoupounithas.'

Col. XXVII.

(1) Another vessel-divination, (to be done) alone, for seeing the bark of Phre. The invocation which you recite: 'Open to me O (?) heaven, mother of the gods! (2) Let me see the bark of Phre going up and going

---

l. 34. **ⲥⲁⲥⲙⲣⲓⲁⲗ**: note **ⲗ** transcribing *mr*.

l. 35. Notice the transcription of the group for 'ass,' here ⲓⲱ, in 26/14 ⲓⲁ-.

Col. XXVI.

l. 8. A gloss to l. 7.

Col. XXVII.

Lines 1–12 are a repetition of 10/22–34; see notes there.

3. e-tbe mt·t ʾr še n t·t ʾy ḥkne·t wr·t nb qnḥ·t tʾ rʿ(?)-št-rd (?) a·wn n-y t nb ʾyḫ·w

4. a·wn n-y t p·t ḥyt·t my wšte-y n n wpt·w z ʾnk Gb ʾrpe ntr·w ʾy p VII stn ʾy p VII

5. Mnt k syt nb šfe·t sḥz t by nn (?) hy rw (?) mʾ rw (?) nn (?) k kke

6. hy ḫnt-ybty·w nwn wr ḫʾw hy by srʾw by ʾmnty·w hy by by·w

7. k kke k k·w sʾ nw·t a·wn n-y ank wbʾ t ʾr pyr n Gb hy ʾnk

8. y·y·y e·e·e· he·he·he h-ʿo h-ʿo h-ʿo ank ʿnep-ʿo myry·p-ʿo-rʿ mʿ·t (?) ʾb thyby

9. ʿo ʾrw·wy wʾw yʿh-ʿo p swḥ-ʾyḫ snfe n smnw snf n qqwpt snf n ʾmwlz

10. ʿnḫ-ʾm·w snw-p·t ʿo-ʾMn qs(?)-ʿnḫ ḫstb n mʿ·t ḫl p-tgs-ʾS·t nt ʾrw m bnn·t nte-k smt

11. yr·t-k nʾm-f ḥr rym·t n by-ʿo-n-p·t n wʿ ḫ n hr n ʾny nge hbyn nte-k mr-k a pe-k qte

12. n wʿ·t pke·t n šn-bn·t ḥwt

13. p ky n ʾr p šn-hne n p ḫbs e·ʾr-k ʾny wʿ ḫbs e-f wʿb e-f wbḫ n wš n t prš mw n qme ar-f e pe-f šʿl n š-stn nte-k mḥ-f n nḥe

14. n mʿ·t nge nḥe n yt·t nte-k mr-f n ʿy IV·t n ʿyw e bnp-w st·t-w nte-k ʿyḫ·t-f a wʿ·t zʿy·t n pr·ybt

15. wʿ·t šmwe·t n ḫ n tphn nte-k t ʿḥ p ḫm-ḫl n pe-f mt a bl e-f wʿb e b·ʾr te-f še erme s-ḥm·t nte-k ḥbs yr·t-f n t·t-k

16. nte-k θ-r p ḫbs nte-k ʿš a ḫry ḫn te-f ʿpe·t šʿ sp VII nte-k t ʾr-f wn yr·t-f nte-k šn·t-f z ʾḫ n-e·nw-k a·ʾr-w

---

l. 8. Note the hieroglyphic transliterations of demotic.

l. 10. *snw-p·t*, possibly *σίναπι*, 'mustard'; it occurs in Louvre dem. mag. iii. 27 with gloss . . . *ροχλου* (?).

l. 14. *st·t-w*, or perhaps *ps·t-w*, which have not been boiled.

l. 15. *tphn*, probably δάφνη, Diosc. i. 106.

A good instance of **ⲙⲡⲉϥⲙⲧⲟ ⲉⲃⲟⲗ**.

down in it; for I am Geb, heir of the gods; prayer is what I make before Phre my father (3) on account of a thing that hath proceeded from me. O Heknet, great one, lady of the shrine, the Rishtret open to me, mistress of spirits, (4) open to me primal heaven; let me worship the angels! for I am Geb, heir of the gods. Hail! ye seven kings; ho! ye seven (5) Mônts, bull that engendereth, lord of strength, that enlighteneth the earth, soul of the abyss (?). Ho! lion as lion of (?) the abyss (?), bull of the night; (6) hail! thou that rulest the people of the East, Noun, great one, lofty one; hail! soul of a ram, soul of the people of the West; hail! soul of souls, (7) bull of the night, bull (?) of (two ?) bulls, son of Nut. Open to me, I am the Piercer of earth, he that came forth from Geb; hail! I am (8) I, I, I, E, E, E, He, He, He, Ho, Ho, Ho; I am Anepo, Miri-po-re, Maat (?) Ib, Thibai (9) great, Aroui, Ouoou, Iaho. The spirit-gathering: blood of a *smune*-goose, blood of a hoopoe, blood of a night jar, (10) *ankh-amu* plant, *senepe* plant, Great-of-Amen-plant, *qes-ankh* stone, genuine lapis-lazuli, myrrh, 'foot-print (?)-of-Isis' plant, pound and make into a ball, and paint (11) your eyes with it upon (?) a goat's tear, with a 'pleasure-wood' of *ani* or ebony; you tie yourself at your side (12) with a strip (?) of male-palm fibre. (13) The way of making the vessel-inquiry of the lamp. You take a clean bright lamp without putting minium (or) gum-water into it, its wick being of fine linen; you fill it with genuine oil (14) or oil of dew; you tie it with four threads of linen which have not been cooked (?); you hang it on an East wall (on) (15) a peg of bay-wood; you make the boy stand before it, he being pure and not having gone with a woman; you cover his eyes with your hand; (16) you light the lamp and you recite down into his head, unto seven times; you make him open

17. e-f z ḥr e-y nw a n ntr·w e-w n p qte n p ḫbs ḫr z-w n-f wḥ a p nt e-w a šn·t-w ar-f e-f ḫp e·ʾr-k wḫ a ʾr-f n t·t-k wʿ·t-k

18. e·ʾr-k mḥ yr·t-k n p kys nt ḥry e·ʾr-k ʿḥ a rt-k wbe p ḫbs e-f mḥ nte-k ʿš ar-f n sp VII e yr·t-k ḫtm e·ʾr-k wḥ e·ʾr-k wn

19. yr·t-k ḫr nw-k a n ntr·w n pe-k pḥ nte-k sze wbe-w ḫr p nt e·ʾr-k wḫ-f e·ḫr ʾr-k-f n wʿ mʿ n kke p ʿš nt e·ʾr-k ʿš-f

20. z-mt·t ank mʿneby ghthethwny ⲭⲁⲃⲁⲭⲉⲗ my wšte-y·t-k p šr n ʾrpythnʾ-

21. pyrʿ pyle·ʾsʾ gnwryph·ʾrysʿ tny-yryssʾ psy psy yrys·sʾ

22. gymythwrw·phws·sʾ ʿo-qmʾtsysʾ **ⲟⲣⲉⲟⲃⲁⲍⲁⲅⲣⲁ** pertʾ-ʿo-mekh

23. perʾg-ʿo-mekh sʿkmeph ʾm n-y a ḫn nte-k šn n-y ḫr p šn nte-y šn ḫrr-f n mt·t mʿ·t n wš

24. n mt·t n ʿze pe-f swḥ-ʾyḫ p kys nt e·ʾr-k ty-f a yr·t-k e·ʾr-k ʾn·nʿ a ʾr . . . . nb n p ḫbs

25. ḫr ʾny-k hyn·w ḥrre n bel n *ⲉⲃⲱⲕ* ḫr gm-k-sw n pr mʿ n p s-trmws e·ʾr-k ʾny·t-w e-w gnn

26. nte-k ty-sw a wʿ lq n yl e·ʾr-k ʿm r-f m šs sp-sn šʿ hw XX n wʿ mʿ e-f hep e-f n kke bn-s

27. hw XX e·ʾr-k ʾny·t-f a ḥry e·ʾr-k wn ar-f ḫr gm-k hyn·w ḫryw erme wʿ mʾz ḫn-f e·ʾr-k ḫʿ-f šʿ hw XL nte-k ʾny·t-f

28. a ḥry nte-k wn ar-f ḫr gm-k-f e·ḥr-f ʾr snf a·ʾre ḫr ʾr-k ty-f a wʿ nk n yl nte-k t p nk n yl a ḫn wʿ nk n blz

29. n mʿ e-f hep n nw nb e·ʾr-k wḫ a ʾr . . . . n p ḫbs

---

l. 19. *n pe-k bl* or *pḥ* (?): cf. l. 30.

ll. 24–29 are a repetition of 5/24–30; see notes there.

l. 24. *wḫe* (?). *šn* stands in the parallel. It seems that *wḫe* (?) is used of *μαντεία αὐτοπτική* (cf. note to 10/22), and *šn-hne*, when opposed to it (l. 34), means divination with a medium.

his eyes; you ask him, saying, 'What are the things which you have seen?' (17) If he says, 'I have seen the gods about the lamp,' then they tell him answer concerning that which they will be asked. If you wish to do it by yourself alone, (18) you fill your eyes with the ointment aforesaid; you stand up opposite the lamp when alight; you recite to it seven times with your eyes shut; when you have finished, you open (19) your eyes; then you see the gods behind (?) you; you speak with them concerning that which you desire; you ought to do it in a dark place. The invocation which you recite, (20) formula: 'I am Manebai, Ghethethoni, Khabakhel, let me worship thee, the child of Arpithna-pira, (21) Pileasa, Gnuriph-arisa, Teni-irissa, Psi, Psi, Irissa, (22) Gimituru-phus-sa, Okmatsisa, Oreobazagra, Pertaomekh, (23) Peragomekh, Sakmeph, come in to me, and inquire for me about the inquiry which I am inquiring about, truthfully without (24) falsehood.' Its spirit-gathering: the ointment which you put on your eyes, when you are about to make any divination by the lamp. (25) You take some flowers of the Greek bean; you find them in the place of the lupin-seller; you take them fresh, (26) and put them into a *lok* of glass; you close its mouth very carefully for twenty days in a hidden dark place; after (27) twenty days you take it forth, you open it; then you find a pair (?) of testicles and a phallus inside it; you leave it for forty days; and you take it (28) forth; you open it; then you find that it has become bloody; you must put it into some thing of glass, and you put the glass thing into a pottery (thing) (29) in a place hidden at all times. When you wish to make a divination (?) by the lamp with it, you

l. 29. *n nw nb*: the parallel 5/29, where this is repeated with the next sentence, shows that it cannot mean 'from all sight.'

n'm-f e·'r-k mḥ yr·t-k n py snf nt ḥry e·'r-k 'n·nʿ a n·q(te)t·k

30. nge e·'r-k ʿḥ wbe p ḫbs e·'r-k ʿš n py ʿš nt ḥry ḫr nw-k a p ntr n pe-k pḥ(?)e·'r-k ʿḥ nge e·'r-k str nfr nfr 'p

31. ḫr sḫ-k py rn a t tys·t n p šʿl n p ḫbs n r'w ḫl ⲃⲁⲭᵧⲭⲥⲓⲭᵧⲭ p-e·z ke zm ⲕⲓⲙⲙⲉⲓⲑⲱⲣⲱ ⲫⲱⲥⲥⲉ

32. py ky nt sḫ ḥry p ky n p . . . . n mʿneby pe e-f ḫp e·'r-k wḫ a 'r-f

33. n šn n p ḫbs py smte ʿn pe ḫr 'r-f 'r šw ʿn a . . . . n mwryby e-f ḫp e·'r-k 'r-f

34. n šn-hne n p ḫbs e·'r-k mḥ p ḫbs nt ḥry ḥr wʿ·t tbe·t nmy nte-k t ʿḥ p ḫm-ḫl a rt-f

35. n p mte n p ḫbs e-f ḥbs a pe-f ḥr nte-k ʿš a te-f(?) ʿpe·t e·'r-k ʿḥ ḥr 't-f n py ʿš n mt·t wʿyʿny e·'r-k wḥ e·'r-k klp

36. ḥr-f ḫr 'r-f z n-k wḥ n mt-t mʿ·t

Col. XXVIII.

1. ke ky n šn-hne wʿe·t z-mt·t 'nk p nb by ʿo-rytsymby s-ʿo-nʿtsyr epysghes emmyme

2. th-ʿo-g-ʿo-m·phrwr phyrym·phwny rn-yk mymy by-byw sp-sn gtheth-ʿo-ny ank Wbst·t pth-ʿo

3. bʿlkhʿm a·ms bynwy sphe phas ank bʿpth-ʿo gʿm·-my·sʿtra rn-yk my·me-ʿo

4. y'nwme pe-f swḥ-'yḫ ḫr š-k a wʿ mʿ e-f wʿb nte-k 'ny wʿ z n ḥmt nte-k yʿ-f n mw n ḥsm nte-k t wʿ lq

5. n nḥe ar-f nte-k wḥ-f ḥr p 'ytn nte-k θ-r wʿ·t lʿmps n ḥmt nte-k θ-s a p 'ytn ḫr t·t p z n ḥmt

6. nte-k ḥbs-k n wʿ·t šnto·t e-s wʿb nte-k erme p hne nte-k ʿš a ḫn p hne e yr·t-k ḫtm šʿ sp VII e·'r-k wn yr·t-k

l. 32. Manebai is the leading word in the invocation, l. 20.

l. 33. Muribai is a leading word in the invocation in the parallel 5/10 to which this evidently refers.

fill your eyes with this blood aforesaid, you proceed to lie down, (30) or you stand opposite the lamp; you recite this invocation aforesaid; then you see the god behind (?) you, while you are standing up or lying down. Excellent (*bis*) and tried (?). (31) You write this name on the strip of the wick of the lamp in myrrh ink, 'Bakhukhsikhukh,' or, as says another book, 'Kimeithoro Phosse'; (32) this method which is written above is the method of the divination of Manebai. If you wish to do it (33) by inquiry of the lamp, this also is the form, it is also profitable for (?) the divination of Muribai. If you do it (34) by vessel-inquiry of the lamp, you fill the lamp aforesaid on a new brick; you make the boy stand upright (35) before the lamp, he having his face covered; you recite to his head, standing over him, this Greek invocation; when you have finished, you uncover (36) his face, then he answers you truthfully.

COL. XXVIII.

(1) Another mode of vessel-inquiry, alone. Formula: 'I am the lord of Spirits, Oridimbai, Sonadir, Episghes, Emmime, (2) Tho-gom-phrur, Phirim-phuni is thy name; Mimi, Bibiu (*bis*), Gthethoni, I am Ubaste, Ptho, (3) Balkham born of Binui, Sphe, Phas, I am Baptho, Gam-mi-satra is thy name, Mi-meo, (4) Ianume.' Its spirit-gathering: you go to a clean place, you take a vessel of bronze, you wash it with water of natron, you put a *lok*-measure (5) of oil to it; you place it on the ground; you light a bronze lamp; you put it on the ground by the bronze vessel; (6) you cover yourself with a clean

---

COL. XXVIII.

l. 1. *epysghes emmyme*: MAX MÜLLER, Rec. trav., viii. 178, reads here *episkhes epimme*, and regards it as a transcription of ἐπίσχες ἐπί με, 'come to me.' The reading is probably *emymme*, but it may still be a corruption of the Greek phrase he has suggested.

l. 5. *θ-s*, ϫoc.

7. e·ʾr-k šn·t-f a p nt e·ʾr-k wḫ̮-f e·ʾr-k wḫ̮ a t ʾre n ntr·w n p hne sze wbe-k n r-w wbe r-k e·ʾr-k ʿš yʾh-ʿo

8. yph e-ʿo-e gynntethwr nephʿr ʾph-ʿo-e ḫ̮r ʾr-w n-k wḥ a mt·t nb nt e·ʾr-k a šn·t-f a·ʾr-w ʿn a·ʾr-w tm z n-k wḥ e·ʾr-k ʿš

9. py ke rn ng-ʿo-ngethygs mʿntwn-ʿo-b-ʿo-e g-ʿo-kšyrhr-ʿo-nt-ʿo-r nt-ʿo-ntr-ʿo-mʿ leph-ʿo-ger

10. gephʿer·s-ʿo-re e·ʾr-k ʿš ny ḫ̮r ʾr-w šn n-k n mt·t mʿ·t

11. ke šn-hne e·ḫ̮r ʾr-k t·t nḥe n sym ar-f e·ḫ̮r ʾr-k-f a ḫ̮ p nt ḥry z-mt·t sze wbe-y sp-sn hʿmst p ntr n n ntr·w n p kk

12. ʾyḫ̮ nb ḫ̮yb·t nb nt ḫ̮n ʾmnt e·ʾr-s p-e·ʾr mw nhse n-y sp-sn py by n ʿnḫ̮ py by n snsn my pry

13. pe hne pe swt ty n p-hw e-tb p hne n ʾS·t wr·t e-s šn m-s py-s hy e-s qte m-s py-s sn ḥwt mnʿš sp-sn

14. mnʿnf sp-sn a·zy-s z mnʿš sp-sn mnʿnf sp-sn ph-ʿo-ny sp-sn n hh n sp nte-k z·t-s n p ḫ̮m-ḫ̮l ze a·zy-s

15. z my š n-k p kke ʾm n-y p wyn nte-k wn yr·t-k ty hte·t ḫ̮r ʾw n ntr·w a ḫ̮n nte-w z n-k wḥ n mt·t nb

Col. XXIX.

1. tey-s ky n šn n p rʿ e-w z nʾm-f z e-f znt m šs sp-sn pe-f swḥ-ʾyḫ̮ ḫ̮r ʾny-k wʿ ḫ̮m-ḫ̮l e-f wʿb nte-k ʾr . . . .

2. ʾyḫ̮ nt sḫ̮ ar-f nte-k ʾny·t-f n p mt ̄n p rʿ nte-k t ʿḥ-f a rt-f ḥr wʿ·t tbe·t nmy n p nw nt e·ʾre

3. p rʿ ne ḫ̮ʿ nʾm-f nte-f ʾy a ḥry tre-f m tre p ʾtn nte-k t ʾw wʿ·t qbe·t n ʿyw nmy n pe-f pḥ (?) nte-k

---

l. 11. *p ntr n n ntr·w*: cf. *φνουθι νινθηρ*, Pap. Bib. Nat. 1643, and *πνουτε νινϭηρ τηρου*, B. M. XLVI. 8.

l. 12. *pr-ʾmnt*, the det. of *ḫ̮n* being the same sign as *pr* that should have followed, one has been omitted.

e·ʾr-s p-e·ʾr mw: their meaning is obscure.

Col. XXIX.

l. 1. The end of the line is quite uncertain after *ʾr t* (?).

l. 3. *qbe·t*: Boh. ⲕⲟⲃⲓ, in the Vienna ritual means a mat (?); in l. 23 we have a parallel passage with *šnt·t*.

linen robe, you and the vessel; you recite into the vessel, your eyes being shut, for seven times; you open your eyes; (7) you ask it concerning that which you wish; if you wish to make the gods of the vessel speak with you with their mouths to your mouth, you cry: 'Iaho, (8) Iph, Eoe, Kintathour, Nephar, Aphoe.' Then they make answer to you concerning everything concerning which you will ask of it again. If they do not tell you answer, you recite (9) this other name: 'Gogethix, Mantounoboe, Kokhir-rhodor, Dondroma, Lephoker, (10) Kephaersore.' If you recite these, then they inquire for you truthfully.

(11) Another vessel-inquiry: you put vegetable oil into it; you must proceed as above. Formula: 'Speak unto me (*bis*), Hamset, god of the gods of darkness, (12) every demon, every shade that is in the West and the East, he that hath died hath done it (?), rise up to me (*bis*), O thou living soul, O thou breathing soul, may (13) my vessel go forth, my knot (?) here to-day, for the sake of the vessel of Isis the Great, who inquireth for her husband, who seeketh for her brother; Menash (*bis*), (14) Menanf (*bis*).' Say, 'Menash (*bis*), Menanf (*bis*), Phoni (*bis*),' a multitude of times; and you say to the boy, 'Say, (15) "Depart, O darkness; come to me O light," and open your eyes at once.' Then the gods come in and tell thee answer to everything.

Col. XXIX.

(1) Behold a form of inquiry of the sun, of which they say it is well tested. Its spirit-gathering: you take a young boy who is pure, you make the spirit-formula (?) (2) which is written for it; you take him before the sun; you make him stand on a new brick at the moment at which (3) the sun shall rise, and it comes up entirely with the entire (?) disk; you put a new mat (?) of linen

4. t ʾr-f ẖtm yr·t-f nte-k ʿḥ a rt-k ḥr ʾ·t-f e·ʾr-k ʿš a ẖry ẖn zz-f e·ʾr-k qlhe a ẖry ẖn

5. zz-f n pe-k tbʿ n p rʿ n te-k·t t·t n wnm bn-s mḥ yr·t-f n p smt a·ʾr-k n ḥ·t

6. nʿsyrʿ ʿo-ʿpkys šfyw(?) sp-sn bybyw sp-sn rn-yk n mʿ·t sp-sn srpt a·wn n-y t p·t n py-s

7. ⟨n py-s⟩ wsẖ py-s mt a·ʾny n-y p wyn nt wʿb my ʾw n-y p ntr nte p wḥ-sḥne n t·t-f nte-f z n-y

8. wḥ a mt·t nb nte ỉw-y šn ẖr-ʾr-w ty n p-hw n mt·t mʿ·t e mn mt·t ʿze ẖn(?)-w ʿrkhnwtsy etʿle tʿl

9. nʿsyrʿ yʿrmekh nʿserʿ ʿmpthw ẖ-ʿo ʿmʿmʾrkʿr tel yʿʾ-ʿo

10. nʿsyrʿ hʿkyʾ srpt ẖzysyphth ʿh-ʿo ʿ-t-ne y·y·e(?)·w bʿlbel my

11. ʾw n-y p wyn e-f wʿb my pẖre p ʿlw my z-f n-y wḥ my ʾw n-y p ntr nte p wḥ-sḥne n t·t-f nte-f z

12. n-y wḥ a mt·t nb nt e-y šn ẖr-ʾr-w n mt·t mʿ·t e mn mt·t n ʿze ẖn-w bn-m-s-s e·ʾr-k ʿš pe-f ḥtr

13. n ke sp VII e yr·t-f ẖtm z-mt·t sy·sy·py·tsyrypy s·ʿ·ʾ·ʿo·nkhʿb

14. hrʿbʿ-ʿo-t phʿkthy-ʿo-p ʿnʿsʿn krʿʿnʿ krʿtrys tmʾ

15. ptʿrʿphne ʿrʿphnw ʾm n p ʿlw my ʾw n-f p ntr nte p wḥ-sḥne n t·t-f nte-f z n-y wḥ a mt·t nb

16. nt e-y šn ẖr-ʾr-w ty n p-hw a·ʾre p wyn ʿsqe a ʾy a ẖn e·ʾr-k z ke ke sʾls-ʿo-ʿthʿ yppel

17. syrbʿ n sp VII e·ʾr-k t *ⲁⲗⲃⲟⲩⲛⲟⲩⲧ* a p ʿẖ e·ʾr-k z py rn ʿo m-s ny tre-w e·ʾr-k ʿš-f

18. n ḥ·t-f a pḥ·t-f θs-pẖr n sp IV ʿueb-ʿo·th·yʿbʿthʿ-bʿyth-ʿo-beuʿ

19. e·ʾr-k z my mʾ p ʿlw p wyn my ʾw p ntr nte p wḥ-sḥne n t·t-f nte-f z n-y wḥ a mt·t nb nt e-y šn

20. ẖr-ʾr-w ty n p-hw n mt·t mʿ·t e mn mt·t n ʿze ẖn-w tey-s ke ky nʾm-f(?) ʿn e·ʾr-k θy p ʿlw a wʿ

---

l. 5. *tbʿ n p rʿ*: possibly the 'Apollo-finger' of modern chiromancy, i. e. the third (ring-) finger. The operation described in 3/12, 16, is the *προκωδωνισας παιδα* of Pap. Bibl. Nat. l. 89.

behind (?) him; you (4) make him shut his eyes; you stand upright over him; you recite down into his head; you strike down on (5) his head with your Ra-finger of your right hand, after filling his eye with the paint which you made before: (6) 'Nasira, Oapkis, Shfe (*bis*), Bibiou (*bis*) is thy true name (*bis*), Lotus, open to me heaven (7) in its breadth and height, bring to me the light which is pure; let the god come to me, who has the command, and let him say to me (8) answer to everything which I am asking here to-day, in truth without falsehood therein (?), Arkhnoutsi, Etale, Tal, (9) Nasira, Yarmekh, Nasera, Amptho, Kho, Amamarkar, Tel, Yaeo, (10) Nasira, Hakia, Lotus, Khzisiph, Aho, Atone, I. I. E. O, Balbel, (11) let the pure light come to me; let the boy be (?) enchanted; let answer be given me; let the god who has the command come to me and tell (12) me answer to everything about which I shall ask, in truth without falsehood therein.' Thereafter you recite his compulsion another (13) seven times, his eyes being shut. Formula: 'Si. si. pi. thiripi S. A. E. O. Nkhab (14) Hrabaot, Phakthiop, Anasan, Kraana, Kratris, Ima-(15) ptaraphne, Araphnu, come to the boy; let the god who has the command come to him, let him tell me answer to everything (16) which I shall ask here to-day.' If the light is slow to come within, you say, 'Ke, Ke, Salsoatha, Ippel, (17) Sirba,' seven times; you put frank-incense (?) on the brazier, you utter this great name after all those, you utter it (18) from beginning to end, and vice versa, four times, Auebothiabathabaithobeua; (19) you say: 'Let the boy see the light, let the god who has the command come in; let him tell me answer to everything about which I shall ask (20) here to-day, in truth without falsehood therein.'

---

l. 8. *ḫn-w*: this seems to be the reading, cf. l. 12.

21. mʿ ḥry e-f θse e·ʾr-k t ʿḥ-f a rt-f n wʿ mʿ e wn wʿ ššt ʿo n pe-f mt e r-f wn a pr-ybt e ḫr [ʾre (?)] p rʿ wbne

22. a ḫn n ḫe·t-f nte-k smt yr·t-f n p ʿlw n p smt nt sḫ ar-f nte-k ʿš ar-f n . . . sp ke-z VII e·ʾr-k ʿḥ ḥr ʾ·t-f nte-k t ʾr-f

23. kšp a ḥr p rʿ e-f mḥ wz·t e-f ʿḥ a rt-f ḥr wʿ·t tbe·t nmy e wn wʿ·t šnto·t n ʿyw nmy n pe-f pḥ(?) e yr·t-f ḫtm

24. e·ʾr-ḳ ʿš a ḥry ḫn zz-f e·ʾr-k qlh a zz-f n pe-k tbʿ nt sḫ ḥry ʿn e·ʾr-k t *ⲁⲗⲃⲟⲩⲛⲟⲩⲧ* a ḥry ne-ḥr-f e·ʾr-k wḥ e·ʾr-k t ʾr-f wn yr·t-f

25. ḫr nw-f a n ntr·w n pe-f pḥ(?) e-w sze wbe-f nt ḫr ʾr-k ty-f a yr·t-f n p ʿlw e-f ʾn·nʿ a šn-hne nb n p rʿ

26. ḫr ʾny-k *ⲓⲓϫ (?)* II n p yʿr e-w ʿnḫ n p II nte-k wš p wʿ nʾm-w n ḫ n elle n p mt n p rʿ nte-k t p snf n p ke a ḥr-f

27. nte-k t nʿ-f erme-f ḥr ḫl nte-k ʾr-w n bnn·t e-w ḫy n tbʿ wʿ(?) e·ʾr-k šʿše(?) t a yr·t-f e·ʾr-k ʾny wʿ ʾb n lyl(?) erme wʿ ḫ n

28. hr n ll ʿn nte-k ḫy ty pḫre ḥr(?) wʿ ḫm n st n t(?)-nḥs ḥr mw n elle n Kmy nte-k mḥ yr·t-k nʾm-f e·ʾr-k

29. mḥ yr·t-k n ty pḫre nte-k q(?)šp a ḥr p rʿ e-f mḥ wz·t e yr·t-k wn a ḥr-f ḫr ʾr-f wnḥ-f ar-k nte-f z(?) n-k(?) wḥ(?)

30. a mt·t nb te-f mt·t ʿo·t(?) wʿb ḫr ʾr-f ʾr šw a ḫm-ḫl nte-f ʾr šw n-k ḥ-k n rm wʿ·t

---

l. 21. *e ḫr p rʿ* should be *e ḫr ʾre p rʿ*; the condition of the MS. is very unsatisfactory in this part of the column.

l. 23. *mḥ wz·t*, i. e. at the summer solstice, Br., Thes., 296.

l. 26. For the use of vine-twigs as fuel for magic purposes, cf. Hyvern., Actes, p. 311; Brit. Mus. Gr. Pap. CXXI. l. 544, &c.

Behold, another form of it again. You take the boy to an upper lofty (21) place, you make him stand in a place where there is a large window before him, its opening looking to the East where the sun shines (22) in rising into it; you paint the boy's eye with the paint which is prescribed for it, you recite to him . . . . . times or seven times; you stand over him; you make him (23) gaze before the sun when it fills the *uzat*, he standing upright on a new brick, there being a new linen robe behind him (?), and his eyes being closed; (24) you recite down into his head; you strike on his head with your finger described above; you offer frankincense (?) before him; when you have finished, you make him open his eyes, (25) then he sees the gods behind him (?) speaking with him.

[The ointment] which you put in the boy's eyes when he goes to any vessel-inquiry of the sun (26). You take two . . . . of the river both alive, you burn one of them with vine-wood before the sun, you put the blood of the other to (?) it, (27) you pound it with it with myrrh, you make them into a pill, they measuring one finger (in length); you . . . . put into his eyes; you take a kohl-pot (?) of . . . . . . and a kohl-stick (?) of (28) *lel* (?). You pound this drug with a little *set*-stone (?) of Ethiopia and with Egyptian vine-water; you fill your eyes with it, you (29) fill your eyes with this drug, you look towards the sun when it fills the *uzat*, your eyes being open towards it; then he appears to you, he gives you answer (?) (30) to everything. Its chief point is purity; it is profitable for the boy, and it is profitable to you yourself as a person (acting) alone.

---

l. 27. *šʿše* or *šʿme*? The reading is uncertain.
l. 29. *qšp* or *kšp*? The latter is the correct form of the word.
l. 30. *mt·t ʿo·t wʿb*: cf. 17/26.

VERSO

Verso Col. I.

1. ʾnḥ n rʿ *οφρυς ηλιου*
2. ʾnḥ n ʿḥ *οφρυς (σεληνης)*
3. hyn·w sym·w ne
4. *ηλιογονον*
5. *σεληνογονον*
6. hyn·w sym·w ne
7. *θιθυμαλος*
8. nte py sym ḫm nt ḫr n km·w pe
9. nt ḫr ʾre t ʾw ʾrte a bl
10. e·ʾr-k t pe-f ʾrt a ḫʿr n rm
11. ḫr ʾr-f blbl

Verso Col. II.

1. *χαμεμελον* thw-wʿb rn-f
2. *λευκανθεμον* šq-ḥtr rn-f
3. *κριναθεμον* mn p nfr a ḥr-y rn-f
4. *χρυσανθεμον* nfr ḥr rn-f ke-z a t ḥrr·t nb

Col. I.

l. 1. *ὀφρὺς ἡλίου* is a synonym of the *σχοῖνος ἐλεία* in Diosc. iv. 52.

l. 4. *ηλιογονον*: cf. *ελιογωνον* as synonym of ϭⲟⲩϭ in Peyr. Lex. 422 along with *κνίκος* (carthamus tinctorius, Diosc. iv. 187), *ἀτρακτυλίς* (ib. iii. 97), &c.; so apparently a sort of thistle.

l. 5. *σεληνογονον*: the name given by *προφῆται* to the *παιονία* (the modern paeonia) according to the synonyms in Diosc. iii. 147. The plant-names ascribed to the *προφῆται* are naturally connected with deities, heavenly bodies and the like. Sprengel (Praefat., p. xvi) identifies the *προφῆται* with those of Egypt, but this is perhaps too precise.

l. 9. The grammatical construction seems confused: one would expect ⲉϣⲁϥ or ⲉⲧⲉϣⲁϥ, St., §§ 426, 427. The writer has given the form of the relative ⲉⲧⲥⲱⲧⲉⲙ, but has inserted *ḫr*, which seems to be an anomaly.

l. 10. Galen, de Simpl. medic., viii. 19/7, makes the same remark about the juice of the *τιθύμαλλος* (Diosc. iv. 162), viz. that if dropped on the skin it burns it.

VERSO

Verso Col. I.

(1) Eyebrow of Ra: ὀφρὺς ἡλίου. (2) Eyebrow of the moon. ὀφρὺς σελήνης. (3) These are some herbs.

(4) *Heliogonon.* (5) *Selenogonon.* (6) These are some herbs.

(7) Spurge, (8) which is that small herb that is in the gardens (9) and which exudes milk. (10) If you put its milk on a man's skin, (11) it causes a blister.

Verso Col. II.

(1) *Chamaemelon.* 'Clean-straw' is its name.

(2) *Leucanthemon.* 'Prick-horse' (?) is its name.

(3) *Crinanthemon.* 'None is better than I' is its name.

(4) *Chrysanthemon.* 'Fine-face' is its name, otherwise

Col. II.

l. 1. χαμαίμηλον, chamomile (synonym of ἀνθεμίς in Diosc. iii. 144, of παρθένιον, ib. 145).

thw-wꜥb = ⲧⲟϩ + ⲟⲩⲏⲃ (?), 'clean hay,' probably on account of the scent. According to Apul. c. 24 *thaboris* (MS. var. *tuoris*) was the Egyptian name of the plant χαμαίμηλον (Wiedemann, Altaeg. Wörter v. Klass. Aut. umschr., p. 22).

l. 2. λευκανθεμον: synonym of ἀνθυλλίς, ἀνθεμίς, παρθένιον, Diosc. iii. 143–145, but none of these plants seem to suit the Egyptian name *šq ḥtr*, 'prick(?)-horse.' Cf. ϣⲱⲕ, fodere, and Ar. شاك, 'prick.'

l. 3. κρινάνθεμον is said to be the houseleek; perhaps its occurrence in Diosc. iii. 127, as synonym of ἡμεροκαλλίς, gives a better explanation.

l. 4. χρυσάνθεμον, Diosc. iv. 58 = Chrysanthemum coronarium. The name also occurs as a synonym for ἀρτεμισία (ib. iii. 117) χρυσοκόμη, ἑλίχρυσον, and ἀείζωον τὸ μέγα (ib. iv. 55, 57, 88).

t ḥrr·t nb: cf. Lemm, Cypr. v. Ant., 12 a, 13, and p. 64, ⲡⲉϩⲣⲏⲣⲉ (*sic*) ⲙⲡⲛⲟⲩⲃ. The Hawara wreaths contained specimens, Petrie, Hawara, p. 53.

5. n p s-qlm te-f gbe·t nẖt pe-f ẖ ʿkf
6. te-f ḥrre·t n nb te-f gbe·t m qty grynʿthemwn
7. p mʿknesyʿ
8. *μανεσια*
9. wʿ ʾny n ty e-f km m qty
10. stem e·ʾr-k nt-f e-f km
11. *μαγνης* p mʿknes nt ʿnẖ ẖr ʾn-w-f
12. *μακνης* e·ʾr-k ẖyt-f e-f km
13. p mʿnes n rm ẖr ʾn-w-f
14. n t ʿn-tsyke e·ʾr-k ẖyt-f
15. ẖr ʾr-f t ʾw snf a bl
16. a t . . . . . pe-k zz
17. wʿ·t *ⲉⲡϣⲉ* nte-k wš[-s (?)] n *ⲛⲉⲛⲉⲉⲃ(?)*
18. nte-k nt-s erme qt I·t n *ϫⲡⲱϩ*
19. erme wʿ·t *ⲃ(?)ⲉϩⲱⲗ* nte-k . . .
20. nte-k t wʿ·t . . . . .

Verso Col. III.

1. pẖre[·t a . . . . sẖy n fy]
2. pr·w zpẖ n(?) pr(?)-ʾmnt sym(?) n *ⲕⲗⲟ*
3. nt-w n wʿ sp ʾr m bnn t a p ʾrp(?)
4. *φηκλης*
5. wʿ ʾny e-f wbẖ pe e-f m qty
6. gʿrbʾnʿ wn ke wʿ e·ẖr ʾr-w ʾr-f

---

l. 7. *mʿknesyʿ* is magnetic iron ore: cf. Diosc. v. 147; Plin., H. N., 36. 25.

l. 10. *e-f km*: here *km* is probably pseudo-participle, but in l. 12 infinitive.

l. 11. *mʿknes nt ʿnẖ* = *μάγνης ζῶν*, frequently referred to by Alexander Trallianus (ap. Fabricius, Bibl. gr. Hamburg, 1724, t. xii), e. g. p. 640 in prescriptions.

ẖr ʾn-w-f: cf. l. 13, it is probably an imperfect sentence, unless it means 'it is imported.'

l. 13. *mʿnes n rm*: perhaps 'human magnes,' on account of the blood. Cf. Plin., H. N., 36. 25, where the haematites magnes of Zimiris in Aethiopia is described as sanguinem reddens si teratur. He also said 'the gold flower' (5) of the wreath-seller; its leaf is strong, its stem is cold (?), (6) its flower is golden; its leaf is like *crinanthemon.*

(7) Magnesia, (8) *manesia.* (9) A stone of . . . . black like (10) stibium; when you grind it, it is black.

(11) *Magnes.* Magnesia viva; it is brought (i.e. imported ?).

(12) *Maknes.* When you scrape it, it is black.

(13) *Maknes* of man. It is brought (14) from India (?); when you scrape it (15) it exudes blood.

(16) To drug (?) your enemy; (17) an *apshe*-beetle (?); you burn it with styrax (?), (18) you pound it together with one drachma of apple (19) and a . . . . and you . . . . (20) and you put a . . . .

Verso Col. III.

(1) Medicament [for a catalepsy (?). Gall of ceras]tes, (2) pips (?) of western apples, herb of *klo.* (3) Grind them together, make into a ball, put it into wine (?), and drink (?).

(4) Lees of wine. (5) It is a white stone like (6) gal-

---

speaks of magnes mas and femina, the former being strongly magnetic and of reddish colour; and W. Max Müller has suggested to us that *n rm* may here be for ἀνδρεῖος.

l. 14. *ʿn-tsyke* = 'Ινδική (Max Müller). For Coptic forms of the name cf. Lemm., Kl. Kopt. Stud. ii. (Bull. de l'Acad. St. Petersbourg, x. 405).

l. 16. Probably the word is that in 23/1.

l. 17. ⲉⲡϣⲉ: cf. the beetle *ʿpšʾy·t* of ch. xxxvi of the Book of the Dead.

ll. 19–20. Reuvens' tracing and the facsimile show many scraps in the last lines, but they are too vague to be legible.

Col. III.

l. 1. Restored from 24/27.

l. 4. φέκλη, 'lees of wine,' 'salt of tartar' (Reuvens, Lettres, i. p. 51, who gives references).

l. 6. *gʿrbʾnʿ*: probably χαλβάνη, galbanum, the resinous sap of Bubo galbanum L., a plant of the fennel tribe used in medicine: see Diosc. iii. 87. Cf. also ϫⲁⲣⲃⲁⲛⲓ, Costum dulce, قسط حلو, Kircher, 186.

7. n sgewe p ky n rḫ-s
8. ar-f z nte-f n mʿ·t pe e-ʾr-k nt wʿ ḫm
9. ḥr mw nte-k ths-f a p ḫʿr
10. n wʿ rm n wʿ·t hte ḫm ḫr ʾr-f
11. ḫt(?) p ḫʿr
12. pe-f rn n mt·t wynn(?) *αφροσεληνον*
13. zʾḫ n ʿḥ wʿ ʾny pe e-f wbḫ
14. pḫr·t a ty ʾre s-ḥm·t mr ḥwt *θθ*·t n šnt·t
15. nt ḥr ʾby ths ḥnt-f (*sic*) nʾm-f
16. nte-k str erme t s-ḥm·t
17. zʾḫ n ʿḥ wʿ ʾny e-f wbḫ pe e-f m qty
18. yl e-f ḫyt n pke sp-sn m qty ʾrsenygwn

Verso Col. IV.

1. pḫre·t n msze e-f n mw
2. ḥm zf ḥr ʾrp e-f nfr
3. nte-k t ar-f bn-s šty n ḥ·t
4. nte-k ḫy(t ?) ḥm wʿ·t(?) zf(?) ḥr ʾrp
5. nte-k t ar-f a hw IV
6. *σαλαματρα*
7. wʿ·t ḥflelʿ ḫm
8. e-s n ʾwn n kʿrʿyne
9. e mn-te-s rt·t
10. tp n sr *κεφαλεκη* rn-f
11. wʿ sym e-f m qty wʿ·t bw n šmr ḥwt

---

l. 7. *sgewe.* Max Müller (Rec. tr., viii. 174) suggests that *σκευή* may have the meaning 'quick-lime,' though this sense is not found in the dictionaries.

l. 12. *wynn* (?): cf. 4/7.

αφροσεληνον = *ἀφροσέληνος*, Diosc. v. 158, another name for *σεληνίτης λίθος*, selenite or foliated sulphate of lime (Reuvens, Lettres, i. p. 51, with reffs.).

ll. 14–16. These lines are repeated in V. 13/10–11.

l. 18. *ʾrsenygwn* = *ἀρσενικόν*, yellow orpiment, i. e. sulphide of arsenic: cf. Diosc. v. 120. Alex. Trall., u. s., p. 632, mentions it in a prescription for gout.

banum. There is another sort which is made (7) into lime (?). The way to know it (8) that it is genuine is this. You grind a little (9) with water; you rub it on the skin (10) of a man for a short time; then it (11) removes the skin. (12) Its name in Greek (?) *ἀφροσέληνον*, (13) 'foam of the moon.' It is a white stone.

(14) A medicament for making a woman love a man: fruit (?) of acacia; (15) grind with honey, anoint his phallus with it, (16) you (*sic*) lie with the woman.

(17) 'Foam of the moon'; this is a white stone like (18) glass, (when ?) it is rubbed into fragments like orpiment.

VERSO COL. IV.

(1) Medicament for an ear that is watery. (2) Salt, heat with good wine; (3) you apply to it after cleansing (?) it first. (4) You scrape salt, heat with wine; (5) you apply to it for four days.

(6) *σαλαμάνδρα*, (7) a small lizard (8) which is of the colour of chrysolite. (9) It has no feet.

(10) 'Ram's horn,' *κεφαλική* is its name, (11) a herb which is like a wild fennel bush; (12) its leaf and its stem

---

COL. IV.

l. 1. The cross × at the beginning of sections in this and the next column seems intended to catch the eye in the crowded writing on the original—see the facsimile.

Flux from the ears: cf. Pap. Eb. 91/3.

l. 7. *wᶜ·t* (?). The sign in the original is like *ḥmt*, 'bronze,' and scarcely like *wᶜ·t*.

l. 8. *kᶜrᶜyne* = *καλαΐνη*, chrysolite, greenish-yellow: cf. GOODWIN, Cambridge Essays, 1852, p. 44 (B. M. Gr. Pap. XLVI. 197), and KRALL, Pap. Rain. Mitth., iv. 141.

l. 9. The *σαλαμάνδρα* of DIOSC. ii. 67 has feet.

l. 10. *tp n sr*: probably *κριός* DIOSC. ii. 126 = Cicer arietinum, PLINY, Nat. Hist. xviii. 32. See SPRENGEL, ad loc.

l. 11. *šmr ḥwt* = ϣⲁⲙⲁⲣϩⲟⲟⲩⲧ, شمار برى, TATTAM, Lex. from MS. Par. 44, p. 340. The Semitic word is interesting.

12. te-f gbe·t pe-f ẖ zqʿ m qty
13. p mr-rm e·ʾr-k nt-f e-f šwy nte-k sʿl-f(?)
14. nte-k ʾr-f n kser-ʿo-n nte-k ty-f a sẖ nb
15. ẖr lk-f ταμονιακη
16. ẖr rt-s m qty slom(?)
17. n te-f gbe·t ne-f pr·w t-qty·t
18. m qty tp n sr e-f θ
19. swre·t ẖm n pe-f pḥ(?)

Verso Col. V.

1. pẖre·t a(?) ʿrz snf mw n ḥʿp(?)-ʿo
2. ḥr ḥnqe nte-k t swr-s t s-ḥm·t nʾm-f n twe
3. e b-ʾr te-s wm ẖr ʿḥ-f
4. p ky a rẖ-s n s-ḥm·t z e-s ʾwr·t e·ʾr-k t ʾre
5. t s-ḥm·t ty-s mʾ a ḥr py sym nt ḥry ʿn
6. ḥr rhwe a·ʾre twe ẖp nte-k gm p sym
7. e-f šhlʿlt bn e-s a ʾwr·t e·ʾr-k gm·t-f
8. e-f wtwt e-s a ʾwr·t
9. pẖre·t a ẖt(?) snfe gbe·t n šyšʿ
10. gbe·t n ḥmt-ʿf e-f knn nt t
11. ar-k e·ʾr-k str erme t s-ḥm·t k·t ẖl
12. ẖzn sẖy n *ϭϩⲁⲥ* nt ḥr
13. ʾrp ʾs n sty t ar-k e·ʾr-k str erme-s
14. *ασφοδελος*
15. ke-z a mzwl hwt

---

l. 13. *p mr rm*: cf. φιλάνθρωπος, synonym of ἀπαρίνη, Diosc. iii. 94, a bedstraw 'cleavers' (προσέχεται δὲ καὶ ἱματίοις, Diosc. ib.).

šl-f (?): cf. ϣⲗϣⲉⲗ, cribrare (?).

l. 14. *kseron* = ξηρόν, as suggested by Max Müller, Rec. tr., viii. 173.

l. 15. ἀμμωνιακή: cf. Diod. iii. 88, and above.

l. 16. *slom*: perhaps = ϣⲗⲱⲙ, μολόχη, a mallow.

Col. V.

l. 1. *ḥʿp*(?)-*ʿo*, 'great Nile,' as name of some perhaps very juicy plant: cf. V. 33/5 for the reading.

ll. 4–8. A similar prescription in the nineteenth dynasty, Br., Rec., ii. pl. 107: cf. Renouf, A. Z., 1873, 123, for recent parallels.

are incised like (13) the 'love-man' plant; you pound it when it is dry, you gather (?) it, (14) you make it into a dry powder; you apply it to any wound; then it is cured.

Styrax, (16) it grows like *slom* (?) (17) as to its leaf; its seed is twisted (18) like the 'ram's horn' plant, it bearing (19) a small spine at its end.

Verso Col. V.

(1) A medicament to stop blood: juice of 'Great Nile (?)' plant (2) together with beer; you make the woman drink it in the morning (3) before she has eaten; then it stops.

(4) The way to know it of a woman whether she is enceinte: you make the woman (5) pass her water on this herb as above again (6) in the evening; when the morning comes and if you find the plant (7) scorched (?), she will not conceive; if you find it (8) flourishing, she will conceive.

(9) A medicament to stop blood: leaf of *sheisha*, (10) leaf of 'fly-bronze,' fresh; pound, put (it) (11) on you, you lie with the woman. Another: myrrh, (12) garlic, gall of a gazelle; pound with (13) old scented wine; put (it) on you, you lie with her.

(14) Asphodelos, (15) otherwise called 'wild onion.'

---

l. 4. *rḫ-s . . . ẕ*: a characteristic construction in demotic: cf. II Kham. vi. 21. 27.

l. 9. *ḫt* (?). This seems a curious use of the word.

l. 10. *ḥmt-ʿf*. This looks like the literal translation of some foreign name. It is clearly a plant-name; but χαλκόμυια, which it suggests, is found only as the name of a kind of fly: cf. our 'corn-bluebottle.'

l. 13. *ʾrp ʾs*, 'old wine,' frequently prescribed in Alex. Trall.: cf. Corp. Pap. Rain. II. 183.

n sty = οἶνος εὐώδης, Pap. Bibl. Nat. l. 1837.

l. 14. ἀσφοδελός, φύλλα ἔχων πράσῳ μεγάλῳ ὅμοια, Diosc. ii. 199.

l. 15. χελκεβε: evidently some bulbous plant like the last; called βοτανην χελκβει in Brit. Mus. Gr. Pap. XLVI. 70. Cf. perhaps γέλγις.

16. χελκεβε

17. ke-z ẖzn hwt

Verso Col. VI.

1. pẖre·t a t ꜥlk mw ḫr s-ḥm·t t ḥyt·t n pẖre·t ḥm ḥr nḥe nt . . . n-s(?) hw(?) II

2. bn-s p hw II pẖr n mḥ II·t psymytsy nte-k nt-f erme wꜥ ẖm n ꜣnzyr n s-nḥe

3. m šs sp-sn nte-k t nḥe n mꜥ·t ar-f e-f nfr erme wꜥ·t swḥ·t nte-k nt-w nte-k ꜣny wꜥ ꜥꜣl(?)

4. n ḥbs(?) n ꜥyw e-f šmꜥt nte-k sp-f n ty pẖre·t nte-s zqm n t s·t-eywe·t nte-s

5. yꜥ n ꜣrp e-f ⟨ne-⟩nfr nte-k t p ꜣ-ꜥo-l n pẖre·t a ḥry nꜣm-s nte-k sꜥ-ꜣy nꜣm-f n ẖn

6. a bl ẖn ty-s ꜥte·t n wꜥ·t hte·t ẖm n p smt n p mz n p ḥwt šꜥ nte t pẖre·t

7. ẖlẖl nte-k ꜣny·t-f a bl nte-k ḫꜥ-s šꜥ rhwe a·ꜣre rhwe ẖp e·ꜣr-k sp wꜥ·t qlme·t n ꜣby

8. n mꜥ·t nte-k ty-f a ḥry nꜣm-s šꜥ twe šꜥ hw III ke-z IV

Verso Col. VII.

1. k·t m-s-s mw n šwbe e-f lẖm znf wꜥ mw n msz n qle·t znf wꜥ a ẖ p znf

2. n wꜥ z nte-k t wꜥ wth n ꜣrp e-f ⟨ne-⟩nfr a ẖe t·w nte-s swr-f n mre·t e bnp-s

3. wm nt nb n p t bn-s zqm n t s·t-eywe·t a·ꜣr-s t ḥ·t a·ꜣre rhwe ẖp e·ꜣr-k t p ꜣl n

4. ꜣbye a ḥry nꜣm-s a ẖ p nt ḥry šꜥ hw VII k·t m-s-s e·ꜣr-k ꜣny wꜥ·t lwps nmy e·ꜣr-k t

---

Col. VI.

l. 1. The last signs must be *hw II*, 'two days': cf. l. 2. The group before this is unusual. The first sign may be ♈, the uterus, reading *k·t* or *ḥm·t* (?) (Kah. Pap. V. 2 note), and the last two might stand for *n-s*, 'to her,' or for *n mn*, 'daily.'

(16) Khelkebe, (17) otherwise called 'wild garlic.'

VERSO COL. VI.

(1) A remedy to cure water in a woman. The first remedy: salt and oil; pound; apply to the vulva (?) daily (?) two days.

(2) After the two days, the second remedy: white lead, you pound it with a little pigment from an oil-dealer (3) very carefully; you put true oil of fine quality to it, together with an egg and pound them; you take a strip (4) of linen cloth which is fine-spun (?); you dip it in this medicament. She must bathe in the bath, she must (5) wash in good wine; you put the medicated strip on her; you draw (?) it in (and) (6) out of her vulva for a short time, like the phallus of a man, until the medicament (7) spreads (?); you remove it, you leave her till evening; when evening comes, you dip a bandage (?) in genuine honey, (8) you put it on her until morning, for three, otherwise said four, days.

VERSO COL. VII.

(1) Another to follow it: juice of a cucumber which has been rubbed down, one ladleful (?), water of the ears of a *kle*-animal, one ladleful (?) like the ladle (2) of a (wine-) cup; you add a *uteh*-measure of good wine to them; and she drinks it at midday, before she has (3) eaten anything whatever, after bathing in the bath, which she has done before; when evening comes, you put the rag (?) (4) with honey on her as above for seven days.

---

l. 2. *psymy'tsy*, as REVILLOUT pointed out, is ψιμύθιον, 'white lead': cf. ZOEGA, 626; DIOSC. v. 103.

5. X n wth n ʾrp ʾs e-f hlk ar-s e·ʾr-k t wʿ·t ½qt·t n bšwš e-f knn a ḫ·t-f n *θ*

6. n twe šʿ mre·t nte-s zqm n t s·t-eywe nte-s ʾy a bl nte-s swr-f a·ʾre rhwe

7. ḫp e·ʾr-k t ʾbye a ḥry nʾm-s a ḫ p nt ḥry ʿn šʿ hw VII

VERSO COL. VIII.

1. *ποδακραν*
2. e·ʾr-k t ḥms p rm nte-k t š sʿn ḫr rt-f n p rm
3. nte-k t š . . . m-s-f a rt-f ḥr ʾ·t-f e·ʾr-k šn
4. p rm z ḥr-f stm šʿ hw III m-s-s e·ʾr-k ʾny qpqp
5. e·ʾr-k psy·t-f ḥr nḥe n qwpre e·ʾr-k ths rt-f
6. nʾm-f e·ʾr-k wḥ e·ʾr-k ʾny qntʾe Rʿqt ḥr ell šw
7. ḫr sym n gyz e·ʾr-k nt-w ḥr ʾrp e·ʾr-k slk-f n p bl
8. ny nte-k nyf m-s-f n r-k

VERSO COL. IX.

1. k·t
2. *ευφορβιου* I·t qt·t
3. *πεπτερεως* ½ qt·t
4. *περηθου* sttr·t(?) I·t
5. *αυταρχες* sttr·t ?) I·t
6. sttr·t(?) I·t *διοναπερον*
7. mn ʾrp sttr·t(?) VI

COL. VIII.

l. 5. *nḥe n qwpre* = *ἔλαιον κύπρινον*, DIOSC. i. 65; PLIN., H. N., 12. 51; 13. 1, 2; 23. 46, made from the seeds or leaves of *ἡ κύπρος*, ⲭⲟⲩⲡⲉⲣ, KIRCHER, p. 179, Lawsonia inermis, the henna of the Arabs. The red dye made from the leaves is now the commonest cosmetic in the East, but was perhaps little known anciently. The oil frequently occurs in prescriptions in ALEX. TRALL.

l. 7. *sym n gyz*: lit. 'hand-plant,' with gloss ⲡⲛⲧⲁⲕⲧⲁⲗⲟⲥ, which no doubt stands for *πεντεδάκτυλος*, DIOSC. iv. 42 = *πεντάφυλλον* (potentilla). According to LENZ, p. 702, it is still called in Greece by both names. Cf. PARTHEY, Zauberpap., ii. 34. 40; Pap. bibl. nat. 287.

ll. 7–8. *n p bl ny*: a curious construction, if correct.

COL. IX.

l. 3. *πεπτερεως* for *πεπέρεως*, 'pepper' (REUVENS, Lettres, i. p. 50), cf.

Another to follow: you take a new dish; you put (5) ten *uteh*-measures of old sweet wine on it; you put a half *kite* of fresh rue on it from (6) dawn till midday; let her bathe in the bath, and come out and drink it. When it is evening (7) you put honey on her as above again for seven days.

VERSO COL. VIII.

(1) Gout. (2) You make the man sit down; you place clay under the feet of the man; (3) you put .... to it (?), his feet resting on it; you ask (4) the man, saying, 'Has it hearkened?' for three days. Thereafter you take an ant (?), (5) you cook it in oil of henna; you anoint his feet (6) with it. When you have finished, you take Alexandrian figs and dried grapes (7) and potentilla; you pound them with wine; you anoint him besides (?) (8) these; and you blow on him with your mouth.

VERSO COL. IX.

(1) Another: (2) 1 *kite* of Euphorbia, (3) ½ *kite* of pepper, (4) 1 stater (?) of pyrethrum (?), (5) 1 stater (?) of adarces, (6) native sulphur, 1 stater (?), (7) any wine 6

Diosc. ii. 188; and for its use as a magico-medical ingredient, WESSELY, N. Gr. Zauberpap., p. 25; and below V. 14/3; SIGISMUND, Aromata, p. 41.

l. 4. *περηθου* = *πυρέθρου*, apparently an umbellifer hot to the taste: cf. Diosc. iii. 78.

l. 5. *αυταρχες* = *ἀδάρκης*, Diosc. v. 136, a salt efflorescence on marsh plants. It is noteworthy that these four ingredients, spurge, pepper, *πύρεθρον*, and *ἀδάρκης*, are all found with many others in a prescription for gout given by ALEX. TRALL., lib. xi. p. 628.

l. 6. *διονιαπερον* = *θεῖον ἄπυρον* (REUVENS, Lettres, i. p. 50), native sulphur. For its use cf. Brit. Mus. Gr. Pap. CXXI. l. 168; ZOEGA, 626 **ⲑⲏⲛ ⲡ̄ⲁⲧⲱϣⲙ**. The **ⲟⲛⲁⲡⲉⲣⲟⲛ** of KIR. 203 = sulphur rubrum, is doubtless a corruption of the above.

8. nḫe n mᶜ·t . . . ntek nt-w
9. nte-k ᵓr-w n wᶜ·t splelyn t a p mᶜ
10. nt šn n p rm

Verso Col. X.

1. ke s a(?) rt-f n p-etᵓgrwn
2. e·ᵓr-k sẖ ny rn-w a wᶜ pq
3. n ḥt nge tren e·ᵓr-k ty-f
4. a wᶜ ẖᶜr n ᵓywr nte-k mr-f a rt-f
5. n p rm n rn-f *δερμα ελαφιον* n t rt·t II·t
6. **ⲑⲉⲙⲃⲁⲣⲁⲑⲉⲙ**
7. **ⲟⲩⲣⲉⲙⲃⲣⲉⲛⲟⲩⲧⲓⲡⲉ**
8. **ⲁⲓⲟⲭⲑⲟⲩ**
9. **ⲥⲉⲙⲙⲁⲣⲁⲑⲉⲙⲙⲟⲩ**
10. **ⲛⲁⲓⲟⲟⲩ** my lk mn a·ms mn
11. n šn nb nt ẖn ne-f pt·w te-f rt·w II·t
12. ẖr ᵓ -k-f e ᶜḥ my

Verso Col. XI.

1. pẖre·t n rt(?) . . .
2. ẖzn ᵓlbwnt
3. . . . . . ᵓs
4. nḫe n mᶜ·t nt ths-f
5. nᵓm-f e-f šwy e·ᵓr-k yᶜ-f
6. n mw qbe ẖr lk-f
7. pẖre·t n rt·t e-f sk m šs sp-sn nfr sp-sn
8. e·ᵓr-k yᶜ rt-f n mw n šwbe·t
9. nte-k ẖyt-f m šs sp-sn ḥr rt-f
10. k·t ᵓlqw n . . . *θθ* n šnt·t
11. šew nt t ar-f

---

l. 9. *splelyn*: cf. Zoega, 630 **ⲥⲡⲉⲗⲉⲗⲓⲛ**, apparently a 'plaster' or 'poultice,' probably = *σπλήν, σπληνίον*.

staters(?); (8) genuine oil . . . . you pound them, (9) you make them into a poultice; apply to the part (10) which is painful of the man.

Verso Col. X.

(1) Another talisman for the foot of the gouty man: (2) you write these names on a strip (3) of silver or tin; you put it (4) on a deer-skin; you bind it to the foot (5) of the man named, *δέρμα ἐλάφιον*, with the two feet. (6) '*θεμβαραθεμ* (7) *ουρεμβρενουτιπε* (8) *αιοχθου* (9) *σεμμαραθεμμου* (10) *ναιοου*. Let N. son of N. recover (11) from every pain which is in his feet and two legs.' (12) You do it when the moon is in the constellation of Leo.

Verso Col. XI.

(1) Remedy for a . . . . foot(?): (2) garlic, frankincense, (3) old . . . . (4) genuine oil; pound (together); anoint him (5) with it. When it is dry, you wash it (6) with cold water; then he recovers.

(7) Remedy for a foot which is much sprained(?); very excellent. (8) You wash his foot with juice of cucumber; (9) you rub it well on his foot.

(10) Another: sycomore figs(?) of . . .; fruit(?) of acacia, (11) persea fruit(?); pound (together); apply (it) to him.

Col. X.

l. 1. *p-ei'grwn* = *ποδαγρῶν*.

l. 2. Cf. Alex. Trall, lib. xi. p. 656, for a similar method of dealing with gout. Such charms are as common in ancient times as in modern.

l. 3. Tin is frequently used for similar purposes: cf. Wessely, N. Gr. Zauberpap., p. 11.

l. 5. *n t rt·t II·t*, that is with the two feet of the skin.

l. 12.  the knife is the sign of the Zodiac for Leo (Brugsch, Nouv. Rech., p. 22, Stobart tables, &c.): cf. 5/11 and note 1/12.

Col. XI.

l. 10. *twne* is perhaps the reading of the imperfect group.

Verso Col. XII.

1. ke-z wr šer'y(?)

2. 'nk pe wr š'(?)-'y nt 'r ḥyq a t rpy·t 'o·t nb qwow(?)

3. ll mw ll p mw n sn-t(?) p nt n r-y p 't n Ḥ·t-ḥr·t šw mr

4. p nt n ḥt-y ḥt-y pz pe ḥt mr p(?) wḫe e·ḫr 're 'm·t

5. 'y-f a 'm-mw wḫe e·ḫr 're wnš·t 'y a wnš wḫe e·ḫr 're wḥr·t 'y·t-f

6. a wḥr p wḫ nt a p ntr šr spd(?) 'y-y·t-f a mw-s·t-s e-f 'n·n' a t sbt·t n nyn're-t-s

7. a wḥ mw n [p]e-f ntr pe-f ḥry pe-f y'h-'o s'b'h-'o pe-f glemwr' mwse plerwbe s my

8. 'br's'ks senkl'y my 're mn a·ms mn 'y-f a mn a·ms mn

9. my 'r-s w' pz w' mr w' lyb 'o . . . . . e-s qte m-s-f a m' nb p ḫyt

10. n y'h-'o s'b'hw h-'o-ry-'o-n(?) p'n-t-rg'-t-r 'n-t-rg'-t-r 'rb'

11. nth'l' th'l-'o th'l'ks z te-y ḥwy ḫyt a·'r-tn

Verso Col. XIII.

1. n n ntr·w 'y·w n Kmy mḥ t·t-tn n st·t sḥt·t ⟨bk-f⟩ ḥwy·t-f a p ḥt n mn a·ms mn

2. hbq n'm-s nge 'yḫ θ n ty-s qt·t mge rm 'mnt my 're p 'y

Col. XII.

l. 1. A gloss on l. 2.

l. 2. *qwow* (the first *w* may be a determinative ᒣ). Brugsch, Dict. Geog., 819, identifies this with the modern Qau (Antaeopolis). But Qau is derived from Copt. ⲧⲕⲱⲟⲩ, which in its turn is perhaps from the hierogl. *dw-q'*.

l. 3. *p 't*: obesity is a mark of beauty in the East.

l. 5. *'y-f*: cf. note 21/35. *'y* in this line must be an error for *'y-f*. *'y·t-f* at the end of the line must be the same word: cf. Boh. ⲁⲓϥ and ⲁⲓⲧⲟⲩ, and *ḥsy-k* 20/20, beside *ḥsy·t-k* 20/19.

VERSO COL. XII.

(1, 2) 'I am the great Shaay (otherwise said, the great Sheray ?), who makes magic for the great Triphis, the lady of Koou (?) (3) Lol Milol, the water of thy brother (?) is that which is in my mouth, the fat of Hathor, worthy of love, is (4) that which is in my heart; my heart yearns, my heart loves. The (?) longing such as a she-cat (5) feels for a male cat, a longing such as a she-wolf feels for a he-wolf, a longing such as a bitch feels for (6) a dog, the longing which the god, the son of Sopd (?), felt for Moses going to the hill of Ninaretos (7) to offer water unto his god, his lord, his Yaho, Sabaho, his Glemura-muse, Plerube . . S Mi (8) Abrasax, Senklai—let N. daughter of N. feel it for N. son of N.; (9) let her feel a yearning, a love, a madness great . . . . . ., she seeking for him (going) to every place. The fury (10) of Yaho, Sabaho, Horyo . . Pantokrator, Antorgator, (11) Arbanthala, Thalo, Thalax: for I cast fury upon you

VERSO COL. XIII.

(1) 'of the great gods of Egypt: fill your hands with flames and fire; employ it, cast it on the heart of N. daughter of N. (2) Waste her away, thou (?) demon; take her sleep, thou (?) man of Amenti; may the house

---

l. 6. Cf. Μωσῆς ὁ μέγας φίλος ὑψίστοιο, quoted from the Orac. Sibyll. 2. 247 by PARTHEY, 2 Gr. Zauberpap., p. 58. *s·t* is ***ch**, 'seat.'

l. 7. *wḥ mw*: very common as a title equivalent to χοαχύτης.

[*p*]*e-f*: this correction of the text seems almost certain.

plerwbe perhaps = πλήρωμα.

COL. XIII.

l. 2. *nge . . . mge* must be **ⲛϭⲓ : ⲛϫⲉ** before the subject, though here before the imperative, which is not allowed in Coptic (W. MAX MÜLLER, Rec. tr., xiii. 151).

3. n py-s yt ty-s mw·t n ny-s mʿ nte e-s n ḫe·t-w . . . ʿš e h-ʿo-h n st·t

4. ar-s e-s z ze n-ny e-s ⟨ʿḥ⟩ qrmrm n bl z ne-ʾy z ʾnk wʿ·t ryt·t n Gb

5. Ḥr r(?)-ʿo-n p rʿ rn-yt prq rn-s a bl n Kmy šʿ hw XL ʾbt XXXIII CLXXV n hw p zq-r n VI n ʾbt

6. gyre thee(?) pysytw ek-ʿo(?)-ymy ʾtʿm sp VII hs n ***ⲙⲉⲥⲉϩ*** wʿ ḫm n mw·t n ʿo·t

7. ḥnʿ sʾsmrym(?) ʾp·t VII·t n hs n ***ϭϩⲉⲥ*** sḫy n ***ⲃⲉⲉⲙⲡⲉ*** n ḥwt ḥ·t n yp·t n nḥe

8. nte-k st·t-w n glm n mḥ nte-k ʿš ar-f n sp VII n hw VII nte-k ths ḥn·t-k

9. nʾm-f nte-k str erme t s-ḥm·t nte-k ths ḥt-s n t s-ḥm·t ʿn

10. a t ʾre s-ḥm·t mr py (*sic*) hy *θθ*·t n šnt·t nt ḥr ʾbye nte-k ths ḥn·t-k nʾm-f

11. nte-k str erme t s-ḥm·t a t ʾre s-ḥm·t mr nq-s hbete n r-f n wʿ ḫtr ḫwt nte-k ths

12. ḥn·t-k nʾm-f nte-k str erme t s-ḥm·t

Verso Col. XIV.

1. a t . . . . . .
2. ʾbn (*δραχμη*) I
3. ***ⲡⲓⲡⲓⲣ*** (*δραχμη*) I
4. mḥ n knwt(?) e-f šwy (*δραχμη*) IV
5. sʾterw (*δραχμη*) IV
6. nt n pḫre šwy a·ʾry yp·t nʾm-f
7. a ḫ p nt e·ʾr-k swne nʾm-f erme s-ḥm·t nb

---

l. 3. *n ḫe·t-w.* Note this Coptic form **ⲛϧⲏⲧⲟⲩ** instead of the usual demotic *ḫn-w* lost in Coptic. In this particular phrase, however, *nʾm-w*, not *ḫn-w*, is usual.

l. 4. *n-ny . . . ne-ʾy.* It is suggested that, in spite of the strange orthography, **ⲛⲁⲓ** misereri is here intended.

l. 5. It is difficult to see what is intended by the numbers.

l. 6. The first words of this line have been read by Pleyte (P. S. B. A.,

(3) of her father and her mother (and) the places where she is .....; call out "There is flame of fire (4) to her," while she speaks, saying, "Have mercy(?)," she standing outside and murmuring "Have mercy (?)." For I am an agent (?) of Geb, (5) Horus Ron Phre is my name, tear her name out of Egypt for forty days, thirty-three months, 175 days, the complement of six months, (6) Gyre, Thee, Pysytu, Ekoimi, Atam.' Seven times. Dung of crocodile, a little placenta (?) of a she-ass, (7) together with sisymbrium, seven *oipi* of antelope's dung, the gall of a male goat, and first-fruits of oil; (8) you heat them with stalks of flax. You recite to it seven times for seven days; you anoint your phallus (9) with it, you lie with the woman; you anoint the breast (?) of the woman also.

(10) To cause a woman to love her husband: pods of acacia, pound with honey, anoint your phallus with it (11) and lie with the woman.

To make a woman *amare coitum suum.* Foam of a stallion's mouth. Anoint your phallus with it and lie with the woman.

VERSO COL. XIV.

(1) To make ...... (2) alum, 1 drachm, (3) pepper, 1 drachm, (4) *mhnknwt*, dried, 4 drachms, (5) satyrium, 4 drachms. (6) Pound together into a dry medicament; do your business with it (7) like that which you know with any woman.

---

v. 152) as κύριε θεῖε πιστὲ ἐξίημι Ἀδάμ, 'O divine faithful Lord, I cast out Adam.'

l. 10. *py*: error for *py-s*.

COL. XIV.

l. 5. *s'terw* = σατυρίου, MAX MÜLLER, Rec. tr., viii. 176–177. For the plant (which is not identified) see DIOSC. iii. 133. It is a venereal stimulant.

VERSO COL. XV.

1. n rn·w n n ntr·w nt ḫr wḫe-k-s e·ʾr-k ʾn·nʿ(?) a ʾny ʿze a ḫn swr(?)

2. mʿskelly mʿskell-ʿo phnwgentʿbʾ-ʿo

3. hreks(?)sygth-ʿo perygthe-ʿo-n perypegʿneks

4. ʿre-ʿo-bʿsʿgrʿ ke-zm ʿo-bʾsʿgrʿ

5. py rn ḫr z-k-f ḥr t ḥ·t n zy e-f n·nʿ a byk e-tbe n rn·w

6. n **ⲇⲓⲟⲥⲕⲟⲣⲟⲥ** nt n ḫn nte-f wzy e·ʾr-k ʿš-w a p z(?) n **ⲁⲇⲱⲛⲁⲓ** nt sḫ

7. n bl e-f a ʾr wʿ·t bkʿy·.(?) ʿo·t e-f ʾny ʿze a ḫn

VERSO COL. XVI.

1. ʾrmy-ʿo-wt (ke-zm **ⲁⲣⲙⲓⲟⲩⲑ**) sythʿny wthʿny

2. ʾryʾmwsy s-ʿo-br-tt byrbʾt my[s]yrythʿt

3. a·ms-thʿrmythʿt a·wy mn a·ms mn a bl ḫn ny-s ʿy·w

4. nt e-s nʾm-w a ʿy nb nte mn a·ms mn nʾm-w e-s mr[·t]-f e-s lby m-s-f

5. e-s ʾr n p šp n ḥt-f n nw nb e·ʾr-k sḫ ny n rʾw ḫl a wʿ·t tys·t

6. n š-stn e-s wʿb nte-k ty-s a wʿ ḫbs nmy e-f wʿb e-f mḥ n nḥe n mʿ·t n ⟨p⟩

7. pe-k ʿy n θ n rhwe a twe e·ʾr-k gm p fʿe n t s-ḥm·t a ty-f a ḫn p sʿl nfr-f (*sic*)

COL. XV.

l. 1. GROFF has written an elaborate study on this column in Mém. de l'Inst. Égypt. iii. 377; many of his readings are wrong, but it remains very difficult to read and interpret.

wḫe-k (?): the second sign is imperfect; *wšte-k* (?).

ʾn-nʿ (?): cf. l. 5, *n-nʿ* (?).

ʿze: cf. 3/29.

swr (?). Can this be really a trace of *hn*, to be restored *n šn hn*, 'by vase-questioning.'

l. 2. For a similar list of names see Pap. Gr. Lugd., Pap. V., col. 9, l. 10.

l. 5. Can **ⲉⲧⲃⲉ** have the meaning 'instead of'?

l. 6. The Dioscuri were the patron gods of sailors.

VERSO COL. XV.

(1) The names of the gods whom you want (?) when you are about (?) to bring in a criminal [by vase-questioning?] (2) Maskelli, Maskello, Phnoukentabao, (3) Hreksyktho, Perykthon, Perypeganex, (4) Areobasagra, otherwise Obasagra.

(5) This name you utter it before a ship that is about (?) to founder on account of the names (6) of Dioscoros, which are within, and it is safe.

You recite them to the bowl (?) of Adonai, which is written (7) outside. It will do a mighty work (?) bringing in a criminal.

VERSO COL. XVI.

(A row of figures, viz. 3 scarabs, 3 hawks, and 3 goats.)

(1) 'Armioout (otherwise Armiouth), Sithani, Outhani, (2) Aryamnoi, Sobrtat, Birbat, Misirythat, (3) Amsietharmithat: bring N. daughter of N. out of her abodes (4) in which she is, to any house and any place which N. son of N. is in; she loving him and craving for him, (5) she making the gift of his desire (?) at every moment.' You write this in myrrh ink on a strip (6) of clean fine linen, and you put it in a clean new lamp, which is filled with genuine oil, (7) in your house from evening till morning. If you find a hair of the woman to put in the wick, it is excellent.

Bowl (?) of Adonai. Perhaps reference may be made to the familiar story of Nectanebus and the magic bowl in Pseudo-Callisthenes.

l. 7. *n bl*: see note on 18/6.

COL. XVI.

l. 7. For the use of hair in Egyptian magic, cf. the actual specimen mentioned by CHABAS, Pap. Mag. Harris, p. 184.

nfr-f or *nfr pe*: cf. 23/8.

VERSO COL. XVII.

1. wʿ r a ʾny [s-ḥm·t?] n ḥwt a hb rswe·t ke-z a pre rswe·t ʿn

2. . . . .

3. e·ʾr-k sẖ ny a wʿ·t gbe·t n ʾqyr nte-k ẖʿ ẖr zz-k e·ʾr-k n·q⟨te⟩·t·k ẖr

4. ʾr-f rswe·t nte-f hb rswe·t e-f ẖp e·ʾr-k a ʾr-f a hb rswe·t e·ʾr-k ty-s a r-f n wʿ qs

5. ẖr ʾr-f ʾny s-ḥm·t ʿn e·ʾr-k sẖ py rn a t kbe·t n ʿqyr n snf n *ⲛⲁ* nge *ⲕⲟⲩⲕⲟⲩet* (*sic*)

6. nte-k t p fʿe n t s-ḥm·t a ẖn t gbe·t nte-k ty-s a r-f n p qs nte-k sẖ n p ʾytn n py rn z a·wy

7. mn t šr·t n mn a p ʿy n p mʿ n str nte mn p šr n t mn nʾm-f

8. *εστι δε και αγωγιμων*

VERSO COL. XVIII.

1. ⲏⲣⲟⲩⲃⲓⲑⲟⲩ

2. ⲉⲕⲧⲟⲩⲗⲁ

3. ⲏⲣⲣⲉⲫⲉⲁⲓ

4. wnḥ-k aʾr-y t mn p ntr

5. nte-k sze erme-y ẖr p nt e-y šn·t-k

6. ẖrr-f n mt·t mʿ·t e bnp-k z n-y

7. mt·t n ʿze *ⲕⲣⲟⲕⲟⲥ* . . . II

8. *ⲥⲧⲏⲙⲙⲛⲕⲃⲧ* . . . II

9. nt ḥr snf n *ϩ(?)[ⲁ]ⲛⲧⲟⲩⲥ*

10. ʾr m bnn·t nte-k ḥyt-f ḥr ʾrte

11. n ms-ḥwt t a yr·t-f n wnm nte-k ʿš(?) ar-f(?)

12. a ḥr ⟨p⟩ ẖbs nb nge p ẖpš n rhwe

VERSO COL. XIX.

1. wʿ r n ʾny s-ḥm·t(?) a bl n py-s ʿy ẖr ʾny-k wʿ *. . . . ⲥⲉ*

COL. XVII.

l. 8. *αγωγιμων* = *ἀγώγιμον*. Cf. REUVENS, Lettres, i. p. 50 and refs. there; also Brit. Mus. Gk. Pap. CXXI. 295, 300, and p. 115.

VERSO COL. XVII.

(1) A spell to bring [a woman] to a man (and ?) to send dreams, otherwise said, to dream dreams, also.

(2) (A line of symbols or secret signs.)

(3) You write this on a rush-leaf and you place (it) under your head; you go to sleep; then (4) it makes dreams and it sends dreams. If you will do it to send dreams, you put it (the leaf) on the mouth of a mummy. (5) It brings a woman also; you write this name on the rush-leaf with the blood of a . . . . or a hoopoe (?); (6) and you put the hair of the woman in the leaf, and put it on the mouth of the mummy; and you write on the earth with this name, saying: 'Bring (7) N. daughter of N. to the house in the sleeping-place in which is N. son of N.' (8) Now it is also an *αγωγιμον*.

VERSO COL. XVIII.

(1) '**ⲏⲣⲟⲩⲃⲓⲑⲟⲩ** (2) **ⲉⲕⲧⲟⲩⲗⲁ** (3) **ⲏⲣⲣⲉⲫⲉⲇⲓ.**

(4) 'Reveal thyself to me, god N., (5) and speak to me concerning that which I shall ask thee, (6) truthfully, without telling me (7) falsehood.' Saffron, 2 (measures), (8) stibium of Koptos, 2 (measures), (9) pound together with blood of a lizard, (10) make into a ball, and rub it with milk (11) of one who has born a male child. Put (it) in his right eye; you make invocation (?) to him (?) (12) before any lamp or the 'Shoulder' constellation in the evening.

VERSO COL. XIX.

(1) A spell for bringing a woman out of her house.

COL. XVIII.

l. 8. ***ⲥⲧⲏⲙⲙⲛⲕⲃⲧ*** = *στιμμὶ κοπτικόν.* Cf. Brit. Mus. Gk. Pap. XLVI. 67, CXXI. 336; Pap. Bibl. Nat. l. 1071.

l. 10. *rte n ms-ḥwt*: common in Old Egyptian prescriptions. Cf. *γάλα ἀρρενοτόκου γυναικός*, Diosc. v. 99, likewise in connexion with *στιμμί.*

2. n ʾm·t (*sic*) n ḥwt nte-k t šwy-f nte-k ʾny wʿ qbḥ(?) . . . .

3. n ḥsy nte-k mnqe wʿ kswr e ḫ·t-f šfe n nb . . . .

4. n my e(?) r-w wn e ḥr-f n wn a wn nʾm-w e·ʾr-k t n(?) nk . . . . ḥr(?)-f

5. e·ʾr-k wḫ a ʾny s-ḥm·t n-k n nw nb e·ʾr-k wḥ p kswr n p ḥrw n wʿ ḫbs

6. e-f mḥ e·ʾr-k z ar-f(?) z a·wy mn t šr mn a py mʿ

7. nt e-y nʾm-f n tkr ḫn ny wne·t·w n p-hw ḫr ʾw-s ty hte·t

VERSO COL. XX.

1. a ty lk yr·t-bn(?) n rm . . . . ʾMn py ḥwt ḫy py ḥwt ʾkš ʾr ʾy a ḫry

2. n mrwe a Kmy gm Ḥr pe šr e-f fy·t-f a hn rt-f a·e-f škʿ-f

3. a zz-f n III r n mt·t ʾkš e-f gm mn a·ms mn a·e-f fy·t-f a hn

4. rt-f a·e-f škʿ-f a zz-f n III r n mt·t ʾkš g(?)ntyny·-tnty

5. nʾ qwqwby . . . khe ʾkhʾ

6. a wʿ ḫm n nḫe nte-k t ḥm ḫlyn ar-f nte-k ths p rm nt ḫr yr·t-bn(?) nʾm-f

7. nte-k sḫ ny ʿn a wʿ zm nmy nte-k ʾr-f n mze a ḫe·t-f nte-k py byl n t p·t n n sḫ . . . .

COL. XIX.

l. 2. *qbḥ*: the reading of the first sign is doubtful. The determinative would lead one to expect *ʾbḥ*, 'tooth,' but it is difficult to read so. *qbḥ* would perhaps be **κοϩϩ**, 'tendo,' or it may be the name of some animal which is to be drowned.

COL. XX.

l. 1. *yr·t* (?), followed by det. or word-sign for evil, 'bad eye,' which might be either ophthalmia or 'evil-eye,' **ειερϩοονε**. The prescription perhaps favours the former.

l. 2. Amon was the god of Meroe: cf. II Kham. iv. 15.

You take a . . . . (2) of a wild she-cat; you dry it; you take a heel-tendon (?) [of a (?) . . . . which has been (?)] (3) drowned; you fashion a ring, the body (? bezel) of which is variegated (?) with gold [in the form of two (?)] (4) lions, their mouths being open, the face of each being turned to the other; you put some . . . . its face (?). (5) If you wish to bring a woman to you at any time, you place the ring on the upper part of a lamp, (6) which is lighted; you say, 'Bring N. daughter of N. to this place (7) in which I am, quickly in these moments of to-day.' Then she comes at once.

VERSO COL. XX.

(1) To heal ophthalmia (?) in a man. '[Ho ?] Amon, this lofty male, this male of Ethiopia, who came down (2) from Meroe to Egypt, he finds my son Horus betaking himself as fast as his feet move (?), and he injured (?) him (3) in his head with three spells in Ethiopian language, and he finds N. son of N. and carries him as fast as his feet move (?), (4) and injures his head with three spells in Ethiopian language: Gentini, Tentina, (5) Kwkwby, [Ak]khe, Akha.' (6) (Say it) to a little oil: add salt and nasturtium seed to it, you anoint the man who has ophthalmia (?) with it. (7) You also write this on a new papyrus; you make it into a written amulet on his body:—'Thou art this eye of heaven' in the writings (followed by an eye with rays, as drawn in the papyrus).

The spell seems very corrupt, but some sense may be made of it by supplying *e-f* before *gm*.

l. 3. *a hn rt-f*, 'according to the movement (?) of his feet.'

l. 6. *ḫlyn*, ϣⲗⲁⲉⲓⲛ, Sah. in Peyron = *κερδαμων* (*κάρδαμον*, DIOSC. ii. 184) *κερδαμωμο* (*καρδάμωμον*, ib. i. 5).

l. 7. *mze*: cf. II Kham. ii. 26; P. S. B. A., 1899, p. 269; perhaps connected with *μαγία*.

Verso Col. XXI.

1. . . . .
2. . . . . . .
3. . . . . . .
4. . . . . t-nḥs(?) ʿnḫ-ʾm
5. nt ʾr(?) . . . . n p yʿr
6. . . . . smt yr·t-k nʾm-f

Verso Col. XXII.

1. . . . . . . [e-f] znt
2. tey-s [p kys nt ḫr ʾr-k (?)] ty-f a yr·t-k e·ʾr-k ʾn-
3. nʿ a p hn n šn wʿe·t-k wyt
4. ms-tme qs(?)-ʿnḫ s(?) . . . ḥrrw n šr-ʿo·t(?)
5. km nte *ⲉⲣⲉⲕⲟ(?)ⲥ* pe snf n qwqwpt
6. nt . . . m bnn nte-k smt yr·t-k nʾm-f ḥr mw
7. n elle n(?) Kmy(?) ḥr st n t(?)-nḥs ḫr
8. nw-k a t ḫyb·t n ntr nb ntr·t nb
9. . . . . . -f te-y ʿš n-tn n ntr-w ʿy nt ḫʿ-w erme p rʿ t(?)semwks
10. ʾmp(?) . . . . p-yʿm·enpʿyʿ yb-ʿo-th yʿe sʿbʿ-ʿo-th
11. a·[wn] n-y sp-sn n ntr·w ʿy nt ḫʿ-w erme p rʿ my wn yr·t a p
12. [wy]n nte-y mʾ p ntr nt šn n p-hw ys sp-sn ze p s . . . . ʾblʿ
13. n[ʿth]ʿnʿlbʿ p ntr wr mʿrʿrʿ ʿn-t-ne ʾbyʾth
14. n . . . . snn(?) . . ʿe n-t-sʿtrʿperqmʿe Wsr ly
15. l[ʾ]m rn-f a·wn n-y sp-sn n ntr·w ʿy my wn yr·t a p wyn
16. nt[e-y] mʾ p ntr nt šn n p-hw a·wn n-y sp-sn te-y ḥwy ḫyt a·ʾr-tn n p ntr ʿo sp-sn
17. . . . nte(?) ne-ʿy(?) te-f pḥt·t nt ʿnḫ šʿ z·t my pḥt·w sp-sn n p rnn

---

Col. XXII.

l. 4. *šr-ʿo·t km·t* = the edible seed *šr·t km·t*, E. E. F. Paheri, Pl. III. top line; Brugsch, Wtb., 1405: cf. the white *šr·t ḥz·t* from which beer was

Verso Col. XXI.

(1–3) (Fragments) (4) . . . . . of Ethiopia (?), *ankh-amu* flowers, (5) pound, make (?) . . . . of the river, (6) . . . . paint your eye with it.

Verso Col. XXII.

(1) . . . . tested. (2) Behold [the ointment which you] put on your eye when you (3) approach the vessel of inquiry alone: green eye-paint, (4) stibium, *qes-ankh* (?), amulet of . . . . , flowers of black *sher-o* (?) (5) which are beans (?), blood of hoopoe, (6) pound, [make] into a ball, and paint your eye with it, together with juice (7) of Egyptian (?) grapes, and *set*-stone (?) of Ethiopia; then (8) you see the shadow of every god and every goddess.

(9) Its . . . . . . 'I invoke you (plur.), ye great gods who shine with the sun, Themouks (10) Amp . . . Piam, Enpaia, Eiboth, Eiae, Sabaoth, (11) open (?) to me (*bis*), ye great gods who shine with the sun, let my eyes be opened to the (12) light, and let me see the god who inquires to-day, hasten (*bis*); for the protection . . . . (13) Ablanathanalba, the mighty god, Marara, Atone, Abeiath, (14) N . . . . Senen (?), [Psh]oi, Zatraperkemei, Osiris, (15) Lilam is his name. Open to me (*bis*), ye great gods, let my eyes be opened to the light, (16) and let me see the god who inquires to-day. Open to me (*bis*). I cast the fury on you (plur.) of the great (*bis*) god, (17) . . . . whose might is great (?),

---

prepared, ib., Suppl., 1200. Here the former is made equivalent to ***ерекос***, presumably *ἄρακος* (= Vicia cracca L., common vetch according to Lenz, Bot. d. alten Griechen u. Römer, p. 726), which was a common cultivated plant in Egypt. Cf. Oxyrhynchus Pap. II. cclxxx. 16, Tebtunis Pap. pass.; in Coptic Corp. Pap. Rain. II. p. 176 (**аракı**), Crum Copt. MSS. Fay. p. 78 verso, l. 35 (**арака**).

l. 7. *elle n*(?) *Kmy*(?): cf. **ελελκημε**, 'black grapes,' but see 29/28, which is practically a parallel.

18. . . . . sp-sn p rn n p [ntr ?] . . . . a·wn n-y sp-sn

19. [n ntr·w] ʿy nt ḫʿ-w erme p rʿ my wn [yr·t a p wyn nt]e-y

20. [mʾ p ntr] nt šn n p-hw ys sp-sn . . . sp . . .

Verso Col. XXIII.

1. . . . .
2. nt . . . . .
3. ḫr(?) . . . . .
4. ke . . . . .
5. . . . ⲛⲁϫ . . . .
6. ʾny . . . . .
7. pr·w . . . .
8. . . . .
9. ke . . . . . ʿn
10. hs . . . . . šwy e-f wš . . . II
11. nt [ḥr nḥe(?) n q]wpr ḥr ʾby
12. ths [ḥn·t-k(?)] nʾm-f nte-k str erme-s

Verso Col. XXIV.

1. . . . .
2. . . . . . ar-f nte-k . . . .
3. . . . . . n š-stn ar-f e py(?) rnn III sḫ ar-f
4. . . . . ḥr ḫl nte-k θ-r-f nte-k wḥ-f
5. . . . . . zz-k nte-k ʿš-w ar-f ʿn n sp IX
6. . . . . . ḫbs ḫr ʾr-k-f n p nw n p θ III n rhwe
7. . . . . . ·t-k z-mt·t y-ʿo-bʾsʾwmpth-ʿo
8. [ghr-ʿo-me lw]ghʿr my wn yr·t a bl
9. [n mt·t] mʿ·t ḫr t mn t mt·t nt e-y šll ḫrr-s ty
10. [n p-hw n] mt·t mʿ·t n wš n z n-k mt·t n ʿze
11. ⲓⲱⲃⲁⲥⲁⲟⲩⲙⲡⲧⲑⲱⲭⲣⲱⲙⲉⲗⲟⲩⲭⲁⲣ
12. my wn yr·t a bl n mt·t mʿ·t ḫr t mn t mt·t nt e-y šll
13. ḫrr-s ty n p-hw

who lives for ever, give power to the name (?) (18) .... the name of the god (?) .... open to me (*bis*), (19) ye great [gods] who shine with the sun, let [my eyes] be opened [to the light, and let] me (20) [see the god] who answers to-day, hasten (*bis*) ... times ...'

Verso Col. XXIII.

(Lines 1–9 fragments.) (10) dung ..... dried and burnt, 2 (measures), (11) pound (with oil of) henna and honey, (12) anoint [your phallus] therewith, and lie with her.

Verso Col. XXIV.

(1) .... (2) .... on it, and you ...... (3) ...... of fine linen on it (? him); these three names being written on it, (4) .... with myrrh; you light it and place it (5) .... your head; you recite them to it again nine times. (6) .... the lamp; you do it at the time of the third hour (?) of evening (7) [and you] lie down (?). Formula: 'Iobasaoumptho (8) [Khrome(?) Lou]khar; let my eyes be opened (9) in truth concerning any given matter which I am praying for here (10) [to-day, in] truth without telling thee (*sic*) falsehood.'

(11) 'Iobasaoumptthokhromeloukhar, (12) let my eyes be opened in truth concerning any given thing which I am praying (13) for here to-day.'

Col. XXIII.

l. 1. Probably some five or six short lines have completely disappeared before the beginning of the existing fragments of this column.

Col. XXIV.

Following this on Leyden, Pl. XIV., there are several scraps of Greek, &c., numbered 1–7. They are written on pieces of papyrus used for patching worn places, and have no necessary connexion with the text.

Verso Col. XXV.

1. . . . .
2. hs n bk ḥm ʾsy
3. bel nt n wʿ sp ths
4. ḥn·t-k nʾm-f nte-k str erme
5. t s-ḥm·t e-f ḫp nte-f šwy e·ʾr-k
6. nt wʿ ḫm nʾm-f ḥr *ⲉⲣⲡ* nte-k
7. ths ḥn·t-k nʾm-f
8. nte-k str erme t s-ḥm·t nfr sp-sn

Verso Col. XXVI.

1. e·ʾr-k [wḫ a t ʾre n] ntr·w n p hne(?) sze wbe-k
2. a·ʾre n ntr·w ʾy a ḫn e·ʾr-k z py rn [a·ʾr-w] sp IX
3. yʾ-ʿo yph e-ʿo-e gynntʾthwr nephʿr
4. ʾph-ʿo-e ḫr ʾr-f wḥ-sḥne n-k a p nt e·ʾr-k a šn·t-f ar-f a·ʾr θ-ḥr
5. ḫp a tm z n-k wḥ e·ʾr-k z py ke rn a·ʾr-w n sp IX šʿ
6. nte-w šn n-k n mt·t mʿ·t ng-ʿo-ngetsyks mʿntw
7. n-ʿo-b-ʿo-e g-ʿc-ghyr hr-ʿo-n-t-r nt-ʿo-ntr-ʿo-mʿ
8. leph-ʿo-ger gephʿers-ʿo-re sp VII
9. ⲓⲁⲩⲱ · ⲉⲓⲫⲏ · ⲱⲛ · ⲕⲓⲛⲇⲁⲑⲟⲩⲣ · ⲛⲉⲫⲁⲣ · ⲁⲫⲟⲉ

Verso Col. XXVII.

1. a ḫ p nt ḥry ḫn z ank pe syt-tʾ-k stm rn-yt
2. stm pe pe rn n mt ank gʾnthʿ gyn-tw gyry-tw
3. ḥry-ntr ʾrynwte lʿbtʾthʿ lʾptwthʿ
4. lʿksʿnthʿ sʿrysʿ mʿrkhʿrʿhwt-tw
5. ʾrsyngʿ·ghlʿ k-zm ʾrsy·ngʿlʿbel b-ʿo-l-b-ʿo-el
6. b-ʿo-el sp-sn l-ʿo-tery gl-ʿo·gʾsʿntrʿ yʿh-ʿo
7. rn-yt yʿh-ʿo pe pe rn n mt bʾlkhʿm p šft n t p·t

Col. XXVI.

l. 1. This column is a reproduction of 28/7–10 with slight variations.

l. 4. *θ-ḥr* = Boh. ϭⲓϩⲟ, 'delay.' This phrase is omitted in the parallel.

VERSO COL. XXV.

(1) . . . . . . (2) hawk's dung, salt, *asi* plant, (3) *bel*, pound together, anoint (4) your phallus with it and lie with (5) the woman. If it is dry, you (6) pound a little of it with wine, and you (7) anoint your phallus with it (8) and you lie with the woman. Excellent (*bis*).

VERSO COL. XXVI.

(1) If you wish [to make] the gods of the vessel (?) speak with you, (2) when the gods come in, you say this name to them nine times: (3) 'Iaho, Iphe, Eoe, Kintathour, Nephar, (4) Aphoe.' Then he makes command to you as to that which you shall ask him about. If delay (5) occur, so that answer is not given you, you recite this other name to them nine times until (6) they inquire for you truthfully: 'Gogethix, Mantou, (7) Noboe, Khokhir, Hrodor, Dondroma, (8) Lephoker, Kephaersore.' Seven times. (9) Iaho . Eiphe . On . Kindathour . Nephar . Aphoe.

VERSO COL. XXVII.

(1) According to that which is above within, saying, 'I am this Sit-ta-ko, Setem is my name, (2) Setem is my correct name. I am Gantha, Ginteu, Giriteu, (3) Hrinoute, Arinoute, Labtatha, Laptutha, (4) Laksantha, Sarisa, Markharahuteu, (5) Arsinga-khla ; another volume (says) Arsinga-label, Bolboel, (6) Boel (*bis*), Loteri, Klogasantra, Iaho, (7) is my name, Iaho is my correct name,

---

l. 9. Repeats the invocation names in ll. 2–3.

COL. XXVII.

l. 1. This column is parallel to 1/13–16.

nt ḥry (*n* ?) *ḫn*: *ḫn* must refer to the recto. Cf. *n bl* = 'verso,' 18/6, V. 15/7.

8. ʾblʿnʿthʿnʿlbʿ srrf n t qnḥ·t n p ntr nt ʿḥ n p·hw(?)

Verso Col. XXVIII.

1. e·ʾr-k ne t š(?) syw(?) . . m(?) a ḫry(?) . . .
2. e ʿḥ zl·t(?)

Verso Col. XXIX.

1. . . . ty lb rm nb nge s-ḥm·t nb
2. e·ʾr-k θ p fʿe n p rm nt e·ʾr·k wḫ-f erme p fʿe
3. n wʿ rm e-f *ⲙⲁⲟⲩⲧ* nte-k mr-w erme ne-w ʾre-w
4. nte-k mr-w a ḫe·t-f n wʿ *ⲃⲉϭ* nte-k wrḥ-f
5. e-f ʿnḫ e-f ḥp e·ʾr-k wḫ a ʾr-f n hyn·w hw·w
6. e·ʾr-k ḫʿ p *ⲃⲉϭ* n wʿ mʿ e·ʾr-k s·ʿnḫ nʾm-f n pe-k ʿy

Verso Col. XXX.

1. e·ʾr-k . . . . . . hs n *ⲥⲙⲟⲩⲛⲉ*
2. ḫr hy ḫe·[t]-s
3. k·t e·ʾr-k ths ḥn·t-k n hs n
4. *ⲕⲉⲗ* nte-k str erme s-ḥm·t ḫr ʾr-s mr·t-k
5. e·ʾr-k nt hs n *ⲥⲓϫ(?)ⲁⲥ* ḥr ʾby
6. nte-k ths ḥn·t-k nʾm-f a ḫ p nt ḥry ʿn
7. ke hs n *ϩⲁⲓⲧⲉ* ḥr sknn n
8. wrt a ḫ p nt ḥry ʿn
9. ke e·ʾr-k qp s-ḥm·t n hs n *ϩⲁⲧⲟⲩⲗ*
10. e p snf ḫrr-s ḫr lk-s
11. hs n *ⲉⲟ* ʿn py smte

Col. XXVIII.

l. 1. This short column appears to be the only part of the papyrus written in a different hand from the rest. It is very obscure, and the words seem much abbreviated. The group elsewhere reading *nk* (ⲛⲕⲁ) is conspicuous, but is without the determinative, and perhaps has another meaning here.

l. 2. Cf. V. 10/12. The zodiacal sign  ★ stands for Scorpio (Brugsch, Nouv. Rech., p. 22). For the reading *zl·t* (?), cf. O. L. Z., 1902, V. col. 6, 223.

Balkham, the mighty (?) one of heaven, (8) Ablanathanalba, gryphon of the shrine of the god which stands to-day (?).'

VERSO COL. XXVIII.

(1) You shall cause a star (?) to go . . . place (?) under the earth (?) (2) when the moon is in the constellation of Scorpio.

VERSO COL. XXIX.

(1) [Spell to] make mad any man or any woman.

(2) You take the hair of the man whom you wish, together with the hair (3) of a dead (murdered ?) man; and you tie them to each other, (4) and tie them to the body of a hawk, and you release (?) it (5) alive. If you wish to do it for some days, (6) you put the hawk in a place and you feed it in your house.

VERSO COL. XXX.

(1) If you . . . . dung of a *smoune*-goose, (2) then her body falls.

(3) Another: you anoint your phallus with dung of (4) a *kel*, and you lie with (the) woman, then she feels thy love (i.e. for thee). (5) You pound dung of . . . . . . with honey, (6) and you anoint your phallus with it as above again.

(7) Another: dung of hyaena (?) with ointment of (8) roses as above again.

(9) Another: you fumigate a woman with ichneumon's dung (10) when the menstruation is on her; then she is cured.

(11) Ass's dung also—this method (of treatment).

COL. XXIX.

l. 5. *n hyn·w hw·w.* Does this mean 'for several days' or 'after several days'?

COL. XXX.

l. 2. *hy ḫe·t-s*: perhaps of abortion, ϩⲟⲩϩⲉ : ⲟⲩϫⲉ.

VERSO COL. XXXI.

1. **ⲥⲓⲥⲓⲩⲱⲟⲩⲧ**
2. ke-z **ⲁⲣⲙⲓⲱⲩⲑ**
3. p ntr nt ʿwḫ p ḫbs nt *θ*-
4. r-yt ʾm a ḫn
5. ḫr zz-y nte-k z n-y wḥ
6. ḫr p nt e-y šn ḫrr-f ty n p-hw

VERSO COL. XXXII.

1. a t ʾre . . . . . ***ⲗⲓⲃⲉ***(?) m-s ḥwt
2. e·ʾr-k ʾny wʿ ***ⲉⲙⲙⲓⲙ*** e-f ʿnḫ
3. nte-k ʾny pe-f ***ⲥⲉ[ϩ]ⲉ*** a bl nte-k ḫʿ-f n wʿ mʿ
4. nte-k ʾny pe-f ***ϩⲉ[ⲧ]*** nte-k ḫʿ-f n ke mʿ e·ʾr-k
5. fy pe-f swmʿ tre-f e·ʾr-k nt-f m šs sp-sn
6. e·ʾr e-f šwy nte-k fy wʿ ḥm n p nt nt·yt erme wʿ
7. ḥm n snf n pe-k tbʿ n mḥ II n p sʿlʿpyn
8. n te-k t·t n gbyr nte-k ty-f a wʿ z n ʾrp
9. nte-k t swr-s t ḥm·t ḫr ʾr-s ***ⲗⲓⲃⲉ*** m-s-k
10. e·ʾr-k t pe-f ***ⲥⲉϩⲉ*** a wʿ z n ʾrp ḫr ***ⲙⲧⲉⲥ***
11. ty hte·t nge ty-f a ef nge nk n wm
12. e·ʾr-k t pe-f ***ϩⲉⲧ*** a wʿ ḫtm n nb nte-k ty-f
13. a t·t-k ḫr ty-f n-k ḥs·t ʿo·t mr·t šfe·t

VERSO COL. XXXIII.

1. a Ḥr . . . . [e-]f mšʿ a ḥry ḥr tw n mre·t n ʾḫ e-f t ʿlʿyt a wʿ ḥtr ḥt . . . . . . a wʿ ḥtr km

2. e n zm . . . [ḫr ʾ·]t-f na p wr-ty ḫn qne-f a·e-f gm n n ntr·w tre-w e-w ḥms·t a ḥry a t s·t wype·t

3. e-w wm [n p rt] n ḥʿp pe wr ḫr-w Ḥr ʾm n e·ʾr-k wm Ḥr ʾm n e·ʾr-k ne wm ḫr-f ʿl·wt-tn a ḥr-y

---

COL. XXXII.

l. 1. This column is a paraphrase of 13/17–21.

l. 6. *e·ʾr e-f*: possibly for ⲉⲁϥ. The parallel has *e-f šwy*.

COL. XXXIII.

l. 1. *a Ḥr*. *a* in this papyrus appears as the auxiliary of the past ⲁ-, but not of the present ⲉ-.

Verso Col. XXXI.

(1) 'Sisihoout (2) otherwise Armiouth, (3) the god who liveth, the lamp which is (4) lighted, come within (5) before me, and give me answer (6) concerning that which I ask about here (7) to-day.'

Verso Col. XXXII.

(1) To make . . . . rave for a man. (2) You take a live shrew-mouse (?), (3) and take out its gall and put it in one place, (4) and take its heart and put it in another place. You (5) take its whole body, you pound it very much; (6) when it is dry, you take a little of the pounded stuff with a (7) little blood of your second finger, (that) of the heart, (8) of your left hand, and put it in a cup of wine (9) and you make the woman drink it. Then she has a passion for you.

(10) You put its gall into a cup of wine, then she dies (11) instantly; or put it in meat or some food.

(12) You put its heart in a ring of gold and put it (13) on your hand; then it gives you great praise, love, and respect.

Verso Col. XXXIII.

(1) Horus . . . . he was going up a hill at midday in the verdure season, mounted on a white horse . . . . on a black horse, (2) the papyrus rolls [of . . .] being on (?) him, those of the Great of Five in his bosom. He found all the gods seated at the place of judgement (3) eating [of the produce ?] of the Nile (?), my (?) Chief.

[*e*?-] *f mšʿ*, &c.: cf. O. C. in A. Z., 1883, 100; 1900, 90 **ⲡⲉⲧⲛⲏⲟⲩ ⲛ̄ⲛⲧⲟⲟⲩ ⲛ̄ⲙⲉⲣⲉ ⲛ̄ϭⲱⲙ**.

For Horus on horseback, cf. Plut., de Is. et Osir., c. 19.

l. 2. *ḥms·t*: probably as Ach. **ϩⲙⲁⲥⲧ** (as used for infinitive in l. 6) rather than **ϩⲉⲙⲥⲏⲟⲩⲧ**.

l. 3. *ḥʿp* (?): cf. l. 6 and V. 5/1. A feminine word similarly spelt is found in connexion with embalming in Brugsch, Thes., 893, 895.

4. mn [ky ?] n'm-y n wm te-y šn zz-y te-y šn ḫe·t a wᶜ gᶜwmᶜ θy·t a wᶜ tw rs ty ᶜh-y

5. ne 'S·t [lk]-s e-s šte ne Nb-ḥt lk-s e-s s·wze ne p XVI n Ne-tbew·w ne pe(?) wᶜ n nḫt

6. n ntr n[e p? 3 ?]65 n ntr ḥms·t a ḫry a wm n p rt n t sḫ·t n ḥᶜp pe wr šᶜ nte-w šte n p gᶜwmᶜ

7. n zz[-f n p] šr n 'S·t n zz-f n mn a·ms mn n n gᶜwmᶜ n grḥ n n gᶜwmᶜ n mre·t p šn zz py srrf

8. py ḫmm [n n gᶜ]wmᶜ·w n ne 'r . . . . n rt-f šte a bl n zz-f n mn a·ms mn 'h nḥe n mᶜ·t

9. n sp VII [nte-k th]s t·t-f ḫe·t-f rt-f nte-k mt·t ar-f

Probably the word here, with divine determinative, is different, and may well represent *Ḥᶜp*, 'the Nile.' The same group occurs in Pap. Insinger 16/21.

pe wr is difficult, 'belonging to the Great,' or 'son of the Great,' or 'my Great one.'

ⲁⲣⲁⲉⲓ: cf. note 1/20.

l. 5. *ne*: probably fut. neg. ⲛⲛⲉ.

XVI n Ne-tbew·w: cf. 2/9 note; perhaps *οι δεκαεξ γιγαντες* of Berl. Pap. (PARTHEY), II. 102. There were also the 16 cubits of the Nile, and according to one account the body of Osiris was torn into sixteen pieces, Rec. tr., iii. p. 56, v. p. 86; other texts give fourteen parts (PLUTARCH) or seventeen (Rhind. bil. i. p. 3).

l. 6. [3]65 gods, i.e. one for each day of the year. Cf. the 365

Said they, 'Horus, come, art thou eating? Horus, come, wilt thou eat?' He said, 'Take yourselves from me; (4) there is no [desire?] in me for eating. I am ill in my head; I am ill in my body; a fever hath taken hold of me, a South wind hath seized me. (5) Doth Isis [cease] to make magic? Doth Nephthys cease to give health? Are the sixteen Netbeou, is the one Power (6) of God, are [? the 3]65 gods seated to eat the produce of the fields of the Nile (?), my (?) Chief, until they remove the fever (7) from the head of the son of Isis (and) from the head of N. born of N., the fevers by night, the fevers by day, the headache, this burning, (8) this heat of the fevers of . . . . . . of his feet, remove from the head of N. born of N.' (Say it) over genuine oil (9) seven times, and anoint his hand, his body, his feet, and pronounce the words to him.

---

names of the great god in Leyd. Pap. Gr. V. 4, 32, and the 365 gods, ib. W. 3, 13.

n t sḫ·t: erased in original.

l. 7. *srrf*: probably for *srf*.

l. 8. *ne 'r*  (?).

šte: a participle resuming the idea of *šte* in l. 6 after the long parenthesis.

CORRESPONDENCE OF COLUMNS

Recto.

	Old No.		New No.
LONDON	I	=	I
,,	II	=	II
,,	III	=	III
,,	IV	=	IV
,,	V	=	V
,,	VI	=	VI
,,	VII	=	VII
,,	VIII	=	VIII
,,	IX	=	IX
,,	X }	=	X
LEIDEN	I }		
,,	II–III	=	XI
,,	IV–V	=	XII
,,	VI	=	XIII
,,	VII	=	XIV
,,	VIII	=	XV
,,	IX	=	XVI
,,	X	=	XVII
,,	XI	=	XVIII
,,	XII	=	XIX
,,	XIII	=	XX
,,	XIV	=	XXI
,,	XV	=	XXII
,,	XVI	=	XXIII
,,	XVII	=	XXIV
,,	XVIII	=	XXV
,,	XIX	=	XXVI
,,	XX	=	XXVII
,,	XXI	=	XXVIII
,,	XXII	=	XXIX

Verso.

	Old No.		New No.
LEIDEN	I	=	I
,,	II	=	II
,,	III	=	III
,,	IV	=	IV
,,	V	=	V
,,	VI	=	VI
,,	VII	=	VII
,,	VIII	=	VIII
,,	IX	=	IX
,,	X	=	X
,,	XI	=	XI
,,	XII	=	XII
,,	XIII	=	XIII
,,	XIV	=	XIV
,,	XV	=	XV
,,	XVI–XVII	=	XVI
,,	XVIII	=	XVII
,,	XIX	=	XVIII
,,	XX	=	XIX
,,	XXI	=	XX
,,	XXIII	=	XXI
,,	XXII, XXIV	=	XXII
,,	XXV, XXVI	=	XXIII
,,	XXVII	=	XXIV
LONDON	I	=	XXV
,,	II	=	XXVI
,,	III	=	XXVII
,,	IV	=	XXVIII
,,	V	=	XXIX
,,	VI	=	XXX
,,	VII	=	XXXI
,,	VIII	=	XXXII
,,	IX	=	XXXIII

It has been found necessary to make some changes in the numbering of the lines in Leid. I–V, XVII, and Verso Leid. III, VIII, XXII–XXVI.

A CATALOG OF SELECTED

DOVER BOOKS

IN ALL FIELDS OF INTEREST

BRASS INSTRUMENTS: Their History and Development, Anthony Baines. Authoritative, updated survey of the evolution of trumpets, trombones, bugles, cornets, French horns, tubas and other brass wind instruments. Over 140 illustrations and 48 music examples. Corrected and updated by author. New preface. Bibliography. 320pp. 5⅜ x 8½. 27574-4 Pa. $9.95

HOLLYWOOD GLAMOR PORTRAITS, John Kobal (ed.). 145 photos from 1926-49. Harlow, Gable, Bogart, Bacall; 94 stars in all. Full background on photographers, technical aspects. 160pp. 8⅜ x 11¼. 23352-9 Pa. $11.95

MAX AND MORITZ, Wilhelm Busch. Great humor classic in both German and English. Also 10 other works: "Cat and Mouse," "Plisch and Plumm," etc. 216pp. 5⅜ x 8½. 20181-3 Pa. $6.95

THE RAVEN AND OTHER FAVORITE POEMS, Edgar Allan Poe. Over 40 of the author's most memorable poems: "The Bells," "Ulalume," "Israfel," "To Helen," "The Conqueror Worm," "Eldorado," "Annabel Lee," many more. Alphabetic lists of titles and first lines. 64pp. 5³⁄₁₆ x 8¼. 26685-0 Pa. $1.00

PERSONAL MEMOIRS OF U. S. GRANT, Ulysses Simpson Grant. Intelligent, deeply moving firsthand account of Civil War campaigns, considered by many the finest military memoirs ever written. Includes letters, historic photographs, maps and more. 528pp. 6⅛ x 9¼. 28587-1 Pa. $11.95

AMULETS AND SUPERSTITIONS, E. A. Wallis Budge. Comprehensive discourse on origin, powers of amulets in many ancient cultures: Arab, Persian Babylonian, Assyrian, Egyptian, Gnostic, Hebrew, Phoenician, Syriac, etc. Covers cross, swastika, crucifix, seals, rings, stones, etc. 584pp. 5⅜ x 8½. 23573-4 Pa. $12.95

RUSSIAN STORIES/PYCCKNE PACCKA3bl: A Dual-Language Book, edited by Gleb Struve. Twelve tales by such masters as Chekhov, Tolstoy, Dostoevsky, Pushkin, others. Excellent word-for-word English translations on facing pages, plus teaching and study aids, Russian/English vocabulary, biographical/critical introductions, more. 416pp. 5⅜ x 8½. 26244-8 Pa. $8.95

PHILADELPHIA THEN AND NOW: 60 Sites Photographed in the Past and Present, Kenneth Finkel and Susan Oyama. Rare photographs of City Hall, Logan Square, Independence Hall, Betsy Ross House, other landmarks juxtaposed with contemporary views. Captures changing face of historic city. Introduction. Captions. 128pp. 8¼ x 11. 25790-8 Pa. $9.95

AIA ARCHITECTURAL GUIDE TO NASSAU AND SUFFOLK COUNTIES, LONG ISLAND, The American Institute of Architects, Long Island Chapter, and the Society for the Preservation of Long Island Antiquities. Comprehensive, well-researched and generously illustrated volume brings to life over three centuries of Long Island's great architectural heritage. More than 240 photographs with authoritative, extensively detailed captions. 176pp. 8¼ x 11. 26946-9 Pa. $14.95

NORTH AMERICAN INDIAN LIFE: Customs and Traditions of 23 Tribes, Elsie Clews Parsons (ed.). 27 fictionalized essays by noted anthropologists examine religion, customs, government, additional facets of life among the Winnebago, Crow, Zuni, Eskimo, other tribes. 480pp. 6⅛ x 9¼. 27377-6 Pa. $10.95

FRANK LLOYD WRIGHT'S HOLLYHOCK HOUSE, Donald Hoffmann. Lavishly illustrated, carefully documented study of one of Wright's most controversial residential designs. Over 120 photographs, floor plans, elevations, etc. Detailed perceptive text by noted Wright scholar. Index. 128pp. 9¼ x 10¾. 27133-1 Pa. $11.95

THE MALE AND FEMALE FIGURE IN MOTION: 60 Classic Photographic Sequences, Eadweard Muybridge. 60 true-action photographs of men and women walking, running, climbing, bending, turning, etc., reproduced from rare 19th-century masterpiece. vi + 121pp. 9 x 12. 24745-7 Pa. $10.95

1001 QUESTIONS ANSWERED ABOUT THE SEASHORE, N. J. Berrill and Jacquelyn Berrill. Queries answered about dolphins, sea snails, sponges, starfish, fishes, shore birds, many others. Covers appearance, breeding, growth, feeding, much more. 305pp. 5¼ x 8¼. 23366-9 Pa. $8.95

GUIDE TO OWL WATCHING IN NORTH AMERICA, Donald S. Heintzelman. Superb guide offers complete data and descriptions of 19 species: barn owl, screech owl, snowy owl, many more. Expert coverage of owl-watching equipment, conservation, migrations and invasions, etc. Guide to observing sites. 84 illustrations. xiii + 193pp. 5⅜ x 8½. 27344-X Pa. $8.95

MEDICINAL AND OTHER USES OF NORTH AMERICAN PLANTS: A Historical Survey with Special Reference to the Eastern Indian Tribes, Charlotte Erichsen-Brown. Chronological historical citations document 500 years of usage of plants, trees, shrubs native to eastern Canada, northeastern U.S. Also complete identifying information. 343 illustrations. 544pp. 6½ x 9¼. 25951-X Pa. $12.95

STORYBOOK MAZES, Dave Phillips. 23 stories and mazes on two-page spreads: Wizard of Oz, Treasure Island, Robin Hood, etc. Solutions. 64pp. 8¼ x 11. 23628-5 Pa. $2.95

NEGRO FOLK MUSIC, U.S.A., Harold Courlander. Noted folklorist's scholarly yet readable analysis of rich and varied musical tradition. Includes authentic versions of over 40 folk songs. Valuable bibliography and discography. xi + 324pp. 5⅜ x 8½. 27350-4 Pa. $7.95

MOVIE-STAR PORTRAITS OF THE FORTIES, John Kobal (ed.). 163 glamor, studio photos of 106 stars of the 1940s: Rita Hayworth, Ava Gardner, Marlon Brando, Clark Gable, many more. 176pp. 8⅜ x 11¼. 23546-7 Pa. $12.95

BENCHLEY LOST AND FOUND, Robert Benchley. Finest humor from early 30s, about pet peeves, child psychologists, post office and others. Mostly unavailable elsewhere. 73 illustrations by Peter Arno and others. 183pp. 5⅜ x 8½. 22410-4 Pa. $6.95

YEKL and THE IMPORTED BRIDEGROOM AND OTHER STORIES OF YIDDISH NEW YORK, Abraham Cahan. Film Hester Street based on Yekl (1896). Novel, other stories among first about Jewish immigrants on N.Y.'s East Side. 240pp. 5⅜ x 8½. 22427-9 Pa. $6.95

SELECTED POEMS, Walt Whitman. Generous sampling from *Leaves of Grass*. Twenty-four poems include "I Hear America Singing," "Song of the Open Road," "I Sing the Body Electric," "When Lilacs Last in the Dooryard Bloom'd," "O Captain! My Captain!"–all reprinted from an authoritative edition. Lists of titles and first lines. 128pp. 5$\frac{5}{16}$ x 8¼. 26878-0 Pa. $1.00

MY BONDAGE AND MY FREEDOM, Frederick Douglass. Born a slave, Douglass became outspoken force in antislavery movement. The best of Douglass' autobiographies. Graphic description of slave life. 464pp. 5⅜ x 8½. 22457-0 Pa. $8.95

FOLLOWING THE EQUATOR: A Journey Around the World, Mark Twain. Fascinating humorous account of 1897 voyage to Hawaii, Australia, India, New Zealand, etc. Ironic, bemused reports on peoples, customs, climate, flora and fauna, politics, much more. 197 illustrations. 720pp. 5⅜ x 8½. 26113-1 Pa. $15.95

THE PEOPLE CALLED SHAKERS, Edward D. Andrews. Definitive study of Shakers: origins, beliefs, practices, dances, social organization, furniture and crafts, etc. 33 illustrations. 351pp. 5⅜ x 8½. 21081-2 Pa. $8.95

THE MYTHS OF GREECE AND ROME, H. A. Guerber. A classic of mythology, generously illustrated, long prized for its simple, graphic, accurate retelling of the principal myths of Greece and Rome, and for its commentary on their origins and significance. With 64 illustrations by Michelangelo, Raphael, Titian, Rubens, Canova, Bernini and others. 480pp. 5⅜ x 8½. 27584-1 Pa. $9.95

PSYCHOLOGY OF MUSIC, Carl E. Seashore. Classic work discusses music as a medium from psychological viewpoint. Clear treatment of physical acoustics, auditory apparatus, sound perception, development of musical skills, nature of musical feeling, host of other topics. 88 figures. 408pp. 5⅜ x 8½. 21851-1 Pa. $10.95

THE PHILOSOPHY OF HISTORY, Georg W. Hegel. Great classic of Western thought develops concept that history is not chance but rational process, the evolution of freedom. 457pp. 5⅜ x 8½. 20112-0 Pa. $9.95

THE BOOK OF TEA, Kakuzo Okakura. Minor classic of the Orient: entertaining, charming explanation, interpretation of traditional Japanese culture in terms of tea ceremony. 94pp. 5⅜ x 8½. 20070-1 Pa. $3.95

LIFE IN ANCIENT EGYPT, Adolf Erman. Fullest, most thorough, detailed older account with much not in more recent books, domestic life, religion, magic, medicine, commerce, much more. Many illustrations reproduce tomb paintings, carvings, hieroglyphs, etc. 597pp. 5⅜ x 8½. 22632-8 Pa. $11.95

SUNDIALS, Their Theory and Construction, Albert Waugh. Far and away the best, most thorough coverage of ideas, mathematics concerned, types, construction, adjusting anywhere. Simple, nontechnical treatment allows even children to build several of these dials. Over 100 illustrations. 230pp. 5⅜ x 8½. 22947-5 Pa. $7.95

DYNAMICS OF FLUIDS IN POROUS MEDIA, Jacob Bear. For advanced students of ground water hydrology, soil mechanics and physics, drainage and irrigation engineering, and more. 335 illustrations. Exercises, with answers. 784pp. 6⅛ x 9¼. 65675-6 Pa. $19.95

SONGS OF EXPERIENCE: Facsimile Reproduction with 26 Plates in Full Color, William Blake. 26 full-color plates from a rare 1826 edition. Includes "The Tyger," "London," "Holy Thursday," and other poems. Printed text of poems. 48pp. 5¼ x 7. 24636-1 Pa. $4.95

OLD-TIME VIGNETTES IN FULL COLOR, Carol Belanger Grafton (ed.). Over 390 charming, often sentimental illustrations, selected from archives of Victorian graphics–pretty women posing, children playing, food, flowers, kittens and puppies, smiling cherubs, birds and butterflies, much more. All copyright-free. 48pp. 9¼ x 12¼. 27269-9 Pa. $5.95

EARLY NINETEENTH-CENTURY CRAFTS AND TRADES, Peter Stockham (ed.). Extremely rare 1807 volume describes to youngsters the crafts and trades of the day: brickmaker, weaver, dressmaker, bookbinder, ropemaker, saddler, many more. Quaint prose, charming illustrations for each craft. 20 black-and-white line illustrations. 192pp. 4⅝ x 6. 27293-1 Pa. $4.95

VICTORIAN FASHIONS AND COSTUMES FROM HARPER'S BAZAR, 1867–1898, Stella Blum (ed.). Day costumes, evening wear, sports clothes, shoes, hats, other accessories in over 1,000 detailed engravings. 320pp. 9⅜ x 12¼. 22990-4 Pa. $14.95

GUSTAV STICKLEY, THE CRAFTSMAN, Mary Ann Smith. Superb study surveys broad scope of Stickley's achievement, especially in architecture. Design philosophy, rise and fall of the Craftsman empire, descriptions and floor plans for many Craftsman houses, more. 86 black-and-white halftones. 31 line illustrations. Introduction 208pp. 6½ x 9¼. 27210-9 Pa. $9.95

THE LONG ISLAND RAIL ROAD IN EARLY PHOTOGRAPHS, Ron Ziel. Over 220 rare photos, informative text document origin (1844) and development of rail service on Long Island. Vintage views of early trains, locomotives, stations, passengers, crews, much more. Captions. 8⅞ x 11¾. 26301-0 Pa. $13.95

THE BOOK OF OLD SHIPS: From Egyptian Galleys to Clipper Ships, Henry B. Culver. Superb, authoritative history of sailing vessels, with 80 magnificent line illustrations. Galley, bark, caravel, longship, whaler, many more. Detailed, informative text on each vessel by noted naval historian. Introduction. 256pp. 5⅜ x 8½. 27332-6 Pa. $7.95

TEN BOOKS ON ARCHITECTURE, Vitruvius. The most important book ever written on architecture. Early Roman aesthetics, technology, classical orders, site selection, all other aspects. Morgan translation. 331pp. 5⅜ x 8½. 20645-9 Pa. $8.95

THE HUMAN FIGURE IN MOTION, Eadweard Muybridge. More than 4,500 stopped-action photos, in action series, showing undraped men, women, children jumping, lying down, throwing, sitting, wrestling, carrying, etc. 390pp. 7⅞ x 10⅝. 20204-6 Clothbd. $25.95

TREES OF THE EASTERN AND CENTRAL UNITED STATES AND CANADA, William M. Harlow. Best one-volume guide to 140 trees. Full descriptions, woodlore, range, etc. Over 600 illustrations. Handy size. 288pp. 4½ x 6⅜. 20395-6 Pa. $5.95

SONGS OF WESTERN BIRDS, Dr. Donald J. Borror. Complete song and call repertoire of 60 western species, including flycatchers, juncoes, cactus wrens, many more–includes fully illustrated booklet. Cassette and manual 99913-0 $8.95

GROWING AND USING HERBS AND SPICES, Milo Miloradovich. Versatile handbook provides all the information needed for cultivation and use of all the herbs and spices available in North America. 4 illustrations. Index. Glossary. 236pp. 5⅜ x 8½. 25058-X Pa. $6.95

BIG BOOK OF MAZES AND LABYRINTHS, Walter Shepherd. 50 mazes and labyrinths in all–classical, solid, ripple, and more–in one great volume. Perfect inexpensive puzzler for clever youngsters. Full solutions. 112pp. 8⅛ x 11. 22951-3 Pa. $4.95

PIANO TUNING, J. Cree Fischer. Clearest, best book for beginner, amateur. Simple repairs, raising dropped notes, tuning by easy method of flattened fifths. No previous skills needed. 4 illustrations. 201pp. 5⅜ x 8½. 23267-0 Pa. $6.95

A SOURCE BOOK IN THEATRICAL HISTORY, A. M. Nagler. Contemporary observers on acting, directing, make-up, costuming, stage props, machinery, scene design, from Ancient Greece to Chekhov. 611pp. 5⅜ x 8½. 20515-0 Pa. $12.95

THE COMPLETE NONSENSE OF EDWARD LEAR, Edward Lear. All nonsense limericks, zany alphabets, Owl and Pussycat, songs, nonsense botany, etc., illustrated by Lear. Total of 320pp. 5⅜ x 8½. (USO) 20167-8 Pa. $6.95

VICTORIAN PARLOUR POETRY: An Annotated Anthology, Michael R. Turner. 117 gems by Longfellow, Tennyson, Browning, many lesser-known poets. "The Village Blacksmith," "Curfew Must Not Ring Tonight," "Only a Baby Small," dozens more, often difficult to find elsewhere. Index of poets, titles, first lines. xxiii + 325pp. 5⅝ x 8¼. 27044-0 Pa. $8.95

DUBLINERS, James Joyce. Fifteen stories offer vivid, tightly focused observations of the lives of Dublin's poorer classes. At least one, "The Dead," is considered a masterpiece. Reprinted complete and unabridged from standard edition. 160pp. 5³⁄₁₆ x 8¼. 26870-5 Pa. $1.00

THE HAUNTED MONASTERY and THE CHINESE MAZE MURDERS, Robert van Gulik. Two full novels by van Gulik, set in 7th-century China, continue adventures of Judge Dee and his companions. An evil Taoist monastery, seemingly supernatural events; overgrown topiary maze hides strange crimes. 27 illustrations. 328pp. 5⅜ x 8½. 23502-5 Pa. $8.95

THE BOOK OF THE SACRED MAGIC OF ABRAMELIN THE MAGE, translated by S. MacGregor Mathers. Medieval manuscript of ceremonial magic. Basic document in Aleister Crowley, Golden Dawn groups. 268pp. 5⅜ x 8½. 23211-5 Pa. $8.95

NEW RUSSIAN-ENGLISH AND ENGLISH-RUSSIAN DICTIONARY, M. A. O'Brien. This is a remarkably handy Russian dictionary, containing a surprising amount of information, including over 70,000 entries. 366pp. 4½ x 6⅛. 20208-9 Pa. $9.95

HISTORIC HOMES OF THE AMERICAN PRESIDENTS, Second, Revised Edition, Irvin Haas. A traveler's guide to American Presidential homes, most open to the public, depicting and describing homes occupied by every American President from George Washington to George Bush. With visiting hours, admission charges, travel routes. 175 photographs. Index. 160pp. 8¼ x 11. 26751-2 Pa. $11.95

NEW YORK IN THE FORTIES, Andreas Feininger. 162 brilliant photographs by the well-known photographer, formerly with *Life* magazine. Commuters, shoppers, Times Square at night, much else from city at its peak. Captions by John von Hartz. 181pp. 9¼ x 10¾. 23585-8 Pa. $12.95

INDIAN SIGN LANGUAGE, William Tomkins. Over 525 signs developed by Sioux and other tribes. Written instructions and diagrams. Also 290 pictographs. 111pp. 6⅛ x 9¼. 22029-X Pa. $3.95

AUTOBIOGRAPHY: The Story of My Experiments with Truth, Mohandas K. Gandhi. Boyhood, legal studies, purification, the growth of the Satyagraha (nonviolent protest) movement. Critical, inspiring work of the man responsible for the freedom of India. 480pp. 5⅜ x 8½. (USO) 24593-4 Pa. $8.95

CELTIC MYTHS AND LEGENDS, T. W. Rolleston. Masterful retelling of Irish and Welsh stories and tales. Cuchulain, King Arthur, Deirdre, the Grail, many more. First paperback edition. 58 full-page illustrations. 512pp. 5⅜ x 8½. 26507-2 Pa. $9.95

THE PRINCIPLES OF PSYCHOLOGY, William James. Famous long course complete, unabridged. Stream of thought, time perception, memory, experimental methods; great work decades ahead of its time. 94 figures. 1,391pp. 5⅜ x 8½. 2-vol. set.
Vol. I: 20381-6 Pa. $12.95
Vol. II: 20382-4 Pa. $12.95

THE WORLD AS WILL AND REPRESENTATION, Arthur Schopenhauer. Definitive English translation of Schopenhauer's life work, correcting more than 1,000 errors, omissions in earlier translations. Translated by E. F. J. Payne. Total of 1,269pp. 5⅜ x 8½. 2-vol. set. Vol. 1: 21761-2 Pa. $11.95
Vol. 2: 21762-0 Pa. $11.95

MAGIC AND MYSTERY IN TIBET, Madame Alexandra David-Neel. Experiences among lamas, magicians, sages, sorcerers, Bonpa wizards. A true psychic discovery. 32 illustrations. 321pp. 5⅜ x 8½. (USO) 22682-4 Pa. $8.95

THE EGYPTIAN BOOK OF THE DEAD, E. A. Wallis Budge. Complete reproduction of Ani's papyrus, finest ever found. Full hieroglyphic text, interlinear transliteration, word-for-word translation, smooth translation. 533pp. 6½ x 9¼.
21866-X Pa. $10.95

MATHEMATICS FOR THE NONMATHEMATICIAN, Morris Kline. Detailed, college-level treatment of mathematics in cultural and historical context, with numerous exercises. Recommended Reading Lists. Tables. Numerous figures. 641pp. 5⅜ x 8½.
24823-2 Pa. $11.95

THEORY OF WING SECTIONS: Including a Summary of Airfoil Data, Ira H. Abbott and A. E. von Doenhoff. Concise compilation of subsonic aerodynamic characteristics of NACA wing sections, plus description of theory. 350pp. of tables. 693pp. 5⅜ x 8½. 60586-8 Pa. $14.95

THE RIME OF THE ANCIENT MARINER, Gustave Doré, S. T. Coleridge. Doré's finest work; 34 plates capture moods, subtleties of poem. Flawless full-size reproductions printed on facing pages with authoritative text of poem. "Beautiful. Simply beautiful."—*Publisher's Weekly.* 77pp. 9¼ x 12. 22305-1 Pa. $6.95

NORTH AMERICAN INDIAN DESIGNS FOR ARTISTS AND CRAFTSPEOPLE, Eva Wilson. Over 360 authentic copyright-free designs adapted from Navajo blankets, Hopi pottery, Sioux buffalo hides, more. Geometrics, symbolic figures, plant and animal motifs, etc. 128pp. 8⅜ x 11. (EUK) 25341-4 Pa. $8.95

SCULPTURE: Principles and Practice, Louis Slobodkin. Step-by-step approach to clay, plaster, metals, stone; classical and modern. 253 drawings, photos. 255pp. 8⅛ x 11.
22960-2 Pa. $10.95